Solutions

Intermediate Student's Book

Tim Falla, Paul A Davies

OXFORD
UNIVERSITY PRESS

UNIT	A VOCABULARY AND LISTENING	B GRAMMAR	C CULTURE
1 On camera	**p4 Fashion** Describing clothes (*baggy, creased, stylish, trendy*, etc.) Clothes (*combat trousers, hoody*, etc.) Compound adjectives (*high-heeled, short-sleeved*, etc.) Grammar: Order of adjectives 🎧 Fashion show commentary	**p5 Present tense contrast** State and dynamic verbs	**p6 Stereotypes?** Maybe it's because I'm a Londoner 🎧 Talking about national characteristics
Get ready for your EXAM p12	Lesson 1 *Listening* True/False/Not stated *Use of English* Multiple-choice gapfill *Speaking* Picture-based discussion Lesson 2 *Reading* Multiple matching *Speaking* Situational role-play			
2 Memories	**p14 How did you feel?** Feelings (*disappointed, irritated, relieved*, etc.) Noun formation (*embarrassed/embarrassment, confused/confusion, nervous/nervousness*, etc.) 🎧 Memories	**p15 Past tense contrast**	**p16 Remembering the past** Poppy Day 🎧 Attitudes to remembrance days Vocabulary: Adjective prefixes (*dis-, in-, un-*, etc.)
	• **Language review** Units 1–2 **p22** • **Skills round-up** Units 1–2 **p23**		
3 Nine to five	**p24 The world of work** Jobs and gender (*architect, estate agent, surgeon*, etc.) Places of work (*office, studio*, etc.) Activities at work (*answer the phone, do paperwork*, etc.) Describing work (*menial, stressful*, etc.) 🎧 What's my job?	**p25 Defining relative clauses**	**p26 Working abroad** Reading: All in a day's work 🎧 Life for immigrants in the UK Vocabulary: Expressing an opinion Vocabulary: Agreeing and disagreeing Vocabulary: Agent nouns: suffixes (*-er, -or, -ist*, etc.)
Get ready for your EXAM p32	Lesson 3 *Listening* Multiple-choice statements *Use of English* Open cloze *Speaking* Situational role-play Lesson 4 *Reading* True/False statements and finding evidence *Speaking* Picture-based discussion			
4 Body and mind	**p34 The human body** Parts of the body (*ankle, eyebrow, wrist*, etc.) Inside the body (*muscle, spine, vein*, etc.) Idioms with parts of the body (*to be head over heels, to get something off your chest*, etc.) 🎧 Idioms with parts of the body	**p35 Past simple and present perfect contrast** Time expressions (*yesterday, this morning, yet*, etc.)	**p36 Fast food addicts** Obesity – who is to blame? Vocabulary: Legal terms (*to sue somebody*, etc.) 🎧 American teenagers and diet and lifestyle
	• **Language review** Units 3–4 **p42** • **Skills round-up** Units 1–4 **p43**		
5 Our future	**p44 Computing** Computing (*get online, log onto*, etc.) Grammar: Zero conditional 🎧 In a computer shop Noun prefixes (*mega-, multi-*, etc.)	**p45 Talking about the future** *could, may (not), might (not), will,* first conditional Vocabulary: Phrases for agreeing and disagreeing (*I (don't) think that's true*, etc.)	**p46 A greener future?** Going green Vocabulary: Politics and the state (*campaign*, etc.) 🎧 Environmental issues Vocabulary: Compound nouns (1)
Get ready for your EXAM p52	Lesson 5 *Reading* Missing sentences *Use of English* Word formation gapfill *Speaking* Debate Lesson 6 *Listening* Matching statements to speakers *Speaking* Picture-based discussion			
6 Telling tales	**p54 Murder in the library** House and garden (*balcony, drainpipe, hedge, lawn*, etc.) 🎧 Interviews with a police inspector Grammar: *must have, might have, can't have*	**p55 Reported speech (statements)** *say* and *tell*	**p56 Myth or reality?** The Loch Ness Monster 🎧 Sasquatch
	• **Language review** Units 5–6 **p62** • **Skills round-up** Units 1–6 **p63**		
7 True love?	**p64 Relationships** Dating and relationships (*get married, split up*, etc.) 🎧 Stages of a relationship Time expressions (*after a few days, in the end*, etc.) Three-part phrasal verbs	**p65 Comparison** Comparative and superlative adverbs *less* and *least* Comparatives and clauses Superlatives and the present perfect	**p66 W B Yeats** 🎧 The life of W B Yeats When you are old
Get ready for your EXAM p72	Lesson 7 *Listening* Completing statements *Use of English* Open cloze *Speaking* Picture-based discussion Lesson 8 *Reading* Multiple matching *Speaking* Situational role-play			
8 Travel	**p74 Getting from A to B** Travel and transport (*backpacking, customs, platform*, etc.) 🎧 A disastrous journey	**p75 The passive**	**p76 Tourism and travel** The British on holiday Vocabulary: Holidays, trips and excursions (*city break, cruise, package holiday*, etc.) Vocabulary: Tourism and travel 🎧 People speaking about their holiday preferences
	• **Language review** Units 7–8 **p82** • **Skills round-up** Units 1–8 **p83**		
9 Spend, spend spend!	**p84 Money and finance** Money and payment (*cheque, currency, PIN number*, etc.) 🎧 Talking about money Prepositions + noun phrases	**p85 *have something done*** Reflexive pronouns	**p86 Advertising in schools** Reading: Young minds for sale 🎧 Pros and cons of advertising in schools Vocabulary: Small and large numbers
Get ready for your EXAM p92	Lesson 9 *Reading* Multiple-choice statements *Speaking* Situational role-play Lesson 10 *Listening* Matching statements to speakers *Use of English* Multiple-choice gap-fill *Speaking* Picture-based discussion			
10 Inspiration	**p94 Art and artists** Visual and performing arts (*abstract painting, graffiti, sculpture*, etc.) 🎧 Behind the scenes Artists and artistic activities	**p95 Participle clauses**	**p96 Is it art?** Britart 🎧 Opinions on modern art
	• **Language review** Units 9–10 **p102** • **Skills round-up** Units 1–10 **p103**		

GRAMMAR BUILDER AND REFERENCE p108   **VOCABULARY BUILDER p128**   🎧 Listening (1.01 = disk 1, track 1 / 2.01 = disk 2, track 1, etc).

D GRAMMAR	E READING	F EVERYDAY ENGLISH	G WRITING
p7 Verb patterns Verb + infinitive/*-ing*	**p8** Surveillance Somebody is watching you 🎧 Song: Somebody's watching me	**p10** Talking about photos 🎧 People talking about photos Vocabulary: Expressions with *look* (*look a bit like*, *look as though*, etc.)	**p11** A letter from an exchange student Paragraphing Set phrases in informal letters
p17 *used to* Pronunciation: *used to*	**p18** Lost in New York Unknown white male Vocabulary: Adjectives + prepositions (*bored with*, *excited about*, *proud of*, etc.)	**p20** Narrating events Grammar: Exclamatory sentences (*How interesting!*, etc.) Vocabulary: Sequencing words (*after that*, *later on*, *next*, etc.) 🎧 People speaking about past events Vocabulary: *-ed/-ing* adjectives	**p21** A narrative Conjunctions
p27 Non-defining relative clauses	**p28** Reversing roles Woman's work? A man's world? Vocabulary: Phrasal verbs: separable and inseparable	**p30** A job interview Pronunciation: Intonation in questions 🎧 An interview for a summer job Vocabulary: Expressions to show understanding (*Really? That's great!*, etc.)	**p31** A job application Formal letter expressions
p37 Present perfect continuous Present perfect simple or present perfect continuous?	**p38** All in the mind The memory man Pronunciation: Homophones	**p40** At the doctor's Vocabulary: Symptoms (*shivery*, *swollen*, etc.) Vocabulary: Illnesses (*concussion*, *food poisoning*, etc.) Vocabulary: Aches and pains (*backache*, *earache*, etc.) 🎧 Patients at the doctor's	**p41** An informal letter: giving news Colloquial language (*It was great to hear from you. What have you been up to?*, etc.)
p47 Future perfect and future continuous	**p48** Visions of the future Fifty years on Vocabulary: Verb + noun collocations	**p50** Talking about plans Grammar: *will*, *going to*, present continuous Vocabulary: Making, accepting and declining suggestions (*Do you fancy...? Great idea. I'm afraid I can't.*, etc.) 🎧 Making plans for the weekend	**p51** An essay: for and against Grammar: *I think* + *will* Future time clauses
p57 Reported speech (questions)	**p58** Was he who he said he was? I'm your long-lost son! Vocabulary: Compound nouns (2)	**p60** Deciding what to do Vocabulary: Intransitive phrasal verbs 🎧 Deciding what to do Pronunciation: Intonation when negotiating	**p61** A formal letter: making a reservation Set phrases in formal letters Grammar: Verbs with two objects
p67 Talking about imaginary situations Second conditional *I wish, If only, I'd rather*	**p68** Internet relationships Are Online Relationships Real? 🎧 Song: Hero	**p70** Making conversation Grammar: Question tags 🎧 Making conversation	**p71** An informal letter: reply to an invitation Grammar: *in*, *on* and *at* with time expressions
p77 Indefinite pronouns: *some-*, *any-*, *no-*	**p78** Trip of a lifetime Big Cat Diary Vocabulary: Verbs + prepositions (*smile at*, etc.)	**p80** At the airport: exchanging information 🎧 At the airport Grammar: Indirect questions	**p81** A postcard Grammar: Introductory *it*
p87 Third conditional Pronunciation: *have*	**p88** Giving it all away Thanks a million Grammar: Clauses expressing purpose 🎧 Song: Everything I Own	**p90** Arguing your case 🎧 Arguing your case	**p91** A formal letter: asking for information Indirect questions
p97 Determiners: *all*, *each*, *every*, *few*, *little*, etc.	**p98** Urban art Banksy and Pavement Picasso Vocabulary: Compound nouns (3)	**p100** Evaluating an experience Grammar: *so* and *such* Pronunciation: Emphasising your opinion 🎧 Talking about performances	**p101** A discursive essay Essay plans Grammar: Nominal subject clauses

Get ready for **B2 EXAMS** p104 Lesson 1 • **Reading** Missing sentences **Speaking** Picture-based discussion
Lesson 2 • **Listening** Multiple-choice statements **Use of English** Open cloze **Writing** Essay
Lesson 3 • **Reading** Multiple-choice statements **Speaking** Debate
Lesson 4 • **Listening** Multiple matching **Use of English** Open cloze **Writing** Essay

1 On camera

THIS UNIT INCLUDES
Vocabulary • clothes • describing clothes • compound adjectives • nationalities
Grammar • order of adjectives • present tense contrast • state and dynamic verbs
• verb + infinitive/-ing
Speaking • describing different nationalities • discussing the issue of surveillance
• describing a photograph
Writing • an informal letter

A VOCABULARY AND LISTENING
Fashion
I can describe clothes.

1 Look at the photos. Give your opinions of the outfits using the adjectives in the box.

awful   beautiful   cool   elegant   great
ridiculous   scruffy   smart   stylish   trendy

> I think he looks cool/awful/ridiculous.

2 Look at the words for describing clothes in the box. Make a list of the clothes you can see in the pictures, adding one adjective to each.

a stripy top, a shiny coat, ...

3 🎧 1.01 Listen to a fashion show commentary. Which of the outfits in exercise 1 is described? How many other outfits are also described?

4 🎧 1.01 Complete the phrases from the commentary using words from the box. Then listen again and check.
1 an attractive _____, brown _____ jacket
2 a _____, _____ T-shirt
3 casual, _____, black jeans
4 a _____, grey, _____ jacket
5 a large, _____ scarf
6 a _____, dark, _____ coat.

5 What order are the adjectives in the phrases in exercise 4 in? Complete the rule in the *Learn this!* box with *colour*, *material* and *shape*.

> **LEARN THIS!** When we have more than one adjective before a noun, they usually come in this order: ¹ opinion, ² size or _____, ³ texture, ⁴ pattern or _____, ⁵ _____ + noun

● ● ○ Grammar Builder 1.1: Order of adjectives: p. 108

Speaking tip
Use these phrases when you cannot describe someone's clothes exactly:
it's a kind of / it's a bit like a / it looks like a + noun
it looks / it's sort of + adjective
She's wearing a kind of scarf. Her hat is sort of brown.

6 **SPEAKING** Describe the outfits in exercise 1. Use phrases from the speaking tip above.

> She's wearing elegant, baggy, long trousers. She's also wearing a kind of...

● ● ○ Vocabulary Builder 1.2: Compound adjectives: p. 128

● ● ○ Vocabulary Builder 1.1: Clothes: p. 128

Describing clothes
patterns: check   flowery   plain   spotty   stripy
shape: baggy   long   loose   short   tight
texture: creased   furry   shiny   smooth
materials: cotton   fur   leather   nylon   wool
other: high-heeled   long-sleeved   matching   short-sleeved

4   Unit 1 • On camera

1B GRAMMAR
Present tense contrast

I can use different present tenses to talk about the present and future.

1 SPEAKING Look at the photo of a brother and sister. What are they wearing and doing? Use the verbs in the box to help you.

| arrive | hold | shout | smile | take a photo | wait | wear |

Louis   Hurry up. That's the bus for the cinema. Our film starts in fifteen minutes.
Carol   Just a second. I'm taking a photo of you.
Louis   You're always taking photos. It's really annoying. What do you do with them all?
Carol   I usually send them to my friends.
Louis   Who are you sending that photo to?
Carol   My friend Laura. She lives in New York. She's coming to stay with us next month.
Louis   Why are you sending her a photo of me?
Carol   Don't worry about that. Come on! The bus is leaving!

2 Now read the dialogue. Underline all the examples of the present simple and present continuous.

3 Study the examples you underlined in the dialogue. Then write S (*simple*) or C (*continuous*) for each use in the table. Which two uses refer to the future?

We use the present ...
1 _____ for habits and routines.
2 _____ for something happening now or about now.
3 _____ for describing annoying behaviour (with *always*).
4 _____ for a permanent situation or fact.
5 _____ for arrangements in the future.
6 _____ for timetables and schedules (e.g. cinema programmes).

4 Complete the rest of the dialogue with the present simple or present continuous form of the verbs in brackets.

Carol   Just a moment. My phone [1]_____ (ring). It's Laura! Hi, Laura! ... I'm on the bus. ... We [2]_____ (see) the new Spielberg film this afternoon. ... Yes, I [3]_____ (look) forward to it. Spielberg [4]_____ (make) great films.
Louis   [5]_____ (she / phone) from New York? What [6]_____ (she / say)?
Carol   Be quiet, Louis! Sorry, Laura. My brother [7]_____ (always / interrupt) me when I'm on the phone. It's so annoying!
Louis   Sorry.
Carol   Yes, I [8]_____ (often / go) to the cinema with Louis. ... Ha ha!
Louis   Why [9]_____ (you / laugh)?
Carol   I have to go now, Laura. But the film [10]_____ (finish) at five o'clock. Let's speak later.

●● **Grammar Builder 1.2: Present tense contrast: p. 108**

5 SPEAKING Work in pairs. Complete these sentences with true information about you. Remember that the present continuous can refer to current actions or future arrangements.

1 I wear ...   5 I'm wearing ...
2 I study ...   6 I'm studying ...
3 I go ...   7 I'm going ...
4 I have ...   8 I'm having ...

> I wear shorts when I play football. I'm wearing jeans at the moment.

LEARN THIS!
State verbs
State verbs describe a state or situation, and are not usually used in continuous tenses.
like love hate prefer understand believe remember forget want need belong

6 Read the *Learn this!* box and complete the sentences with the state verbs in the box below.

| belong know like mean prefer remember not understand want |

1 That bike _____ to me.
2 I _____ baggy clothes to tight clothes.
3 My brother _____ to borrow my leather jacket.
4 I _____ this sentence. Can you explain it?
5 I _____ what you _____ .
6 Hello! _____ you _____ me? We met briefly at Susan's party.
7 _____ you _____ meeting people?

●● **Grammar Builder 1.3: State and dynamic verbs: p. 109**

7 SPEAKING Work in pairs. Tell your partner:
1 two things you do every day.
2 two things that are happening in the classroom now.
3 two things you're doing next weekend.
4 two facts about yourself or your family.
5 two things that people are always doing which annoy you.
6 two things that you want but don't need OR two things that you need but don't want.

Unit 1 • On camera   **5**

1C CULTURE Stereotypes?

I can talk about differences between nationalities.

1 Look at the photo and the title of the text. Answer the questions.
1 Where are the people?
2 What are they wearing?
3 What are they doing?
4 What aren't they doing?

2 Read the text. Who has the most negative view of Londoners: Sam, Joanna or Amir?

Maybe It's Because I'm A Londoner

Look at the people in the photograph. They're sitting close together on an underground train, but they aren't smiling or talking to each other. This is how the world usually sees Londoners: quiet, reserved, unfriendly. But how accurate is this impression? We asked three residents of London to give their opinions.

Sam, age 18. British, born in London.
'I don't think Londoners are particularly miserable – in fact, we like a good joke. But we're probably a bit gloomy and pessimistic. When it comes to sport, for example, we cheer on the British competitors and teams, but we aren't really surprised when they lose. We accept underachievement as the norm. I think Americans are different: they expect to win.'

Joanna, age 19. Polish, living in London for a year.
'I think Londoners are really cold and unfriendly. People here don't chat – they don't say hello to their neighbours, and some of them wouldn't even recognise their neighbours in the street. I find it difficult to make friends here. In fact, I spend most of my time with Poles, not English people. People claim that the English are nice when you get to know them, but how can you get to know them when they're so uncommunicative?'

Amir, age 17. British, born in London, Pakistani parents.
'London is a truly multicultural city. I think it's true to say that more than one in three of the city's population belong to an ethnic minority group, and you can hear about 300 different languages here. New people are arriving all the time, so the city is changing day by day. It's a very competitive, fast-moving place. Most Londoners are focused, and aren't afraid of work – they know what they want and how to get it!'

3 Match the opinions about Londoners with the three people. Write S (Sam), J (Joanna) or A (Amir).
1 They aren't very welcoming.
2 They work very hard.
3 They don't talk to each other very much.
4 They've got a good sense of humour.
5 They're ambitious.
6 They aren't optimistic.

4 🎧 1.02 Listen to four teenagers' opinions about people from their own country. What are their nationalities? Choose from the words in the box.

Nationalities
American   Argentinian   Australian   Belgian   Brazilian
Chinese   French   German   Greek   Hungarian
Japanese   Polish   Russian   Spanish   Swiss

	Nationality
Rosanna	
Ethan	
Junko	
Carlos	

5 🎧 1.02 Listen again. Match two opinions (a–h) with each person. Write R (Rosanna), E (Ethan), J (Junko) or C (Carlos) next to each opinion.
a They're usually polite and formal with strangers.
b They're very patriotic.
c They're very talkative.
d They're hard-working.
e They're really cheerful.
f They don't like to show their emotions.
g They're very generous.
h They're quite warm and friendly.

6 Work in pairs. How would you describe people from: (a) your own town or city, (b) from another country you know? Choose adjectives from the box or your own ideas and make notes.

friendly/unfriendly   optimistic/pessimistic
serious/funny   talkative/quiet   hard-working/lazy
rude/polite   ambitious/unambitious   relaxed/tense
mean/generous   reliable/unreliable   arrogant/modest

7 **SPEAKING** Tell the class your ideas from exercise 6. Do they agree?

6   Unit 1 • On camera

1D GRAMMAR
Verb patterns

I can identify and use different verb patterns.

1 Read the text about the paparazzi. Who do you agree with more, the celebrity or the photographer?

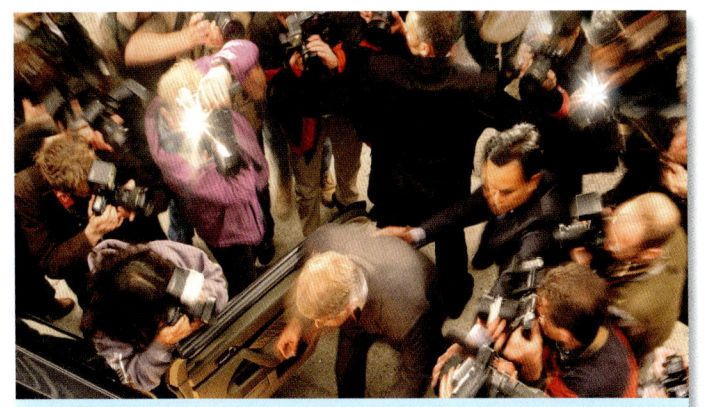

The public enjoy reading about stars in magazines – and they hope to see new photos of them with every article. Who takes these photos? They're called the paparazzi: photographers who spend hours each day following famous people and waiting for them outside clubs, hotels and restaurants.

THE CELEBRITY
'I refuse to co-operate with the paparazzi. I never agree to pose for photos, and I avoid going to clubs and restaurants. Often, I can't face leaving the house because I know that they're waiting for me in the street outside. Of course, I realise that fame has a price, and I don't expect to lead a completely normal life – but imagine having no privacy at all. I can't help thinking it's really unfair.'

THE PHOTOGRAPHER
'Most famous people pretend to hate the paparazzi, but most of them want to be in the magazines – stars need publicity. OK, so they lose a bit of privacy – but they still manage to have a better life than most other people! And a lot of celebrities seem to enjoy the attention. It's the paparazzi who have a bad time. Sometimes we spend all night following celebrities and fail to get one good picture!'

2 Find these verbs in the text. Are they followed by an infinitive or an *-ing* form? Add them to the chart.

agree   avoid   can't face   can't help   enjoy   expect
fail   hope   imagine   manage   pretend   refuse
seem   spend (time)   want

verb + infinitive	verb + *-ing* form
decide	fancy
happen	feel like
mean	can't stand
promise	suggest

● ● Grammar Builder 1.4: Verb patterns: p.109

3 Complete the text with the infinitive or *-ing* form of the verbs in brackets.

THE MAGAZINE EDITOR
'I can't stand ¹_____ (hear) celebrities complain about the paparazzi. If they don't feel like ²_____ (have) their photo taken, they could stay at home. But instead, they decide ³_____ (go) to expensive restaurants. They're only pretending ⁴_____ (hate) the paparazzi. I often phone stars and suggest ⁵_____ (take) some photos of them, and they usually agree ⁶_____ (co-operate). And celebrities sometimes phone me and promise ⁷_____ (be) at a certain place at a certain time – and they expect ⁸_____ (see) photographers there! Stars need publicity, and they enjoy ⁹_____ (be) on the pages of magazines.'

4 Complete the sentences with the infinitive or *-ing* form of the verbs in the box. Which opinions do you agree with?

not be   lead   read   understand   write

1 I enjoy _____ about celebrities, but I think their privacy is also important.
2 Magazines always seem _____ about the same people.
3 I pretend _____ interested in celebrity magazines, but I secretly look at them!
4 I fail _____ why people are so interested in celebrities.
5 I love celebrity magazines. I often imagine _____ that kind of life.

5 🎧 1.03 Listen to four speakers. Match them with four of the opinions from exercise 4.
SPEAKER: 1 ☐   2 ☐   3 ☐   4 ☐

> **LEARN THIS!**
> **Verbs that change their meaning**
> 1 Some verbs can be followed by an infinitive or an *-ing* form, without any difference in meaning.
> 2 Some verbs change meaning depending on whether they are followed by an infinitive or *-ing* form, e.g. *remember   forget   stop   try*

6 Read the *Learn this!* box. Then translate the sentences. How does the meaning of the verbs change?

1 I won't forget to send you a postcard.
2 I'll never forget seeing the Pyramids.
3 He stopped to chat to his friends.
4 He stopped chatting to his friends.
5 I tried skiing but didn't like it.
6 I tried to ski, but I couldn't even stand up on the skis.

7 **SPEAKING** Work in pairs. Tell your partner about something that you:

1 sometimes forget to do.
2 will never forget doing.
3 must remember to do.
4 will always remember doing.
5 tried to do, but couldn't.
6 tried doing, but didn't enjoy.

● ● Grammar Builder 1.5: Verbs that change their meaning: p. 110

Unit 1 • On camera   7

E READING
Surveillance

I can understand an article and a song about surveillance.

1 Look at the photos and answer the questions.
1 What are Closed-Circuit Television (CCTV) cameras?
2 Where do you usually find CCTV cameras? Are there any places you don't find them?

2 Read the text. Match the headings with the paragraphs A–E. There is one heading you do not need.
1 Eyes in the sky
2 What are CCTV cameras for?
3 Internet surveillance
4 They know who you are calling
5 Safety on the streets
6 Watching shoppers

3 Choose the best answers.
1 Today, there are CCTV cameras which
   a know when a crime is in progress.
   b identify people who have committed crimes before.
   c can speak to people if they are getting angry.
   d stop dangerous or illegal behaviour.
2 CCTV cameras record the actions of
   a one in fourteen people in the UK.
   b four million people.
   c criminals in the UK.
   d everybody in the UK.
3 CCTV cameras receive a message from RFID tags when
   a a shoplifter comes into the shop.
   b a shoplifter steals an item.
   c somebody lifts up an item that has got a tag.
   d the camera starts filming.
4 When you use a mobile phone, the phone company can work out
   a the name of the person you are speaking to.
   b what you are saying.
   c how long you have had the phone.
   d where you are.

Somebody is watching you

A The first CCTV cameras appeared in Britain in 1953, and by the 1960s there were already a few cameras in major streets in London. Today, there are more than four million CCTV cameras across the country. That's one camera for every fourteen people. The cameras are there to film dangerous or illegal behaviour. With new software, they can automatically recognise the faces of known criminals, and a new kind of CCTV in the Netherlands can detect angry voices and automatically warn the police of trouble. But these cameras don't just watch criminals; they watch all of us, almost all of the time. Every time we go into a shop, or use a cash machine, or travel on public transport a camera records our actions.

B The amount of surveillance in towns and cities across Britain is increasing. Some goods in shops now have RFID (Radio Frequency Identification) tags attached to them. When you pick up one of these items, the RFID tag sends a radio message to a CCTV camera and the camera starts filming you. Shops say that this technology helps to catch shoplifters – but only by treating everybody as a potential criminal.

C Cameras and tags are not the only ways of monitoring our actions. Every time you make or receive a call on your mobile phone, the phone company knows the number of the phone you are calling and how long the call lasts. It is even possible to work out your exact location. The police often use this information when they're investigating serious crimes.

D And what about satellites? Are they watching us from space? How much can they see? Anybody with a computer can download Google Earth and get satellite photos of the entire world. Perhaps governments are using even more powerful satellites to watch their citizens.

E Even when you are at home, you are not necessarily safe from surveillance. When you use your computer to visit websites, you are probably sending and receiving cookies without realising it. Cookies transfer information from your computer to the website and, in theory, could record which websites you visit. Or perhaps somebody has secretly installed a keystroke logging program on your computer. These record every letter that you type on the keyboard: your passwords, your e-mails, your bank account numbers and more. Modern technology is making it easier and easier to stay in contact, but it is also making it nearly impossible for us to hide.

Unit 1 • On camera

5 You can get photos of the world from space if you
  a work for a government.
  b go to a government website.
  c work for Google.
  d have a computer.
6 When you surf the Internet, cookies
  a record every letter that you type.
  b record your passwords and e-mails.
  c keep you safe from surveillance.
  d exchange information with websites.

4 Match the highlighted words in the text with the definitions below.
1 a machine which gives you money when you type in your code
2 watching
3 secret words that allow you to enter (a place or a website)
4 against the law
5 inhabitants of a state or nation
6 a label which you attach to an item (e.g. a suitcase)
7 transfer from the Internet to your computer
8 computer programs
9 people who steal from shops

5 🎧 1.04 Read and complete the song with the words in the box. Then listen and check.

| dream | hair | home | life | neighbours | phone | price |
| showers | tricks | TV |

6 Find a word in the song, beginning with the letter *P*, which sums up how the singer is feeling. Why do you think some people feel that way about surveillance?

7 Put the sentences into two groups: *Arguments for surveillance* and *Arguments against surveillance*.
1 The police might misuse the information.
2 Surveillance deters people from committing crime.
3 If you don't do anything wrong, then you have nothing to fear from surveillance.
4 Surveillance makes everybody feel guilty.
5 It's the first step towards a police state.
6 Personal privacy is more important than catching criminals.
7 More surveillance means the police can catch more criminals.
8 We rely too much on technology to solve social problems.
9 Public safety is more important than personal privacy.

8 SPEAKING Work in groups. Discuss the questions and give reasons for your opinions. Use the arguments in exercise 7 to help you.
1 Do you think the increase in surveillance in our society is a good thing or a bad thing?
2 Which, if any, of these methods of surveillance do you think are worrying? Give reasons.

| CCTV cameras | cookies | RFID tags | satellites |
| the monitoring of mobile phone calls |

I think … is worrying because …

Somebody's Watching Me

(Who's watching?
Tell me, who's watching?
Who's watching me?)

I'm just an average man
With an average ¹_____
I work from nine to five.
Hey, hell, I pay the ²_____
All I want is to be left alone
In my average ³_____
But why do I always feel
Like I'm in the twilight zone?

And I always feel like somebody's watching me
And I have no privacy
I always feel like somebody's watching me
Tell me, is it just a ⁴_____?

When I come home at night
I bolt the door real tight
People call me on the ⁵_____
I'm trying to avoid
But can the people on ⁶_____ see me?
Or am I just paranoid?

When I'm in the shower
I'm afraid to wash my ⁷_____
'Cause I might open my eyes
And find someone standing there
People say I'm crazy
Just a little touched
But maybe ⁸_____ remind me
Of Psycho too much. That's why

I always feel like somebody's watching me
And I have no privacy
I always feel like somebody's watching me
Who's playing ⁹_____ on me?

Who's watching me?
I don't know anymore
Are the ¹⁰_____ watching me?
(Who's watching?) Well, is the mailman watching me
(Tell me, who's watching?) And I don't feel safe anymore
Oh, what a mess
I wonder who's watching me now? Who? The IRS?

I always feel like somebody's watching me
And I have no privacy
I always feel like somebody's watching me
Tell me, is it just a dream?

I always feel like somebody's watching me
And I have no privacy
I always feel like somebody's watching me
Who's playing tricks on me?

Glossary
twilight zone = a place where everything is strange
bolt = lock
touched = crazy
Psycho is a famous film about a murderer
mailman (NAmE) = postman (BrE)
IRS = Internal Revenue Service, the government agency which collects taxes in the USA

Unit 1 • On camera 9

1F EVERYDAY ENGLISH
Talking about photos

I can describe the people in a photo to someone.

Sarah What's this photo?
Connor It's from our New Year's Eve party.
Sarah You look as though you're having a great time. Who's the girl at the front, the one in the shiny, grey dress?
Connor She's a friend of my sister's.
Sarah Is your sister in this photo?
Connor Yes, she is. She's the girl on the left, the one with long, brown hair.
Sarah Oh, yes. She looks a bit like you. Who's the guy standing at the back in the grey shirt?
Connor That's my cousin, Jeff.
Sarah He looks nice!

1 🎧 1.05 Read and listen to the dialogue. Find Connor's sister in the photo.

2 Complete the phrases for identifying people in photos. Use the prepositions in the box.

| at   in   on   with |

1 the guy _____ the back/front
2 the girl _____ the left/right
3 the man _____ short, black hair
4 the woman _____ the stripy top

3 Read the information in the *Learn this!* box. Then find one example of each expression in the dialogue in exercise 1.

> **LEARN THIS!**
> **Expressions with *look***
> *look (a bit/just) like* + noun/person
> *look* + adjective
> *look as though/as if/like* + clause

4 Complete the sentences with the correct form of one of the expressions with *look* from exercise 3.
1 Did you see Naomi at the party? She _____ beautiful in that long dress.
2 She doesn't _____ an Australian. She _____ Chinese.
3 They don't _____ they're working very hard.
4 You _____ a film star in that jacket.
5 It _____ it's going to rain.

5 **SPEAKING** Work in pairs. Describe somebody from the photo in exercise 1 using an expression from exercise 3. Can your partner identify the person?

> He looks as though he's laughing.

> Is it the boy on the left in the white shirt?

6 🎧 1.06 Listen. Label the people in the photo in exercise 1 with the names in the box. How are they connected to Connor? What else can you remember about them?

Kim   Mike   Sandra

> **Listening tip**
> Don't worry if there are words in the recording that you don't understand. You don't have to understand every word to complete the task.

7 **SPEAKING** Work in pairs. Prepare a dialogue about the photo below.
Student A: You know the people in the photograph. Invent names and decide how they are connected with you/each other (friends? family members?).
Student B: You don't know any of the people in the photograph. Ask Student A about them. Use phrases from exercise 2 to identify who you are talking about.

8 **SPEAKING** Act out your dialogue to the class.

> Who's the guy on the right, the one in the green shirt?

> That's my cousin, Danny.

10   Unit 1 • On camera

1G WRITING
A letter to an exchange student

I can write a letter introducing myself to an exchange student.

A

Dear Luc,

[1] Hi! I'm your exchange student from England. My name is George and I'm 16 years old. I live with my parents and my two sisters in Bournemouth, a town on the south coast of England. ¹☐

[2] I'm enclosing a photo of me and my sisters, Lizzie and Diana. Lizzie is the one on the left with long, blonde hair. ²☐ The other girl is a friend of Diana's from school.

[3] I'm in year 11 at Lidborough School. It's a small, private school just outside Bournemouth. ³☐ I'm studying for twelve GCSEs, including French, of course! My best subject is probably English, and my worst is maths.

[4] I'm really looking forward to visiting you in Bordeaux next month and meeting your family. ⁴☐ What kind of school do you go to? Please write soon and send a photo too!

Best wishes

George Kelp

B

Dear Gloria

[1] I'm Sarah Jones, your new exchange student. I'm 17 and I live on a farm in a small village in central Wales with my mum and dad. ⁵☐ I haven't got any brothers or sisters.

[2] Wales is part of the UK, but it's got its own culture and language. Most people in the village here are Welsh speakers, and my grandparents speak it all the time. ⁶☐

[3] I've got lots of hobbies and interests. I go horse riding a lot, and I play hockey and badminton. I'm into rock music and my favourite bands are the Stereophonics and the Super Furry Animals. ⁷☐

[4] Anyway, that's all for now. Please write soon and tell me about your life in Spain. By the way, do you live near the beach? And what's the weather usually like in May?

Regards

Sarah

P.S. I'm sending you a photo of me and my horse, Cleo.

---

1 Quickly read the letters. Where do Luc, George, Gloria and Sarah live?

2 Identify the topic of each paragraph in the letters. Choose from these topics.
   a   asking for information about the other person
   b   school
   c   sports, hobbies and interests
   d   describing your own country/town/village
   e   introduction and general personal details
   f   friends and girlfriend/boyfriend
   g   describing a photo of your family

3 Match the sentences (a–g) with the gaps in the letters (1–7). Use your answers to exercise 2 to help you.
   a   Have you got any brothers or sisters?
   b   Diana is the one in the blue top.
   c   But don't worry – my parents and I speak English at home!
   d   Both bands are from Wales, of course.
   e   Our house is about 2 km from the sea.
   f   My grandparents live in the same village, so I see them all the time.
   g   There are only about 200 students, and the facilities are really good.

> **Writing tip**
>
> When you write a letter, organise the information or your arguments. Each paragraph should focus on one key topic.

4 Imagine you have a new exchange student. Plan a letter introducing yourself to him or her. Choose topics for paragraphs 2 and 3 from the list in exercise 2. Make notes for each paragraph.

Paragraph 1: Introduction, general personal details

Paragraph 2:

Paragraph 3:

Paragraph 4: Asking for information about the other person

5 Now write a four-paragraph letter of 120–150 words using your plan from exercise 4.

Unit 1 • On camera   11

Get ready for your EXAM 1

1 **Get ready to LISTEN** Choose four adjectives from the box that best describe the clothes you like to wear.

> bright   casual   comfortable   conservative
> exotic   practical   shocking   spotless   vivid

2 🎧 1.07 Do the Listening exam task.

LISTENING exam task

Listen to part of a radio programme. Decide whether the information in each sentence (1–8) is true, false or not stated in the programme.

		True	False	Not stated
1	Everybody's 'wardrobe personality' is one of four types: Dramatic, Classic, Romantic or Natural.	☐	☐	☐
2	Dramatic personalities like to be looked at.	☐	☐	☐
3	Dramatics do not wear designer clothes.	☐	☐	☐
4	Classic personalities enjoy quiet hobbies like gardening.	☐	☐	☐
5	Classics spend the most on clothes of any type.	☐	☐	☐
6	Make-up is not very important for Romantic personalities.	☐	☐	☐
7	Natural personalities are comfortable in either casual or formal clothes.	☐	☐	☐
8	'Extreme Naturals' risk dressing too casually for some situations.	☐	☐	☐

3 Read the text in the Use of English exam task, ignoring the gaps. According to the text, what is the problem with 'size zero' fashion models?

  a They make ordinary clothes look ridiculous.
  b They put their own health at risk and set a bad example to young girls.
  c The top fashion designers do not like designing clothes for models who are very thin.

4 Do the Use of English exam task.

USE OF ENGLISH exam task

Complete the text with the correct words (A, B or C).

Size zero

At the age of 22, Luisel Ramos was [1]_____ a life that many girls and young women would envy. She was a top fashion model who spent her time [2]_____ from country to country to take part in major fashion shows. She was beautiful and [3]_____ , tall and thin. She was earning a lot of money, too. But she was [4]_____ , and wanted [5]_____ an even bigger success in the world of fashion. In the months leading up to Uruguay's Fashion Week in 2006, Luisel followed a strict diet of lettuce leaves and Diet Coke. By the time the fashion show arrived, she weighed around 45 kilos, despite being 1.75 metres [6]_____ . Unfortunately, she didn't stop [7]_____ about the harm the diet was doing to her health.

The audience cheered as Luisel Ramos walked down the catwalk wearing the latest fashions from some of the world's [8]_____ designers. But as she was returning to her dressing room, she collapsed and died. Doctors blamed her death on her very low bodyweight and lack of essential nutrition.

A month [9]_____ Luisel's death, the Madrid Fashion Week banned models who were too thin from taking part, and Italian fashion designers also refused [10]_____ 'size zero' models. People often blame the fashion industry for using unhealthily thin models, thereby encouraging girls to become obsessed with their weight, but perhaps the tragic death of Luisel Ramos was a turning point.

1	A making	B doing	C leading
2	A to fly	B flying	C was flying
3	A styled	B styling	C stylish
4	A relaxed	B ambitious	C modest
5	A be	B being	C to be
6	A height	B of height	C tall
7	A thought	B to think	C thinking
8	A top	B highest	C most
9	A later	B afterwards	C after
10	A to use	B using	C use

5 **Get ready to SPEAK** Describe the first photo in the Speaking exam task below. Say:

- where the women are
- what they are doing
- how they are feeling and why

6 Do the Speaking exam task.

SPEAKING exam task

Compare and contrast the two photos. Answer the questions.

1 Who is buying clothes 'off the peg'? Who is having clothes specially made?
2 What are the advantages and disadvantages of having clothes specially made for you?
3 Which shopping experience would you find more enjoyable, and why?
4 Do you preferring shopping alone or with somebody else? Give reasons.

12 Get ready for your exam 1

Get ready for your EXAM 2

1 Work in pairs. Would either of you like to be famous? Give reasons. Then tell the class.

2 Do the Reading exam task.

Reading exam task

Read the text. Match the headings (A–F) with the paragraphs (1–5). There is one heading that you don't need.

FADING RED CARPET

1 ☐ Any movie fan who is worth their DVD collection knows what a good movie premiere night is like. Cameras flashing, fans cheering, and in the middle – the famous red carpet. One by one, the greatest names of Hollywood get out of their sparkling limousines and walk down this carpet to the most stunning of parties. And, of course, everyone wishes they could be there. Well, except for the stars themselves.

2 ☐ Although it may look like they are going to have a ball, for most movie people a night like this is still work. First of all they are in the public eye, even if the fans and the paparazzi are kept at a distance. The smile still has to be kept fixed on their faces, no matter how exhausted they might be. And, if they have the misfortune to slip on the wet floor, they can be sure to find a snap of that moment in the papers the next day.

3 ☐ Then there is the ever-present gossip. If you arrive together, you're probably dating each other. If you arrive separately, pose for the pictures separately, and finally leave separately, it is absolute proof that you're dating each other. Your every move, smile and gesture will be noticed and commented on, and, most likely, misinterpreted.

4 ☐ The funny thing is that the least important part of the night is the showing of the movie itself. Most of the people present, from the crew to the critics, have already seen it anyway. The premiere night of the movie *The Fantastic Four* had to do without the movie because the film projector broke down, but nobody complained. It is the crowd, the location and the money that you spend that this is really all about.

5 ☐ So why do they do it? Well, nuisance or not, it is good publicity. All the media are there, willing to give you a bit of their airtime or column space. Besides, it is tradition. Bothersome or not, it just has to take place. As one Hollywood director says, 'If my studio told me I couldn't have a premiere for my film, I'd be offended.'

A Reasons to go
B A typical opening night
C On everyone's lips
D All work no fun
E Where to go
F What counts

3 Match the highlighted words in the text with the definitions below.
1 everything that is written or said about somebody or something by the media
2 happy shouting
3 a photo
4 people who write reviews
5 well known to many people because of the media
6 things that are said about somebody's private life which are not always true
7 the people with technical skills involved in making a movie
8 a place where an event takes place
9 the first time a movie is shown

4 Get ready to SPEAK Work in pairs. Talk about your favourite movie stars. Why do you like them? What movies were they in?

5 Do the Speaking exam task.

Speaking exam task

Work in pairs. Imagine you are going to the cinema together this evening. Discuss the list of films and agree which one you would like to see.

The Guns of Gettysburg
7.20
American Civil War epic starring George Clooney. Contains some violence: 15+ only. 205 minutes.

Super Doc
6.15 & 9.15
Jim Carrey comedy about a man pretending to be a doctor who discovers a real talent for saving lives. Suitable for families. 100 minutes.

Space Station Mars
7.30 & 10.30
Sci-fi thriller starring Kirsten Dunst. A space station is under threat, but does the danger come from outside or from inside the station itself? Suitable for 15+. 130 minutes.

La Sonrisa del Diablo (The Devil's Smile)
11.15
Mexican love story about betrayal and forgiveness. English subtitles. Not suitable for young children. 85 minutes.

Get ready for your exam 2 13

2 Memories

THIS UNIT INCLUDES
Vocabulary • feelings • noun formation • adjective prefixes • adjectives + prepositions • sequencing words • -ed/-ing adjectives • phrasal verbs
Grammar • past tense contrast • used to • exclamatory sentences
Speaking • talking about feelings • describing early memories • discussing important days • describing and reacting to a story
Writing • a narrative

A VOCABULARY AND LISTENING
How did you feel?

I can describe how I feel.

1 Look at the photos. How do you think the people feel? Use the adjectives in the box.

> **Feelings** amused bored confused delighted depressed disappointed embarrassed excited fed up guilty homesick irritated jealous nervous pleased relieved scared shocked upset

> I think the man in photo 1 looks …

2 Work in pairs. Mime adjectives from exercise 1. Can your partner guess?

> Are you disappointed?
> No. Try again.
> Are you fed up?
> Yes, I am. Your turn.

3 Choose the best adjective (a, b or c) to describe each person's feelings.
1 It was a difficult and important exam – and I passed it.
   a confused   b relieved   c excited
2 I was away from home and I missed my family.
   a bored   b nervous   c homesick
3 The shop assistant was very rude to me.
   a shocked   b scared   c pleased
4 We lost the match – the other team scored in the last minute.
   a nervous   b confused   c disappointed
5 I forgot to give my brother a message, and he missed his friend's party.
   a jealous   b guilty   c delighted
6 My boyfriend spent the evening talking to another girl.
   a jealous   b amused   c excited
7 My dad decided to dance at my birthday party, but he's a terrible dancer.
   a scared   b embarrassed   c depressed
8 I didn't get an invitation to the party. Everyone else did.
   a upset   b relieved   c bored

4 🎧 1.08 Listen to five people recalling events in their life. Match the speakers (1–5) with five of the events (a–f).
a my first day at primary school
b an argument with a friend
c an important exam result
d getting lost
e receiving a great present
f a family wedding

Speaker 1 ☐   Speaker 3 ☐   Speaker 5 ☐
Speaker 2 ☐   Speaker 4 ☐

5 🎧 1.08 Listen again. How did the people in exercise 4 feel? Choose the best adjective from the box for each speaker.

> delighted embarrassed jealous relieved scared

6 **SPEAKING** Work in pairs. Which of the events in exercise 4 have happened to you? How did you feel at the time?

7 When did you last feel like this? Make notes for each adjective.
1 irritated   4 scared   7 relieved
2 nervous   5 shocked   8 bored
3 delighted   6 confused

1 irritated – sister borrowed MP3 player

8 **SPEAKING** Work in pairs. Ask and answer questions using the adjectives in exercise 7.

> When did you last feel irritated?
> I last felt irritated when my sister borrowed my MP3 player without asking.

●●○ Vocabulary Builder 2.1: Noun formation: p. 129

Unit 2 • Memories

2B GRAMMAR
Past tense contrast

I can describe my earliest memory using different past tenses.

1 Read about one of Tom's early memories. How do you think these people felt?

a Tom   b Tom's aunt and uncle   c Tom's parents

An early memory by Tom

I was about five years old. My aunt and uncle **had come** to visit us with their son, Joshua. While my parents **were chatting** to my aunt and uncle, my cousin and I **went** outside to play. It **was raining** and the sky **was** grey. We **sat** down on the doorstep and **started** throwing stones at a tree in our front garden. I threw a stone, it **bounced** off the tree, **landed** on my aunt and uncle's car and **smashed** the windscreen. I couldn't believe what I **had done**. When my aunt and uncle **came** outside, I **was staring** at the broken windscreen.

2 What tenses are the verbs in blue in the text: past simple, past continuous or past perfect?

3 Read and complete the rules in the *Learn this!* box with the names of the tenses. Find examples of each rule in the text.

LEARN THIS!
Past tenses
When we are narrating events in the past
1 We can use the _____ to set the scene.
   It was raining and the wind was blowing.
2 We use the _____ for actions or events that happened one after another.
   I got home, sat down and turned on the TV.
3 We use the _____ for an action or event that interrupted a background event; we use the _____ for the background event.
   While I was having dinner, the phone rang.
   What were you doing when I saw you?
4 We use the _____ to talk about an event that happened before another event in the past.
   I wasn't hungry because I had already eaten a pizza.

Grammar Builder 2.1: Past tenses: p. 110

4 Work in pairs. Discuss the difference in meaning between the sentences.
1 When I got to the party, Kim opened his presents.
2 When I got to the party, Kim was opening his presents.
3 When I got to the party, Kim had opened his presents.

5 Choose the correct tenses.
1 Dad **broke / was breaking** a glass while he **was doing / had done** the washing up.
2 The ground was wet when I **was leaving / left** the house in the morning. It **rained / had rained** during the night.
3 'Why were you out in the rain?' 'I **brought / was bringing** in the washing.'
4 When I **arrived / was arriving** home, my mum **helped / had helped** me with my homework.
5 After we **worked / had worked** for an hour, we **stopped / were stopping** for a rest.
6 Tom **was driving / had driven** home when he **was crashing / crashed** the car.
7 My dad **was getting up / got up**, **had / was having** breakfast and **went / had gone** to work.
8 I **had / was having** a headache because I **wasn't eating / hadn't eaten** since the day before.

6 Complete the text. Use the past simple, the past continuous and the past perfect form of the verbs in brackets.

Sylvia's earliest memory

It was about a week after my third birthday. My aunt [1]_____ (give) me a new doll as a present, and while I [2]_____ (play) with it, I [3]_____ (notice) that my other dolls were all quite dirty in comparison. I [4]_____ (decide) to give them a bath. When I [5]_____ (wash) them all, I [6]_____ (take) them outside and [7]_____ (put) them on the grass. It was a warm day and the sun [8]_____ (shine). While I [9]_____ (wait) for the dolls to dry, I [10]_____ (hear) a shout from inside, so I [11]_____ (look) in through the window. Water [12]_____ (pour) down from the kitchen ceiling onto the floor. I [13]_____ (not turn) the taps off in the bathroom. I remember that my dad was really angry because he [14]_____ (decorate) the kitchen the previous week.

7 Write notes about one of your earliest memories. Use the questions to help you.
1 How old were you? Where were you? Who were you with? How were you feeling?
2 Describe the scene. What were you/other people doing? What was the weather like?
3 What happened? Describe the events. How did you feel?

8 SPEAKING Tell the class about your earliest memory.

> One day when I was about six years old, ...

Speaking tip
Do not read directly from your notes. You can look at your notes from time to time, but when you are speaking, look at your audience. Always speak slowly and clearly.

Unit 2 • Memories   15

2C CULTURE
Remembering the past

I can discuss the significance of important days.

1 Quickly read the text. Underline the part of the text that talks about the ceremony in the photo.

Poppy Day

Poppy Day, 11 November, is the day when people in Britain remember the soldiers that died in the First World War (1914–18), the Second World War (1939–45) and all other wars since. The first Poppy Day was in 1921. The First World War had ended three
5 years earlier, but it was still very difficult, often impossible, for ex-soldiers in Britain to find employment. So some of them started making and selling red paper poppies. They gave the money that they raised to ex-soldiers who were disabled or unemployed, and to the families of soldiers who had died. The choice of flower
10 was significant. During the war, the soldiers had noticed poppies growing every year on the battlefields in Belgium and the north of France. A well-known poem from that time, written by a Canadian soldier, begins with the lines

In Flanders* fields the poppies blow
15 *Between the crosses, row on row,*
That mark our place*; …

In the days leading up to Poppy Day, about 32 million people in Britain buy and wear small poppies. Some people choose to wear white poppies because they think that white symbolises
20 peace. Then, at 11 a.m. on 11 November (at the moment when the First World War ended) there's a two-minute silence. Many people stop and think quietly about the soldiers who died. There are ceremonies at war memorials in towns and villages all over the country. The most important ceremony is in London, when
25 the Queen and the Prime Minister lay wreaths of poppies at the Cenotaph, a monument to soldiers who died in battle.

*(*Flanders* = the north of Belgium; *our place* = our graves)

2 Read the text. Choose the best answers.
1 On 11 November people remember
  a soldiers who have died since 1921.
  b soldiers who have died in wars since 1914.
  c soldiers who died in the two world wars.

2 Why did ex-soldiers start making poppies?
  a Because they couldn't find a job.
  b Because they were disabled.
  c Because they didn't have families.
3 They chose to make poppies because
  a they had seen poppies growing on the battlefields.
  b a Canadian soldier had written a poem about poppies.
  c poppies are popular in Belgium and the north of France.
4 On Poppy Day
  a 32 million people sell poppies.
  b people wear red or white poppies.
  c people buy and wear 32 million white poppies.
5 During the two-minute silence people
  a walk to a ceremony in their town or village.
  b think about the moment the First World War ended.
  c stop and think about soldiers who have died.

3 🎧 1.09 Listen to people talking about Poppy Day. Tick the people who wear a poppy.

Speaker 1 ☐   Speaker 2 ☐   Speaker 3 ☐

4 🎧 1.09 Complete the sentences. Then listen again and check.
1 I think it's very _____ to remember the soldiers who _____ in wars.
2 They _____ the ultimate sacrifice – they _____ their lives for other people.
3 I think we need to stop thinking about the _____ and think about the _____.
4 We should try to _____ wars, not _____ them.
5 It's important to look after _____ when they come home.
6 Soldiers risk their lives to _____ the people at _____.

5 Say if you agree or disagree with each sentence in exercise 4.

6 **SPEAKING** Work in pairs. Discuss the questions.
1 Is it important to remember soldiers who died fighting for our country? Why?/Why not?
2 Is there a day in your country when people remember soldiers who died in wars?

●●○ **Vocabulary Builder 2.2: Adjective prefixes: p. 129**

16   Unit 2 • Memories

2D GRAMMAR — used to

I can talk about things that were true in the past but aren't now.

1 🎧 **1.10** Read and listen to the conversation. When Julia's grandma was young, did she have:
a a car?   b a radio?   c a TV?

Julia   What was life like in the village when you were young, grandma?
Grandma   Oh, it was very different.
Julia   What did you use to do in the evenings?
Grandma   We used to sit and chat, or listen to the radio.
Julia   Did you use to watch television?
Grandma   No, we didn't have a television. And we didn't have a car.
Julia   Really?
Grandma   No. So we didn't use to leave the village very often.

2 Underline all the examples of *used to* in the conversation in exercise 1.

3 Read the *Learn this!* box. Choose the correct words in the rule and complete the examples.

> **LEARN THIS!**
>
> **used to**
> 1 We use *used to* for **past / present / future** habits or situations that are now **the same / different**.
>   My dad ¹_____ smoke, but he doesn't now.
> 2 The form of *used to* is the same for all persons.
>   **affirmative**
>   My parents ²_____ live in London.
>   **negative**
>   I ³_____ have a DVD player.
>   **interrogative**
>   ⁴_____ you ⁵_____ walk to school? Yes, I did./ No, I didn't.
>   Where ⁶_____ Danny ⁷_____ live?

4 🎧 **1.11** **PRONUNCIATION** Listen and repeat the sentences. How is the 's' pronounced in *used to*: /s/ or /z/? How is *to* pronounced?
1 We used to sit and chat.
2 We didn't use to leave the village very often.
3 Did you use to watch television?

5 Complete the sentences with the affirmative, negative or interrogative form of *used to* and the verbs in the box.

| be do like live speak work |

1 My sister _____ this town, but she hates it now.
2 Where _____ she _____, before she lived in London?
3 She _____ any exercise, but now she goes running every day.
4 She _____ any Italian, but now she's almost fluent.
5 My mum _____ in a bank, but she's unemployed now.
6 _____ she _____ a waitress before she became an actress?

● ● ● **Grammar Builder 2.2:** *used to*: p. 111

6 🎧 **1.12** Listen to a description of a ghost town. Why did it become a ghost town?

7 🎧 **1.12** Listen again. Choose the correct words to complete the sentences about Fairview today.
1 It **has / doesn't** have a population of 2,000 now.
2 People **work / don't work** in the gold mines now.
3 People **eat / don't eat** in the saloon now.
4 People **buy / don't buy** snacks at the coffee shop.
5 Tourists **visit / don't visit** the town now.
6 People **can / can't** stay at the hotel now.
7 There **is / isn't** a road.

8 Rewrite the sentences in exercise 7 so that they are true about Fairview in the past. Use the affirmative or negative form of *used to*.
1 *It used to have a population of 2,000.*

9 Work with a partner. Think about life in your country either 20, 50 or 100 years ago. Make notes using these headings.
1 transport   3 entertainment   5 politics
2 work   4 education   6 food and drink

10 **SPEAKING** Tell the class about your ideas.

> A hundred years ago, there were hardly any cars. People used to walk …

Unit 2 • Memories   17

2E READING
Lost in New York

I can understand a magazine article about a man who lost his memory.

1 Read the text quickly. Which sentence is not true?
1 Doug lost his memory and has never recovered it.
2 Doug lost his memory but later remembered who he was.
3 Doug lost his memory but has found his family and friends again.

2 Put the events in the correct order.
a Staff at the hospital found a phone number in Doug's bag.
b Doug woke up on a subway train in New York.
c The police sent Doug to hospital.
d Doug met his family and old friends.
e Doug worked in Paris.
f An old friend made a documentary about Doug's experiences.
g Nadine took him home.
h Doug went to a police station.
i Doug's ex-girlfriend, Nadine, identified him.

3 Are the sentences true or false?
1 Doug was wearing warm clothes when he woke up on the subway.
2 Very few people have ever had such serious memory loss as Doug.
3 The hospital authorities didn't want to release Doug until they knew who he was.
4 Doug discovered that he was quite rich.
5 Doug recognised his family and friends immediately.
6 Doug's sisters think that his personality has changed since his memory loss.

4 Match the words (1–12), which are highlighted in the text, with their nearest equivalents (a–l).

1 skull   a beach shoes
2 flip-flops   b memory loss
3 rucksack   c confused
4 baffled   d beautiful
5 tag   e send home
6 amnesia   f shown
7 discharge   g accompanied
8 at once   h head
9 escorted   i confident
10 stunning   j bag
11 outgoing   k immediately
12 portrayed   l label

LEARN THIS!
Adjectives + prepositions
Some adjectives are followed by certain prepositions when used before a noun or pronoun.
John is **nervous about** his exams.
I'm **fed up with** this book.
Jane's parents are very **proud of** her.

5 Read the *Learn this!* box. Find the sentences in the text and complete them with the correct prepositions.
1 The doctors were surprised _____ the severity of his memory loss. (*paragraph 3*)
2 He was worried _____ meeting his family and friends. (*paragraph 6*)
3 According to them, he has become much more relaxed and isn't scared _____ showing his feelings. (*paragraph 6*)
4 He's happy _____ his new life. (*paragraph 7*)

● ● ● Vocabulary Builder 2.3: Adjectives + prepositions: p. 129

6 **SPEAKING** Work in pairs. Complete each sentence in three different ways. Use your imagination. Then tell your partner.
1 I was really surprised at …
2 I was worried about …
3 I'm really scared of …
4 I'm very happy about …

18 Unit 2 • Memories

Unknown white male

On 3 July 2003, a 35-year-old Englishman called Doug Bruce walked into a police station in Coney Island, New York, and told the police that he did not know his own name. He had woken up a few minutes earlier on a subway train, with bumps on his skull and a headache, and had found he had no idea where he was going, where he had been, or who he was. 'I was scared,' he said later, when talking about the experience. 'I didn't know anything. It was frightening, it was like being in the darkness.'

Doug went to a police station because he had nowhere else to go. He was wearing a T-shirt, shorts and flip-flops and he had a rucksack with a few possessions in it: a Spanish phrase book, a bunch of keys and a map of New York. The police were baffled. 'We'd never had anything like this before,' says Lieutenant Pete Pena. They sent Doug to Coney Island Hospital. On his name tag, the nurse wrote 'Unknown white male'.

The doctors were surprised at the severity of his memory loss. Although Doug could form sentences without difficulty, he remembered nothing about his own past and seemed to know little about the world. One specialist at the hospital, Dr Leonid Vorobyev, admitted that he had only ever seen such serious amnesia 'in the movies and in my textbooks'. Doug was diagnosed as suffering from 'total retrograde amnesia', which is extremely rare.

The hospital authorities would not discharge Doug until he had been identified. Eventually, hospital staff found a phone number inside the phrase book in his rucksack. It was the number of an ex-girlfriend's mother, but she didn't know who he was. However, when Doug spoke to his ex-girlfriend, Nadine, she recognised his voice at once. 'Is that you, Doug?' she asked. 'I don't know,' came the reply. Nadine went to the hospital, told the doctors who Doug was, and escorted him home.

'Home' turned out to be a stunning apartment in downtown Manhattan, which he shared with two dogs and three parrots. Doug discovered that he had previously lived in Paris, where he had made a lot of money working at the stock exchange.

Now that Doug had discovered his identity, he had to cope with other challenges. He was worried about meeting his family and friends. They seemed like strangers to him. His sisters told him that he had changed: before his memory loss, he had been very sociable and outgoing, but rarely showed his emotions. According to them, he has now become much more relaxed and isn't scared of showing his feelings.

For Doug, life has started all over again. He has tasted chocolate mousse and strawberries for what he believes is the first time. He has seen snow fall, and fireworks explode 'for the first time'. He's happy with his new life. His story has now been portrayed on film. An old friend of his, director Rupert Murray, has made a documentary about Doug's extraordinary experiences called *Unknown White Male*.

2F EVERYDAY ENGLISH
Narrating events

I can describe and react to a story.

Martin	I remember my first date with a girl really well.
Julia	How interesting! Were you excited?
Martin	I was feeling more nervous than excited, to be honest, as I'd asked out the most popular girl in the school. I couldn't believe that she had agreed to go out with me. I was very shy, and not at all confident.
Julia	So what happened?
Martin	At first, nothing. I'd made a list of topics to talk about. But the list was in my pocket and I couldn't remember any of the topics, so we walked to the café in complete silence.
Julia	How embarrassing! What happened next?
Martin	It got even more embarrassing. I got her an orange juice from the bar, and I decided to try to be funny. So I put the juice on a tray, and I carried it over to the table with one hand like a waiter. Then I tripped and I just threw the juice all over her. She was really shocked.
Julia	Oh no! What a disaster!
Martin	In the end, I just took her home – again in silence – and I never had the courage to speak to her again.
Julia	Poor you! But – how funny!

1 🎧 **1.13** Read and listen to the dialogue. In your own words, explain what two things went wrong on Martin's date.

2 Tick (✓) the sequencing words that Julia and Martin use.

after a few minutes ☐	a few minutes later ☐
after that ☐ at first ☐	finally ☐ first ☐
in the end ☐ later on ☐	next ☐ then ☐

LEARN THIS! Exclamatory sentences
1 We can use exclamatory sentences beginning *What ...* or *How ...* to react strongly to something.
2 We use *how* with an adjective.
   How wonderful!   How unpleasant!
3 We use *what* with a noun, even if it has an adjective before it.
   What a singer!   What an amazing goal!

3 Read the *Learn this!* box. Find four exclamatory sentences in the dialogue in exercise 1.

●●○ **Grammar Builder 2.3: Exclamatory sentences: p. 111**

4 🎧 **1.14** Listen to two dialogues. What are they about? Choose from a–e.
a going to a great party   d meeting a new family member
b meeting a celebrity   e staying at an amazing hotel
c starting at a new school

5 🎧 **1.14** Listen again to the dialogues. Choose the best answer.

Dialogue 1
1 Zoe's birthday
   a was fantastic all day.
   b started badly but was fantastic in the end.
   c started well but was terrible in the end.
2 Zoe and her friend saw a film at
   a the first cinema they went to.
   b the second cinema they went to.
   c the third cinema they went to.
3 Johnny Depp
   a sat next to Zoe and her friend in the cinema.
   b gave Zoe and her friend tickets for the film.
   c bought Zoe and her friend drinks and popcorn.

Dialogue 2
4 Who has just had a baby?
   a Emily's sister.
   b Emily Rose.
   c Patrick's sister.
5 When Patrick first saw the baby,
   a he was surprised.
   b he wasn't very interested.
   c he immediately thought she was beautiful.
6 Patrick felt proud because
   a Emily Rose was so cute.
   b his friends are silly.
   c he's Emily Rose's uncle.

6 **SPEAKING** Work in pairs. Make notes about a real or imagined memorable event (e.g. a birthday, a journey, a holiday, your first day at school).
1 Where were you?/What were you doing?/Who were you with?/How old were you?
2 What happened? Describe the events. How did people react?/How did you feel?
3 What happened in the end?

7 **SPEAKING** Work in pairs. Use your notes to prepare a dialogue. Use sequencing words from exercise 2 and exclamatory sentences.

8 **SPEAKING** Act out your dialogue to the class.

●●○ **Vocabulary Builder 2.4: *-ed/-ing* adjectives: p. 129**

20 Unit 2 • Memories

2G WRITING — A narrative

I can write a narrative, telling the story of an event.

1 Read the story. Which of these things did Joe *not* do?
1. go out with two school friends
2. have a fairly quiet evening
3. have dinner in a restaurant
4. meet some girls
5. buy cinema tickets
6. see a film
7. go to a night club
8. hear live music
9. phone Anna
10. bump into Anna again

A great night out
by Joe

Last year, I went out to celebrate my birthday with two other boys from my class. We were planning a fairly quiet evening – a quick pizza followed by a film at the cinema. However, the evening turned out to be much more exciting than we expected!

While we were eating our dinner, a group of three girls came into the restaurant and sat down at the next table. We started chatting and found out that one of them – Anna – was celebrating her birthday that evening too. She suggested going out together – all six of us – after our meal. They seemed really nice, so we agreed. We decided not to go the cinema, even though we already had tickets for the film. Instead, we set off towards the town centre where there's a night club that plays really good music. We turned up just as a live band was starting to play! We danced for hours and had a great time with our new friends.

At the end of the night, Anna gave me her mobile phone number and talked about meeting up again. Unfortunately, I couldn't call her because I lost the number. I think I threw it away by mistake.

I still think about that evening quite often. It's a shame that I lost Anna's number, but maybe I'll bump into her and her friends one evening and we'll all go out again. I hope so!

2 Complete the paragraph plan. Use phrases in the box.

> description of the events   how you feel about it now
> setting the scene   what happened afterwards

Paragraph 1   Introduction: _____
Paragraph 2   Main body: _____
Paragraph 3   Follow-up: _____
Paragraph 4   Conclusion: _____

3 Complete the sentences with phrasal verbs from the story.
1. Let's go ____ for dinner tonight.
2. Out new teacher turned _____ to be from Australia.
3. Sit _____ – I've got some amazing news!
4. Did you find _____ her name?
5. She usually sets _____ for work at 6.00 am.
6. You've turned _____ late for class again!
7. The CD was broken so I threw it _____ .
8. I bumped ____ a friend from primary school yesterday.

● ● ○ **Vocabulary Builder 2.5: Phrasal verbs: p. 130**

Writing tip: conjunctions

We can often join short sentences together by using a conjunction. The simplest conjunction is *and*.

I left school. I walked home.
*I left school **and** walked home.*

Try to use these other conjunctions as well, to join short sentences and improve the style of your writing:

as   because   but   even though   since   so   though   whereas   while

4 Read the writing tip above. Which conjunctions from the list can you find in Joe's story?

5 Use conjunctions from the writing tip to complete the sentences. Sometimes more than one answer is possible.
1. I listened to music _____ I walked to the shops.
2. I'm not going to the night club _____ it's too expensive.
3. My dad gave me a present _____ I passed my exam.
4. He was still hungry, _____ he had eaten a whole pizza.
5. I'll be back late, _____ don't wait up for me.

6 You are going to write a narrative called 'A terrible night out'. In pairs, think of all the things that could possibly go wrong during a night out. Make a list.

7 Plan your narrative. Make notes using ideas from exercise 6 and following the paragraph plan in exercise 2.

8 Write your narrative using your notes from exercise 7. Remember to use conjunctions to improve the style of your writing.

LANGUAGE REVIEW 1–2

Vocabulary

1 Complete the words to make adjectives to describe clothes.

1 st _ _ p _
2 c _ _ _ k
3 s _ _ n _
4 b _ _ _ y
5 c _ _ t _ _
6 m _ _ _ h _ _ g

Mark   /6

2 Choose the correct words.

1 Jacob passed all his exams. He felt **relieved / upset**.
2 We waited for ages. We felt **fed up / pleased**.
3 Leah made her sister cry. She felt **guilty / homesick**.
4 Charlie watched TV all day. He felt **confused / bored**.
5 Amelia went to school wearing different socks. She felt **delighted / embarrassed**.

Mark   /5

Grammar

3 Complete the sentences with the present simple or the present continuous form of the verbs in brackets.

1 Josh _____ (not like) meat. He's a vegetarian.
2 Abigail _____ (catch) the bus every day at 7.30 a.m.
3 I _____ (meet) Liam tomorrow to finish our science project.
4 Can you hear Connor? He _____ (sing) in the shower again.
5 I'm fed up. My sister _____ (always / borrow) my clothes.
6 We _____ (stay) with my grandmother while the builders are in our house.

Mark   /6

4 Complete the sentences with the past simple, past continuous or past perfect form of the verbs in brackets.

1 Lucy was crying because she _____ (lose) her bag.
2 We _____ (call) the police because a strange man was following us.
3 Harry opened the front door and _____ (go) inside.
4 When William fell off his chair, everybody _____ (laugh).
5 Joseph stayed at home because he _____ (break) his leg.
6 Caitlin _____ (do) her homework when her boyfriend called.

Mark   /6

5 Rewrite the sentences using the negative or the interrogative form of *used to*.

1 I used to have a bath every night. (?)
   Did you use to have a bath every night?
2 Mia used to watch cartoons on TV. (?)
   _____
3 We used to go abroad on holiday. (–)
   _____
4 I used to wear flowery dresses. (–)
   _____
5 Alex used to sleep in the same room as his brother. (?)
   _____
6 They used to live in the city centre. (?)
   _____

Mark   /5

Everyday English

6 Complete the dialogue with the words in the box.

| back   from   look like   looks   nice |

Girl What's this photo?
Boy It's ¹_____ our weekend in Berlin.
Girl You ²_____ you're having fun. Who's the boy in the red trousers?
Boy He's my friend George. He ³_____ a bit like Jude Law.
Girl Yes, you're right! Is your girlfriend in the photo?
Boy Yes. She's the one at the ⁴_____ in the yellow top.
Girl She looks ⁵_____.

Mark   /5

7 Put the lines (a–e) in the correct order to complete the dialogue.

a So what did your mum do in the end?
b I got really upset because my mum wouldn't let me take my teddy bear.
c Poor you! What a shame!
d Really? What happened?
e I know. I cried and cried and I refused to leave the house without it.

Boy I remember my first day at school as if it was only yesterday.
Girl ☐
Boy ☐
Girl ☐
Boy ☐
Girl ☐
Boy Well, she had to give in and let me take it, but she wasn't happy.

Mark   /5

Total   /38

EXAM CHALLENGE Workbook pages 94–97

22 Language Review 1–2

Skills Round-up 1–2

Speaking

1 Look at the photo. Describe the people and the clothes.

Reading

2 Read the letter quickly. Find the names of two of the people in the photo in exercise 1. Who are the other two?

3 Read the letter again. Are the sentences true or false?
1 Marek and Sarah have never met face to face.
2 Vlasta used to live with Sarah's family.
3 Sarah's house caught fire during a barbecue in the garden.
4 Marek has nearly finished his university studies.
5 He wants advice about finding a job in England for a year.
6 Vlasta has not always had blond hair.

Listening

4 🎧 1.15 Listen to the phone conversation. Where is Marek going to stay when he arrives in England?

5 🎧 1.15 Listen again and complete the sentences.
1 Marek's sister teaches _____.
2 Sarah's parents work for a _____ law firm.
3 Marek is planning to arrive in England in the month of _____.
4 Marek hopes to find a room or flat on the _____.
5 Sarah's _____ has just left home.
6 Sarah's family live at 46 _____ Gardens.

Writing

6 Imagine you were a guest at the barbecue that Marek mentions in his letter. Write a narrative describing the events. Use the words and phrases below to help you

Verbs			
burn	set fire (to something)	put out a fire	smoulder
Nouns			
fire engine	siren	firefighters	hose	smoke

Dear Sarah

I hope you don't mind me writing to you. You probably don't remember me, but we met about three years ago. My sister Vlasta used to work as an au pair for the family next door to you, and I visited her for a week. We both went to a barbecue at your house. Your dad set fire to a tree in the back garden and had to call the fire brigade. I'm sure you remember that!

Anyway, I'm writing to you now because Vlasta remembers that your parents are both lawyers. I'm studying Law at university here in the Czech Republic. It's a five-year course, and I'm just about to finish my second year. I've decided to spend next year working in the UK, partly to improve my English and partly to earn some money. Could your mum or dad give me any advice about how to get a job in a law firm? I'm prepared to do any kind of work – I don't mind making tea!

I'm enclosing a recent photo of me, Vlasta and two friends of ours. Vlasta is the girl with long, blond hair. (It used to be dark.) I'm the one on the left, with short, dark hair and a long-sleeved T-shirt.

Best wishes

Marek Zeman

3 Nine to five

THIS UNIT INCLUDES
Vocabulary • jobs and gender • places of work • activities at work • describing work • expressing an opinion • agreeing and disagreeing • agent nouns • phrasal verbs: separable and inseparable
Grammar • defining relative clauses • non-defining relative clauses
Speaking • discussing working abroad • discussing work and gender • a job interview
Writing • a job application

A VOCABULARY AND LISTENING
The world of work

I can talk about jobs and work.

1 Make a list of jobs. How many can you think of in two minutes?

2 **SPEAKING** In your opinion, what is the most interesting job on your list, and why? Compare your ideas with the class.

• • Vocabulary Builder 3.1: Jobs and gender: p.130

3 Read the adverts. Use the words in red to complete the vocabulary tables.

We are looking for...
people to work **part-time** in our busy **call** centre. Working **hours** are 5 p.m. to 9 p.m., Monday to Friday. You will work in a small **team**, answering the **phone** and dealing with the **public**. You will **earn** £7.50 an **hour**. The work is **challenging**, but fun.

We need an experienced receptionist to work full-time in our **bank**. You will be in **charge** of the reception desk and your role will be to greet **customers** and answer queries. Applicants must be able to **use** a computer. You will work on your **own**, and will report directly to the **manager**. Salary negotiable.

Labourers needed to work on a building site. 35-hour week. Skilled and unskilled workers required. No experience necessary – on-the-job training will be given.

Places of work

1 _____	office	studio
hospital	restaurant	surgery
2 _____ centre	school	building 3 _____
laboratory	shop	

Activities at work

answer the 4 _____	do manual work
be in 5 _____ of ...	deal with the 6 _____
do paperwork	work on your 7 _____
8 _____ a computer	work in a 9 _____
greet 10 _____	

Describing work

stressful	busy	fun
11 _____	menial	easy
boring	unskilled	12 _____
full-time	13 _____	

4 **SPEAKING** Look at the photos. Describe the jobs, using the words in the vocabulary tables in exercise 3 to help you.

> I think the man in photo 1 is a ...
> He's working in a ...
> His job looks challenging.

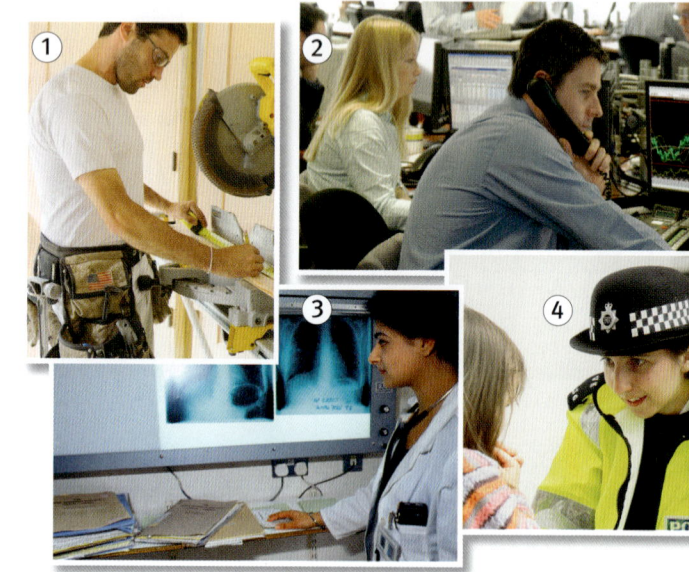

5 🎧 1.16 Listen to the game show, 'What's my job?'. What are the two jobs?

6 🎧 1.17 Complete the questions with the words in the box. Then listen and check.

> anything   clothes   dangerous   earn   hands
> homes   office   outside   sell   travel

1 Do you usually work _____?
2 Do you buy or _____ anything?
3 Do you _____ a lot of money?
4 Do you wear special _____ for your work?
5 Is your job _____?
6 Do you visit people's _____?
7 Do you _____ a lot for work?
8 Do you work with your _____?
9 Do you make _____?
10 Do you work in an _____?

7 **SPEAKING** Work in pairs. Play 'What's my job?'. Remember, you can only answer 'yes' or 'no'. Use the questions in exercise 6 and think of more questions using the vocabulary tables in exercise 3.

Unit 3 • Nine to five

3B GRAMMAR
Defining relative clauses

I can describe a person, thing or place using defining relative clauses.

1 Read the text. What was bad about working as a water caddy?

The worst jobs in history: a water caddy

In 18th century England, there were no water pipes or taps in houses. In the countryside, people got their water from wells or rivers. But at this time, thousands were moving to cities where there was no easy water supply. A water caddy was a person who delivered water to people's homes. It was extremely hard work, and involved carrying a barrel of water which weighed about 30 kilos. And it could be dangerous, too, if you were taking water to somebody whose home was on the top floor!

2 Underline examples of *who*, *whose*, *where* and *which* in the text in exercise 1. Then complete the rules in the *Learn this!* box.

> **LEARN THIS!**
> **Relative pronouns:** *who*, *whose*, *where* and *which*
> 1 We use _____ for things and animals.
> 2 We use _____ for people.
> 3 We use _____ for places.
> 4 We use _____ to indicate possession.

3 Complete the questions with *who*, *whose*, *where* and *which*. Then answer them.
1 What do you call a place _____ people go to watch films?
2 What do you call a person _____ job is to design buildings?
3 What do you call a woman _____ takes orders and serves food in a restaurant?
4 What do you call a camera _____ records video pictures?
5 What do you call a shop _____ you can buy all kinds of food and drink?
6 What do you call a person _____ is in charge of a shop or a company?
7 What do you call a machine _____ records TV programmes?
8 What do you call a person _____ place of work is a surgery?

4 Read the *Look out!* box. In which sentences in exercise 3 could you use *that*?

> **Look out!**
> We often use *that* instead of *which*. In informal English, we can also use *that* instead of *who*.

5 Complete the text with *who*, *whose*, *where* and *which*.

The worst jobs in history: a link boy

In 18th Century London, the areas of the city ¹_____ rich people lived had street lamps. However, poorer areas of the city were full of streets ²_____ had no lights. And streets ³_____ were dark were often full of muggers, murderers and other criminals! Rich people ⁴_____ journey home at night passed through these poor areas needed to take some form of lighting with them. A link boy was a boy ⁵_____ showed rich people the way home through the back streets. The children ⁶_____ did this job needed to have a map of the city in their heads. They also needed to be aware of the dangers ⁷_____ might be around any dark corner. And the money was not good. The rich people ⁸_____ lives the link boys made safer normally paid only one penny per trip.

6 Decide who had the worse job: a water caddy or a link boy. Give reasons for your decision. Can you think of any jobs that are worse than both?

7 Read the *Learn this!* box. Which relative clauses in exercise 5 are in the middle and which are at the end?

> **LEARN THIS!**
> **Defining relative clauses**
> A defining relative clause comes after a noun and tells us which person, thing or place we are talking about. It can be in the middle or at the end of a sentence.
> She's the vet **who looked after my cat**.
> The hospital **where my sister works** is enormous.

● ● ○ Grammar Builder 3.1: Defining relative clauses: p. 111

8 **SPEAKING** Work in pairs. Take turns to define the words in the box. Your partner has to guess what you are defining.

> a dentist   a carpenter   a journalist   a laboratory
> a studio   a building site   an MP3 player   an Italian
> a salary

> It's a person who/whose …
> It's something which/whose …
> It's a place where …

Unit 3 • Nine to five **25**

3C CULTURE
Working abroad

I can discuss the advantages and disadvantages of working abroad.

1 Look at the text and the charts. What is the most popular job for EU migrants in the UK?

All in a day's work

If you walk into a factory or warehouse anywhere in Britain and listen to the conversations among the employees, you are likely to hear not just English but also Czech, Hungarian, Polish and a variety of other European languages. Since the EU welcomed ten new member states in 2004 and a further two in 2007, thousands of people from these countries have decided to come to the UK in search of better job opportunities.

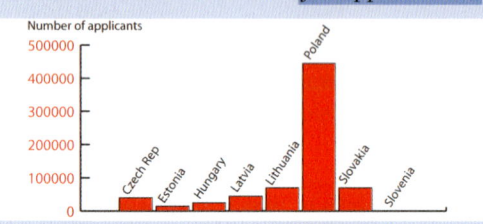

Britain is one of only three EU countries that gave full rights to work to immigrants from the ten countries which joined in 2004. An independent survey of almost 2,200 British companies shows that 12% of employers now employ workers from these new EU states. Many are highly skilled; the stereotypical image of unskilled workers from 'new Europe' is not accurate. A third have taken jobs as administrators and supervisors. Only 4% work in construction.

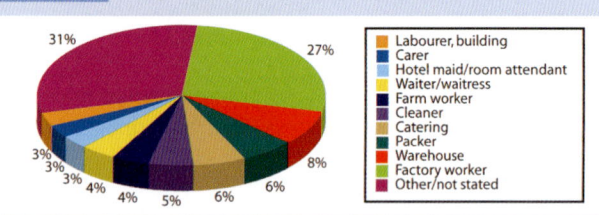

Most of the migrant workers in Britain are young – 82% are aged between 18 and 34. Surveys suggest that the majority are happy with their new lives, but also plan to return to their native country at some point in the future.

2 Answer the questions using the information in the text and the chart.
1 Why can you hear so many different languages in an ordinary British factory?
2 In total, how many countries joined the EU during the period 2004 to 2007?
3 What are three most common nationalities for EU migrants in Britain?
3 Why is it easier for people from new member states to work in Britain than in most other EU countries?
6 What percentage of EU migrants work on farms?
7 What percentage of EU migrants are older than 34?
8 What is the long-term plan for most EU migrants?

3 Complete the definitions with the highlighted words from the text.
1 _____ are people who do paperwork.
2 _____ are chances to find work.
3 _____ are people who work for a person or company.
4 A _____ is a place where goods are stored.
5 _____ are people who are in charge of a team at work.
6 _____ are people or companies who give work to other people.
7 _____ are people who move to a country from another country.

4 🎧 1.18 Listen to three recent immigrants talking about life in the UK. Which speaker (1–3) is having the worst experience?

5 🎧 1.18 Listen again and match each speaker (1–3) with two opinions (a–f).
a You can earn a lot of money in Britain if you are prepared to work hard.
b It's easy to find menial jobs in Britain, but very difficult to find an interesting job.
c Most British people are happy to work with people from other countries.
d British people are impatient if you can't speak good English.
e Renting a flat is very expensive in Britain, so you have to share with other people.
f Some people in Britain are worried that immigrants from EU nations are taking all the jobs.

6 **SPEAKING** Work in pairs. Discuss the advantages and disadvantages of going to work abroad. Would you like to do it?

> You can earn money.

> Yes, but on the other hand, you might be lonely.

Expressing an opinion
I think that …   In my opinion, …   In my view, …
Agreeing and disagreeing
Yes, I agree.   That's right.   I think so too.
I don't agree.   On the other hand …
That may be true, but …

● ● ● **Vocabulary Builder 3.2: Agent nouns: p. 131**

26 Unit 3 • Nine to five

3D GRAMMAR
Non-defining relative clauses

I can correctly use non-defining relative clauses.

1 Read the text quickly. What is Walter O'Rourke's job, and why does he do it?

Walter O'Rourke, who works as a ticket inspector on trains in New Jersey, is a rich man. In fact his salary, which is around $50,000 a year, is just pocket money to Mr O'Rourke, whose investments earn him about $2 million each year. So why does he choose to work? The answer is that Mr O'Rourke, who was born in 1939, has always loved trains. For him, working on a crowded train in New Jersey is more fun than relaxing in Florida, where he has two houses. 'There's no place that I'd rather be,' he says. 'I don't need the money. I need the job.'

2 Read the text again, ignoring the relative clauses in red. Does the text make sense without them?

3 Read the *Learn this!* box and choose the correct words to complete the rules. Use the relative clauses in red in exercise 1 to help you.

> **LEARN THIS!**
> **Non-defining relative clauses**
> 1 A non-defining relative clause comes immediately **before / after** a noun and gives us information about that noun.
> 2 It adds extra information to the sentence. The sentence **makes sense / does not make sense** without it.
> *Macy's department store is one of the largest shops in the world. It's in New York.*
> *Macy's department store, **which is in New York**, is one of the largest shops in the world.*
> 3 It **starts / ends** with a comma, and **starts / ends** with a comma or a full stop.

Look out!
In non-defining relative clauses, we use *who*, *whose*, *where* and *which*, but we do not use *that*.

4 Complete the text with the relative clauses (a–f).
 a which makes toys and games
 b who has worked with Jack since 1975
 c where his son and grandchildren live
 d who will be 90 years old next month
 e which started at just £4 a week
 f who are planning a big 90th birthday party for him

Jack Barnes, ¹____, still gets up at seven o'clock every morning and catches the bus to work. He has been an employee at the J.B. Bates & Sons factory, ²____, for more than 60 years. In that time, his salary, ³____, has increased by 20,000%! Jack's colleagues, ⁴____, do not believe that Jack will ever retire. 'He loves his work too much,' says Bill Tanner, ⁵____. 'He talks about moving to Australia, ⁶____, but he'll never do it.'

● ● **Grammar Builder 3.2: Non-defining relative clauses: p. 112**

5 Combine the two simple sentences to make one sentence. Use a non-defining relative clause.
 1 Her son works in a factory. He lives in Spain.
   Her son, who lives in Spain, works in a factory.
 2 My sister wants to be a musician. She plays the violin.
 3 I'd like to visit Buckingham Palace. The Queen lives there.
 4 I left my new phone on the bus. I bought it last week.
 5 Martin speaks fluent Polish. His mum comes from Warsaw.
 6 Last month, I visited Jamaica. My grandfather was born there.
 7 My uncle earns a lot of money. He works for a bank.
 8 The Ferrari 550 can go at 320 km/h. It has a 5.5 litre engine.
 9 Jake is going to study maths at university. His sister is in my class.

6 Make a list of five famous people. Write a simple sentence about each person.
 Nigel Kennedy has a house in Poland.
 Angelina Jolie …

7 **SPEAKING** Work in pairs. Take turns to be A and B, using your sentences from exercise 6. Student A: Read a sentence to Student B. Student B: Try to expand the sentence with extra information about the famous person.

> Nigel Kennedy has a house in Poland.

> Nigel Kennedy, who is a famous violinist, has a house in Poland.

Unit 3 • Nine to five 27

3E READING: Reversing roles

I can understand and react to a magazine article about gender and work.

1 Read the puzzle. What is the answer?

> A man and his son are in a serious car accident. The man dies and the son is taken to hospital. When he gets there, the surgeon sees the boy and says: 'I can't operate on this boy. He's my son!' How can this be?

2 Why do many people find it difficult to answer this puzzle?

3 Look at the photos. What jobs are the man and woman doing? Choose from the jobs in the box.

labourer   midwife   mechanic   nurse   plumber   surgeon

4 Read the texts quickly. Check your answers to exercise 3. How do you think people react when they find out about these people's jobs?

Woman's work?

In many ways, David Cunningham is a stereotypical Scottish man. In his free time, he plays golf, goes to football matches, and meets his friends in the local pub, all the things you'd expect a young, active man
5 to do. And like many men, he isn't very good at housework. He's untidy, hardly ever hoovers and he's never cooked a meal in his life. However, one thing about him does not fit this stereotype: his job. David Cunningham is a midwife.

10 Although some women are surprised when they find out that their midwife is a man, David has a good reputation in the part of Scotland where he works. In his opinion, it's because of the way he carries out his duties. 'I really care about the women that I look
15 after,' he says. He gets on well with the husbands too. 'Having another man there calms them,' he explains. 'And many of them feel more comfortable asking a man questions.'

'I've been qualified for fourteen years and I've
20 delivered hundreds of babies,' says David, who used to be a coal miner. 'There are only five or six male midwives in Scotland. When I started, I expected more men to join the profession, but the number hasn't really changed. People still see it as a job
25 which only women do.'

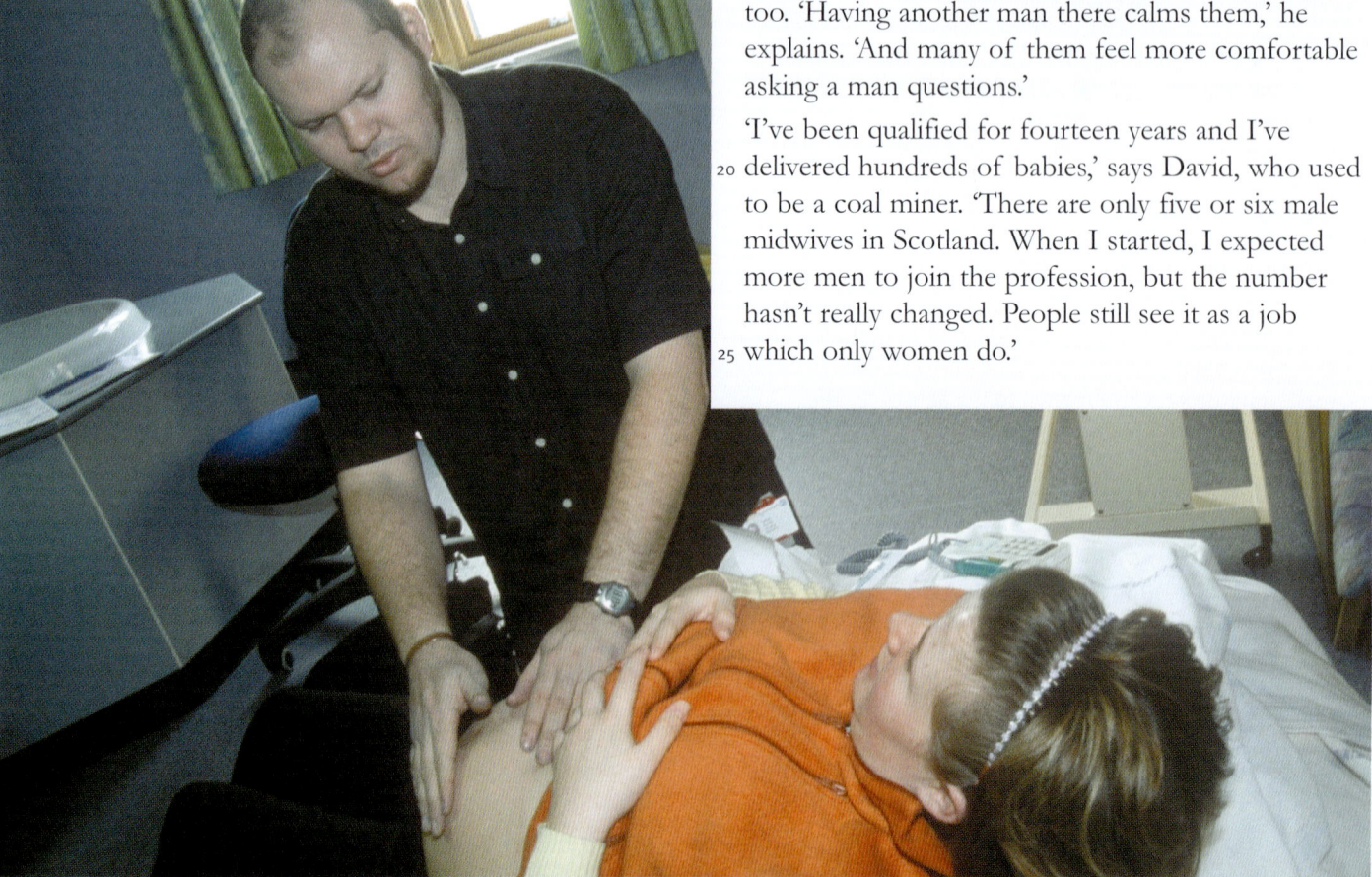

28   Unit 3 • Nine to five

A man's world?

Base 34 is a new garage in Montpellier, in the south of France. Customers who take their cars there for repairs may be surprised to find that all the employees are women.

When Herve Malige advertised for women who wanted to become mechanics, he received 120 applications. After tests and interviews, he chose fifteen. They included a nurse, a secretary, a beauty therapist and two flight attendants. They all wanted a chance to work in this traditionally male environment. 'I think a lot of people instinctively trust women more. And female customers might feel more comfortable with somebody who doesn't treat them as if they don't understand anything!'

Although most car mechanics are still men, the situation is gradually changing. Men are starting to leave the profession, and women are joining it. Why? In a word, technology. In the past, being a mechanic was a physically tough and dirty job. Now, cars are much more complicated than they used to be. You need patience and intelligence to work out what the problem is, not strength. Many people believe that this makes the job more suitable for women than for men.

5 Are the sentences true or false? Correct the false sentences.
1 David Cunningham does not have the same hobbies as most other men in Scotland.
2 Most women that David has worked with think that he is good at his job.
3 David gets on well with the women but not with their husbands.
4 David is not very experienced in his work.
5 There are not many male midwives in Scotland, but the number is increasing.
6 What is surprising about Base 34 is that no men work there.
7 Fifteen women applied to work at the garage.
8 The women had different jobs before working at the garage, but wanted a change.
9 The job of mechanic is changing because cars are getting simpler.
10 Many people think that there will be more female car mechanics in the future.

6 Find the phrasal verbs (1–5) in the texts. Match them with the definitions (a–e).

1 find out   a deduce
2 carry out   b care for
3 look after   c do
4 get on well/badly with   d learn, discover
5 work out   e have a good/bad relationship with

●●○ Vocabulary Builder 3.3: Phrasal verbs: separable and inseparable: p. 131

7 Look at the jobs in the box. Decide which jobs involve:
a helping or looking after people.
b working with small children or babies.
c working with heavy machinery.
d getting dirty.

Jobs aircraft pilot   astronaut   beauty therapist   builder   coal miner   flight attendant   kindergarten teacher   lorry driver   nurse   nanny   secretary

8 SPEAKING Work in pairs. Discuss the questions.
1 Would you expect a man or woman to do the jobs in exercise 7?
2 Do you think men and women are better at different jobs, or equally good at all jobs? Give reasons.
3 Would you mind doing a job that is traditionally carried out by people of the opposite sex? Why?/Why not?

3F EVERYDAY ENGLISH
A job interview

I can ask and answer questions at a job interview.

Manager	How did you find out about the job?
Callum	I saw your advert in the local newspaper.
Manager	Have you worked in a shop before?
Callum	Yes, I have. I used to help out at my uncle's shop.
Manager	Right. What did you do there?
Callum	Everything! I served customers. I cleaned, I stacked shelves ...
Manager	How long did you work there?
Callum	About two years, part-time.
Manager	I see. And why do you think you're the right person for this job?
Callum	Because I'm hard-working and reliable, and I enjoy dealing with the public. I'm also good at working in a team.
Manager	Well, thanks for coming in, Callum. We'll be in touch before the end of the week.

1 🎧 1.19 Read and listen to the dialogue. Then read the three job advertisements below. Which job did Callum apply for?

a
RECEPTIONIST
required for sports club near the city centre. We are looking for a reliable person who can work 10 hours a week (2 hours every evening, Monday to Friday). Computer skills essential.
£6 / hour

b
Waiter / Waitress
A busy café in the town centre needs a confident waiter or waitress to join our friendly, young team. Must have experience.
£6.30 / hour plus tips

c
Electrical store requires a part-time shop assistant for weekends only. Must enjoy dealing with customers.
£5.50 an hour

2 Find 1–3 below in the dialogue in exercise 1.
1 a phrase which means 'to put things on the shelves in a shop'.
2 an adjective which means '(somebody) that you can trust'.
3 a phrase which means 'to contact by phone or letter'.

3 🎧 1.20 **PRONUNCIATION** Listen and repeat the five questions. Copy the intonation. In which question does the voice go up at the end? What is the difference between this question and the others?

4 🎧 1.21 Match the definitions with the four jobs in the box. Then listen to the interview for a summer job. Which of the four jobs is it?

> fruit picker   gardener   life guard   market researcher

a A person who interviews ordinary members of the public to get information for companies.
b A person who takes fruit from trees or plants when it is ready.
c A person who looks after plants and flowers.
d A person who watches to make sure swimmers are safe.

5 🎧 1.21 Listen again. Number the questions in the order that you hear them. How many of the answers can you remember?
a What kinds of things do you do? ☐
b Are you in good physical health? ☐
c When can you start work? ☐
d Do you live locally? ☐
e Have you got any experience of this type of work? ☐
f Why do you want this job? ☐

6 🎧 1.22 **PRONUNCIATION** Read the speaking tip. Then listen and repeat the expressions. Copy the intonation.

> **Speaking tip**
>
> When someone responds to your question or to a statement you've made, show that you've listened to them, and understood what they said. Use these phrases.
> *Really?   That's great!   Right.   I see.   That's interesting. OK.*

7 Work in pairs. Plan an interview for one of the other jobs in exercises 1 or 4. Use questions from this page or invent your own. Include some phrases from the speaking tip.

8 Write your dialogue out. Then practise reading it in pairs.

9 **SPEAKING** Act out your dialogue to the class. The class votes on whether the applicant gets the job!

Unit 3 • Nine to five

3G WRITING
A job application

I can write a letter applying for a job.

1 Read the letter quickly. Answer the questions.
1 What job is Sandra applying for?
2 Where did she work last summer?
3 When can she start work?

The Manager
Lenny's Restaurant
Green Lane
Luton
LU17 9HY

13 Birch Avenue
Luton
LU13 7BU

19 June 2007

Dear Sir or Madam

1 I am writing to apply for the post of kitchen helper at Lenny's Restaurant which was advertised in last Saturday's newspaper.

2 I have considerable experience of working in catering. Last summer, I worked for six weeks as a waitress in my local café. My responsibilities there included taking orders and serving customers as well as cleaning the kitchen and washing up.

3 I consider myself to be reliable, hard-working and enthusiastic. If necessary, I can supply references from the café owner and also from a teacher at my school.

4 I would be very grateful for the opportunity to visit the restaurant and discuss my application with you in person. I am available for interview any day after school or on Saturdays. If my application is successful, I will be available to start work on 25 July, immediately after my exams.

I am enclosing my CV.

I look forward to hearing from you soon.

Yours faithfully,

Sandra Blunt

Sandra Blunt

2 In which paragraph (1, 2, 3 or 4) does Sandra mention:
a references that she can send?
b the job she is applying for?
c when she can start work?
d where she saw the job advert?
e her personal qualities?
f her experience of working in catering?

Writing tip
Avoid using informal expressions in formal letters. Find formal expressions that have the same meaning.

3 Find more formal ways of saying the underlined phrases in Sandra's letter.
1 I am writing to <u>ask you</u> for the <u>job</u> of kitchen helper.
2 <u>I've worked a lot</u> in catering.
3 <u>The things I had to do there</u> included taking orders.
4 <u>I think that I am</u> reliable, hard-working and enthusiastic.
5 I can <u>give you</u> references.
6 <u>I would really</u> like to visit the restaurant ...
7 ... and <u>talk about</u> my application <u>face to face</u>.
8 I <u>can</u> start work on 25 July.
9 <u>I'm sending</u> my CV.

4 Read the job advert. Think about what qualities and experience you might need for the job. Make notes.

Hotel Receptionist

We need an intelligent, friendly, confident person to work at our hotel in Oxford from 15 July to 31 August. Working hours are from 10 a.m. to 6 p.m. Your duties will include greeting guests, checking them in and out, answering the phone and taking bookings.

Please apply in writing to:
Queen Victoria Hotel
84–88 Beecham Rd
Oxford OX4 7UH

5 Write a formal letter of 120–150 words applying for the job. Follow the writing plan below.

Paragraph 1
- Mention the job you are applying for and where you saw the advert.

Paragraph 2
- Talk about why you are right for the job. Mention personal interests, and relevant experience and responsibilities.

Paragraph 3
- List your personal qualities and offer to send references.

Paragraph 4
- Say you would like to come for an interview and when you are available.
- Say when you could start work.

Unit 3 • Nine to five

Get ready for your EXAM 3

1 **Get ready to LISTEN** Work in pairs. Ask and answer the questions.
1 How good is your memory?
2 Do you find it easy to remember things?
3 Can you remember what happened in your last English lesson? Do you and your partner remember the same things?

2 🎧 1.23 Do the Listening exam task.

LISTENING exam task

Listen to a report of an experiment. Choose the correct answers: A, B or C.

1 During the research, some of the participants
  A made an advertisement with Bugs Bunny.
  B drew pictures of Bugs Bunny.
  C did not see Bugs Bunny at all.

2 All the participants
  A had visited Disneyland before.
  B said they wanted to visit Disneyland.
  C told stories of meeting Bugs Bunny.

3 Bugs Bunny
  A sometimes visits Disneyland.
  B can be found at Warner Brothers Six Flags theme park.
  C does not appear at any theme park.

4 The point of the experiment was
  A to show how easily a false memory can be created.
  B to show how false memories can cause serious problems.
  C to explain why some people are more likely than others to have false memories.

5 To create a false memory
  A we have to talk about it.
  B we must admit it could have happened.
  C we must look at some pictures.

6 According to the text, nostalgic advertisements
  A refer to unhappy memories.
  B help you improve your memory.
  C change the way we remember things.

3 How reliable do you think our memories are? Can you think of any examples when people added made-up details to their stories?

4 Do the Use of English exam task.

USE OF ENGLISH exam task

Complete the text with an appropriate word in each gap.

Jobs for lazy people

If you look through the job pages of any newspaper, you find the same adjectives appearing in advert after advert: motivated, ambitious, hard-working, energetic, dynamic ... These are the qualities that you need for all jobs, ¹_____ they? Well, perhaps ²_____ quite all. A few jobs exist which might be suitable for somebody ³_____ is less hard-working – even lazy!

Some furniture companies employ people ⁴_____ job is to test their new sofas and armchairs. ⁵_____ example, the La-z-Boy Company, ⁶_____ makes reclining chairs, has several full-time furniture testers. All they have to ⁷_____ is sit in the chairs for long periods of time and then say ⁸_____ comfortable they are. It's one of the few workplaces ⁹_____ it is OK to fall asleep on the job!

If you are looking for peace and quiet, as well as a job which involves doing nothing ¹⁰_____ long periods, then perhaps you should consider becoming a house sitter. These people are paid just to occupy somebody's home while they are away on holiday or on business. Of course, you have to deal with any problems that arise, but if you are lucky, there won't be any.

5 Do the Speaking exam task.

SPEAKING exam task

Work in pairs. Imagine that you left school ten years ago and that you are now organizing a reunion for members of your class. Agree on:

- where you should hold the reunion (restaurant? school hall? other venue?)
- what the reunion should involve (food? entertainment? speeches?)
- how the reunion will be paid for
- whether you should invite any teachers as well.

Get ready for your EXAM 4

1 `Get ready to READ` Work in pairs. Tell your partner about your dream job. Where would or wouldn't you like to work? What would or wouldn't you like to do at work? Give reasons. Use the vocabulary from page 24 to help you.

2 Do the Reading exam task.

READING exam task

Read the text. Decide if the statements are true or false. For each statement, write the letter of the paragraph where you find evidence for your decision.

A NEW DREAM JOB?

A Mr Lim, 24, is an absolute pro. What used to be his hobby is now a profession earning him about $300,000 only last year. Over the next couple of years he will make much more.

B He lives in a small two-bedroom apartment and, despite making a fortune, shares it with nine other people. There's a computer for everyone but not much room for anything more, except pizza boxes and bags filled with clothes. When, after a ten-hour training session, Mr Lim is ready to get some sleep, he simply rolls out a mattress. Like many of his profession, he prefers to sleep during the day and sit in front of his computer most of the night. His private life is non-existent and he hasn't been on a date for ages.

C So what is Mr Lim's job? He is a professional computer-game player and spends his days wiping out countless armies and annihilating alien species. This profession appeared on the job market only a few years ago, but it's a booming industry. In Korea, thousands of young people try out for the top teams. There are over 200 pros, the best ones joining professional leagues founded in the late 90s. The rules of selection are very strict, but anyone who thinks they've got what it takes can register through a national system and then climb from one level to the next to finally join the national delegation. These compete against each other in Singapore at the world championships.

D Since the championships and online matches are watched by thousands, big money is made on tickets and advertising. Korea even has TV channels covering games round-the-clock and DVDs of famous face-offs proved more profitable than *The Matrix*. The champions are awarded lucrative cash prizes. Most of the players are about 20; however, there are also some in their 30s and 40s.

E It is too early to predict how long a career like this can last. However, with its popularity on the rise, you might be set for life. So bring your favourite mouse, headphones and keyboard if you wish (computers are provided to prevent cheating) and let the games begin.

		True	False	Evidence
1	In Korea, you can watch games any time you want.	☐	☐	____
2	Participants use only their own equipment.	☐	☐	____
3	Mr Lim's apartment is not comfortably furnished.	☐	☐	____
4	There are thousands of top players in Korea.	☐	☐	____
5	The profession is open to everybody.	☐	☐	____
6	Mr Lim does not have a proper bed.	☐	☐	____
7	Computer-game playing may be a good job in the future.	☐	☐	____
8	What Mr Lim does for a living used to be his favourite free-time activity.	☐	☐	____

3 `Get ready to SPEAK` Look at the pictures in the exam task. Do you shop in markets? What kind of things do you buy there? Do you go to a library? Why? Why not?

4 Do the Speaking exam task.

SPEAKING exam task

Compare and contrast the two photos. Answer the questions.

1 What are the main differences between the two places of work: an open-air market and a public library?
2 What could be good or bad about working in a market or a library?
3 What kind of personal qualities do you need to do each job well?
4 Which job would you enjoy more, in your opinion? Why?

4 Body and mind

THIS UNIT INCLUDES
Vocabulary • parts of the body • inside the body • legal terms • homophones • aches and pains • symptoms • illnesses
Grammar • past simple and present perfect contrast • present perfect continuous
Speaking • talking about diet and lifestyle • at the doctor's
Writing • an informal letter: giving news

A VOCABULARY AND LISTENING
The human body

I can talk about parts of the body and injuries.

1 Work in pairs. Match the parts of the body with the words in the box.

Parts of the body	ankle	calf	chest	chin	eyebrow
eyelash	eyelid	heel	hip	lip	neck	nostril	scalp
shin	stomach	thigh	throat	thumb	waist	wrist

2 🎧 1.24 Listen and check your answers.

● ● Vocabulary Builder 4.1: Parts of the body: p. 131

3 **SPEAKING** Work in pairs. Student A: Describe a part of the body using one or more of the phrases below. Student B: Guess what A is describing. Swap roles.

It's part of your (face, leg, hand, etc.)
It's at the front/back of your ...
It's between your ... and your ...

4 **SPEAKING** Work in pairs. Ask and answer questions with *Have you ever* about these injuries. If the answer is 'yes', ask another question using the word in brackets.

1 twisted your ankle? (How?)
2 broken a bone? (Which?)
3 dislocated a finger? (How?)
4 had a stiff neck? (Why?)
5 pulled a muscle? (Which?)
6 had aching feet? (Why?)

> Have you ever twisted your ankle?
> Yes, I have.
> How did you do it?
> I was playing basketball and I lost my balance.

5 Complete the idioms with the words in the box. Then match them with the meanings (a–f) below.

| arm | chest | foot | hairs | heels | leg |

1 to get something off your _____
2 to split _____
3 to twist somebody's _____
4 to be head over _____ in love
5 to put your _____ in it
6 to pull somebody's _____

a to be completely in love
b to persuade somebody to do something
c to upset or embarrass somebody accidentally
d to tease somebody
e to talk about something that has been worrying you for a long time
f to argue about unimportant details

6 🎧 1.25 Listen to six dialogues. Match each dialogue to an idiom in exercise 5.
1 The man is telling the woman that he's head over heels in love.

7 Work in pairs. Write two short dialogues to illustrate the meaning of two idioms from exercise 5.

8 **SPEAKING** Act out your dialogues to the class. Can they guess what the idiom is?

> I think Sally is twisting Jake's arm.

● ● Vocabulary Builder 4.2: Inside the body: p. 132

Unit 4 • Body and mind

4B GRAMMAR
Past simple and present perfect contrast

I can correctly use the past simple and present perfect simple.

1 What is the man in the photo doing? Read the text and answer the questions.
1. In which country did free running start?
2. In which film did Sebastien Foucan appear in 2006?

FREE RUNNING

Sebastien Foucan has taken part in free running since he was 15. The sport began in France in the 1980s. Free runners have to run, climb or jump over obstacles as gracefully as they can. The obstacles could be fences, cars, walls – even buildings. Sebastien once said, 'Free running has always existed, free running has always been there, the thing is that no one gave it a name.'

Sebastien has appeared on TV a number of times, but his big break came in 2006 when he appeared in the James Bond film, *Casino Royale*. Since then, free running has become very popular among extreme sports enthusiasts. It can be quite dangerous although Sebastien has never had a serious accident.

Sebastien has jumped across the rooftops of Paris and London. And he's just announced his latest challenge: the buildings and monuments of New York!

2 Underline all the past simple and present perfect verbs in the text. Read the *Learn this!* box and match them with the uses.

LEARN THIS!
1. We use the **past simple** to talk about completed events in the past (often with words that refer to a finished time: *yesterday, two years ago*).
   I went to London last weekend.
2. We use the **present perfect**
   a. to say how long a current situation has existed (often with *for* and *since*).
      Peter has lived in that house for five years.
   b. to talk about an experience in the past. The exact time of the experience is not important.
      'Have you ever been to Paris?' 'No, I haven't.'
   c. to talk about events that are connected with the present (for example, news and recent events). We sometimes use *already*, *just* and *yet*.
      'Is Jim here?' 'No, he's just gone.'

●●● **Grammar Builder 4.1: Past simple and present perfect: p. 113**

3 🎧 1.26 Complete the interview. Use the past simple or present perfect form of the verbs in brackets. Then listen and check.

Suzie Bowman is a freediver. Freedivers try to dive as deep as possible into the sea on a single lungful of air, without breathing apparatus.

Interviewer When ¹_____ you _____ (start) freediving?
Suzie I ²_____ (make) my first freedive in 2001.
Interviewer How ³_____ you _____ (discover) that you had a talent for freediving?
 Well, I ⁴_____ (be) a good swimmer since a very young age. Later, I ⁵_____ (find) that I could hold my breath for a long time under water.
Interviewer How many world records ⁶_____ you _____ (break)?
Suzie I ⁷_____ (break) three so far. But I hope to break more.
Interviewer ⁸_____ you _____ (have) any scary moments?
Suzie No, not really. Some sharks ⁹_____ (swim) past me on one occasion, but they ¹⁰_____ (not be) interested in me!

4 Find the time expressions in the box in the dialogue in exercise 3. Then add them to the chart below.

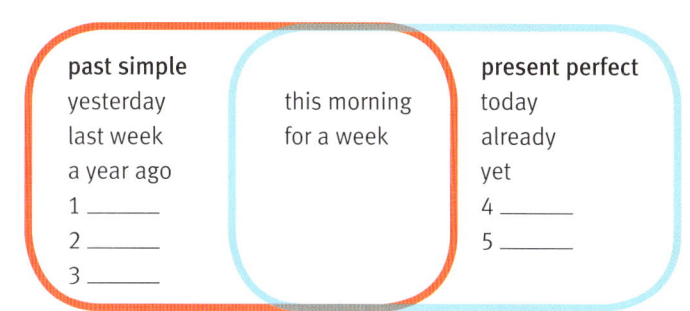

in (2001)   later   on one occasion   since   so far

past simple	this morning	present perfect
yesterday	for a week	today
last week		already
a year ago		yet
1 _____		4 _____
2 _____		5 _____
3 _____		

5 **SPEAKING** Work in pairs. Ask and answer questions about what you have done this week. Use the phrases in the box and your own ideas. Notice which tenses are used to ask the two questions in the example.

go to the cinema?   play computer games?   eat out?
read any good books?   do any homework?   do any sport?

– Have you been to the cinema this week?
– Yes, I have.
– What did you see?
– We saw *Casino Royale*.

Unit 4 • Body and mind   35

4C CULTURE
Fast food addicts

I can understand and react to an article about obesity and diet.

OBESITY – WHO IS TO BLAME?

In 2002, several obese teenagers in the USA sued McDonald's, claiming that the company was responsible for making them fat. ¹ ☐ They claimed that the company had not warned them about the health problems that can result from eating too much salty, high-fat food and drinking too many sugary drinks: diabetes, high blood pressure and obesity. The mother of one of the children, who at the age of 15 weighed more than 180 kilograms, said in her statement: 'I always believed McDonald's was healthy for my son.'

McDonald's rejected the claim that they were responsible for these teenagers' health problems. ² ☐ 'The understanding of what hamburgers and French fries do has been with us for a long, long time,' he added. The judge agreed, and dismissed the case, saying: 'it is not the place of the law to protect people against their own excesses.' In other words, if people choose to eat a lot of unhealthy food, they can't blame the company that sold it to them.

³ ☐ In 2005, the US House of Representatives passed a bill which became known as the 'Cheeseburger Bill'. It made it much harder for obese people to take legal action against the food industry. ⁴ ☐ There is some scientific evidence to suggest that fast food is addictive, and harmful too. So is selling fast food the same, in a way, as drug-dealing?

1 Describe the food in the photo. Which items contain a lot of:
  1 fat?   3 vitamins?   5 protein?
  2 sugar? 4 carbohydrate? 6 salt?

2 Read the text, ignoring the gaps. Explain in your own words why some teenagers in the USA sued McDonald's.

3 Match the sentences (a–e) with the gaps (1–4) in the text. There is one sentence that you do not need.
  a 'People don't go to sleep thin and wake up obese,' said McDonald's lawyer, Brad Lerman.
  b However, the bill has not ended the arguments about responsibility.
  c They argued that McDonald's deliberately misled them into thinking that their cheeseburgers and other products were healthy and nutritious food.
  d These new burgers were larger, and higher in fat, than the standard burgers.
  e Other similar lawsuits against fast food companies in the USA have also failed.

4 Do you think fast food companies are partly to blame for obesity? Justify your answer.

5 Complete the legal words and phrases from the text.
  1 To _____ somebody means to take legal action against somebody.
  2 A law _____ is a legal case against somebody.
  3 To _____ a case is to reject it in court.
  4 To pass a _____ is to make a law.

6 🎧 1.27 Listen to three American teenagers talking about diet and lifestyle. Answer the questions for each person.
  1 How many hours of TV does he/she watch per day?
  2 How many times a week does he/she do exercise?
  3 Does he/she eat healthily?

7 🎧 1.27 Listen again. Are the sentences true or false?
  1 Tony likes watching films.
  2 Tony walks, plays football and goes surfing.
  3 Tony never eats junk food.
  4 Karen doesn't watch TV if there aren't any good programmes on or she has to do a lot of homework.
  5 The only exercise Karen does is at school.
  6 Karen's mum heats up TV dinners for her.
  7 Chris watches TV before and after school.
  8 Chris usually plays basketball at the weekend.
  9 Chris's family sometimes have a takeaway meal in the evening.

8 SPEAKING Work in pairs. Ask and answer the questions. Make a note of your partner's answers.
  1 Do you ever eat junk food? What type? How often?
  2 In your opinion, do you have a healthy diet?
  3 How many hours a day do you spend watching TV?
  4 How often do you exercise? What exercise do you do?
  5 What could you do to make your lifestyle healthier?

9 SPEAKING Tell the class about your partner.

> Chris spends four hours a day watching TV.

Unit 4 • Body and mind

4D GRAMMAR
Present perfect continuous

I can correctly use the present perfect continuous.

1 Read the text quickly. What is unusual about Mark Bolton? What do you think of his ideas?

Students at Medway Secondary School **have been listening** to a lot of Mozart and Bach recently. Teacher Mark Bolton takes a CD player into all his lessons and he plays music while his students are working. But he isn't a music teacher – he teaches maths. Mark **has been teaching** at the school since 2002 but he's **only been playing** music in his lessons for the last two years. 'It helps my students to concentrate,' he says. 'Their marks have improved a lot because they **have been working** much harder.' Mark has discovered that Mozart produces the best results, although any music has a positive effect. 'I've **been playing** rock music to the younger students,' he says. And what do his students think? Julia Marsh, 15, is looking very relaxed when she comes out at the end of the lesson. 'That's because I've **been listening** to James Blunt,' she says. 'I used to hate maths,' she adds, 'but now I love it!'

2 Look at the verbs in blue in the text. Complete the rule.

> We form the present perfect continuous with *have* / _____ + _____ and the *-ing* form of the verb.

LEARN THIS!

Present perfect continuous
We use the present perfect continuous to talk about
1 an action that began in the past and is still in progress. We often use *for* or *since* to say how long it has been in progress.
I've been learning English for six years.
2 an action that has recently stopped and which explains the present situation.
I'm tired. I haven't been sleeping well.

3 Read the *Learn this!* box. Then complete the questions and answers using the present perfect continuous and information from the text in exercise 1.

1 'What _____ students at Medway Secondary School _____ recently?' 'Mozart and Bach.'
2 'How long _____ at the school?' 'Since 2002.'
3 'How long _____ music in his lessons?' 'For the last two years.'
4 'Who _____ rock music to?' 'His younger students.'
5 'Why is Julia looking relaxed?' 'Because she _____ James Blunt.'

4 Complete the sentences with the present perfect continuous form of the verbs in the box. Then match the sentences with the questions (a–f).

> eat   not feel   rain   paint   sit   work

1 I _____ in a traffic jam.
2 I _____ the ceiling.
3 I _____ chocolates all day.
4 I _____ very well.
5 I _____ in the garden.
6 It _____.

a Why are your hands dirty?
b Why aren't you hungry?
c Why is your hair wet?
d Why have you got paint in your hair?
e Why are you late?
f Why are you going to the doctor's?

Look out!

Present perfect simple or present perfect continuous?
We use the present perfect simple **not** the present perfect continuous
1 if the action is **finished and complete**.
   I've written a letter to my cousin. I'm going to post it now.
2 if we want to say **how often** an action has happened.
   She's broken her leg three times.
3 with state verbs (*like, love, know, remember,* etc.).
   I've known Joe for a year. ✓
   I've been knowing Joe for a year. ✗

5 Read the *Look out!* box. Find two examples in the text in exercise 1 of the present perfect simple which describe actions that are finished and complete.

6 Complete the sentences. Use the present perfect simple or continuous form of the verbs in brackets.

1 I _____ (learn) English for five years. I study after school.
2 You can have your book back now. I _____ (read) it.
3 I _____ (know) Tom since May.
4 You look upset. _____ you _____ (cry)?
5 How many times _____ you _____ (see) that film?
6 I _____ (look) for my keys for ages, but I _____ (not find) them yet.
7 Mum _____ (shop) all morning. She _____ (buy) lots of Christmas presents.
8 He _____ (do) his homework, but he _____ (not finish) yet.

> ●● Grammar Builder 4.2: Present perfect simple and present perfect continuous: p.113

7 **SPEAKING** Work in pairs. Student A: Make a comment from the list (1–5). Student B: Give a reason, using the present perfect simple or continuous.

1 You look tired.
2 You look cold.
3 Your clothes are wet and dirty.
4 You look fed up.
5 You look irritated.

> You look tired.
> I've been playing football.

Unit 4 • Body and mind   37

4E READING — All in the mind

I can understand a magazine article about how to improve your memory.

The Memory Man

Can you remember people's faces but not their names? Are you bad at remembering people's birthdays? How many things have you forgotten this week? According to Andi Bell, you needn't be forgetful ever again.

Andi Bell used to be unemployed. Now he is a memory grandmaster who has won the world memory championships three times. He has been training his memory for around fifteen years, ever since he read an article about the amazing memory man, Dominic O'Brien. In 2002, he beat his hero O'Brien at the World Memory Championships for the first time.

Andi has broken many memory records and is currently the speed memory champion. He has correctly memorised the order of a pack of cards in just 31.16 seconds. He can also remember the order of over 1,000 cards in one hour. So how does he do it?

Andi's technique is an unusual but simple one. Journalist Lara Barton met him and wrote an account of his technique.

Today, Andi Bell is going to teach me how to improve my memory. In less than one hour, I will have a working memory of the past 1,000 years in history.

'Right,' says Andi, 'think of ten rooms in a building you know very well.' I think of the house I grew up in. He tells me we're going to call each room a different century. 'What is your first room?' he asks.

'It's my bedroom, Andi.'

'Your bedroom is the 1000s,' he says. 'Imagine the Battle of Hastings in the middle of the room.' Then just before the door I have to imagine a water clock to remind me of Su-Sung's invention in China. I've never seen a water clock, so I imagine something like a sundial in water. By the end of the tour, I've put Marco Polo at the bottom of the stairs, Queen Victoria in the kitchen cupboard, and the Mona Lisa in the dining room. Whatever will my mother say?

The basic idea is that you imagine events, and put them at a particular point in the room, depending upon when they happened during the century. For example, events at the start of a century go near the door.

Essentially, the historical events become like furniture – you learn to associate them with a particular room and place. To me, Mozart now sits, like a table, in the middle of my kitchen, and I have to walk around him to get to Beethoven!

Andi says that everybody can benefit from his techniques. All you have to do is think of the things you want to remember and put them in familiar places in your mind. 'You can apply it to anything, you can apply it to learning,' he says. So, have you have been paying attention? You have no excuse for not passing your exams now.

1 Read the text quickly. Which sentence is false?
1 Andi Bell can remember everything that happened in his life.
2 Andi Bell can memorise things very quickly.
3 Andi Bell thinks that everyone can improve their memory.

2 Choose the best answers.
1 Andi Bell
   a has always had a fantastic memory.
   b was unemployed before he started to train his memory.
   c has been a memory grandmaster for fifteen years.

2 Andi started training his memory because
   a he read an article about Dominic O'Brien.
   b he wanted to meet his hero, Dominic O'Brien.
   c he wanted to win the World Memory Championships.

3 Andi teaches Lara Barton to memorise
   a ten rooms in a building she knows.
   b historical events from the past 1,000 years.
   c ten rooms in the house she grew up in.

4 In order to memorise things, Lara has to
   a visualise them next to the door.
   b pretend they are famous composers.
   c visualise them as furniture in a room.

5 Andi says his technique
   a is best used for studying.
   b is better for some people than others.
   c is good for learning anything you need to remember.

3 Complete the sentences with the highlighted verbs in the text. Use the correct tense and form.
1 Don't _____ to lock the door before you go to bed.
2 Our teacher told us to _____ this poem by tomorrow.
3 I can't _____ his name.
4 Can you _____ me to phone Phillip?
5 Close your eyes and _____ that you are on the beach.
6 I _____ the smell of sun cream with holidays.

> **LEARN THIS!**
> **Homophones**
> A homophone has the same pronunciation as another word, but a different spelling and meaning, for example: *their* and *there*, or *sea* and *see*.

4 Read the *Learn this!* box. Find homophones of these words in the first two paragraphs of the text.

| 1 there | 3 bee | 5 four |
| 2 weak | 4 one | 6 red |

5 **PRONUNCIATION** Say these words aloud. Which two or three words in each group are homophones?

1	a wore	b ware	c war
2	a where	b wear	c ware
3	a two	b too	c to
4	a here	b hear	c hare
5	a through	b throw	c threw
6	a know	b now	c no
7	a howl	b whole	c hole
8	a write	b right	c rite
9	a there	b they're	c their
10	a aren't	b ant	c aunt

6 🎧 1.28 Listen and check your answers to exercise 5.

7 Find four parts of a house in the text. Then work in pairs and brainstorm more parts of a house. How many can you think of?

8 **SPEAKING** Work in pairs. Play a memory game.

- Think of eight words for your partner to remember. Write them down and give them to your partner.
- Look at the eight words that your partner wrote for you. Imagine you are walking round your house or flat. Place each word in a different place on your route.
- Cover the words and start at the beginning of the route. See if you can 'find' all of the words in the places you put them.
- If it was too easy, try it with ten or twelve words.

Unit 4 • Body and mind

4F EVERYDAY ENGLISH — At the doctor's

I can talk about illnesses, their symptoms and treatment.

1 🎧 1.29 Complete the dialogue with the phrases in the box. Then listen and check.

> listen to your chest
> keep warm and get plenty of rest
> I've got a temperature and a bad cough
> for about a week
> three times a day after meals

Patient Good morning, Doctor.
Doctor Good morning. What can I do for you?
Patient Well, I haven't been feeling very well recently. ¹ _____
Doctor How long has this been going on?
Patient ² _____
Doctor Can I ³ _____ ?
Patient Of course.
Doctor I think you've got an infection. I'll prescribe some antibiotics.
Patient Will I get better soon?
Doctor Take the tablets ⁴ _____ and it should clear up in a few days.
Patient OK. Thank you.
Doctor You should ⁵ _____. If you're not feeling better in a week from now, come and see me again.
Patient Thank you, Doctor. Goodbye.
Doctor Goodbye.

• **Vocabulary Builder 4.3: Aches and pains: p. 132**

2 Match the symptoms (1–6) with the illnesses (a–f).

Symptoms
1 I can't stop sneezing and my eyes are watering all the time.
2 I feel shivery, I've got a headache and I'm aching all over. I feel terrible.
3 I banged my head and I feel dizzy and confused.
4 My ankle is swollen and I can't really walk on it.
5 I've got a nasty cough, a temperature and my nose is blocked.
6 I've got stomach ache and I feel sick.

Illnesses
a flu
b a chest infection
c food poisoning
d hay fever
e a twisted ankle
f concussion

3 🎧 1.30 Listen. Which illnesses do the three patients have?

4 🎧 1.31 Complete the doctor's advice. Use the words in the box. Then listen and check.

> avoid   diarrhoea   drink   feel   ice   liquid   plenty of
> prescribe   rest   see   stay   take   walk   work

1 You should _____ as much as possible, and _____ in bed.
2 I don't think you should go to _____. You need _____ rest.
3 If you don't _____ better in three or four days, come back and _____ me again.
4 You must _____ your foot for a couple of days. Try not to _____ on it.
5 I'll _____ some painkillers. You can _____ them every four hours.
6 You can also put _____ on it to keep it cool.
7 Drink lots of _____.
8 When the _____ stops, you can eat a little dry bread – but _____ milk and cheese.

5 **SPEAKING** Work in pairs. Prepare a dialogue between a patient and a doctor. Use the words and phrases in exercises 1, 2 and 4.
• Greet each other.
• Doctor: ask what the problem is.
• Patient: explain your symptoms.
• Doctor: say what you think the illness is.
• Patient: ask for the doctor's advice.
• Doctor: give your advice.
• Patient: thank the doctor.
• Say goodbye to each other.

6 **SPEAKING** Act out your dialogue to the class.

Unit 4 • Body and mind

4G WRITING
An informal letter: giving news

I can write a letter giving news.

1 Read the letters quickly. What illness or injury do Emily and Julie each have?

Dear Rob

How are you? What have you been up to? Sorry I haven't written to you for ages, but I've been really busy recently with end-of-term exams. You know what it's like! I've also been rehearsing for the Christmas show, which starts next week.

Guess what! I'm in hospital! Don't panic, I'm not seriously ill. I fell over when I was playing tennis and broke my arm. Anyway, I'm only in for a day or two. Luckily my injury won't stop me singing in the show.

The family are all fine. Mum's been working really hard. She doesn't get home till late. Dad's bought a new car – well, I say 'new', but actually it's about ten years old. Chris has got a new computer and spends most of the time playing computer games.

That's all for now. I'd better go.

Loads of love

Emily

Dear Graham

Thanks for your letter. I got it last week and it really made me laugh! I'm off school today with a temperature and an upset stomach. I've been sick three times, but I'm feeling a bit better now.

Enough of all that. I bumped into Sally and Dave last weekend. Guess what! They've been going out together since the Halloween party in October. They seem really keen on each other. Susie is fine too. She sends her love. (I think she still fancies you!) We all miss you!

I guess you've started at your new school in London now. How is it? Have you made loads of new friends? Don't forget about your old ones!!! So many questions! Do write again and send me your news.

love

Julie

P.S. Why don't we get together in London one weekend? I can easily get the train down.

---

2 Answer the questions.
1 What has Emily been doing at school?
2 Why doesn't Emily's mum get home until late?
3 What have her dad and her brother bought?
4 What have Dave and Sally been doing?
5 What does Susie think of Graham, in Julie's opinion?
6 Where does Graham go to school now?

3 Write *a* next to the phrases for beginning a letter and *b* next to the phrases for signalling the end of a letter.

Phrases for informal letters
1 Sorry I haven't written for ages.
2 That's all my news for now.
3 It was great to hear from you.
4 Must dash – Mum's calling me for dinner.
5 I'd better finish here as I'm running out of space.
6 Thanks for your letter.
7 I'd better stop here. It's getting late.
8 That's all for now. I'd better go now.
9 How are you?

4 Find the phrases (1–7) in the letters. Then match the phrases with the functions (a–g).
1 Enough of all that.
2 Why don't we … ?
3 Guess what!
4 Loads of love
5 What have you been up to?
6 Do + verb (e.g. Do write)
7 She sends her love.

a introducing surprising news
b making a suggestion
c asking for news of the other person
d ending the letter
e changing the subject
f making a strong request
g sending greetings from someone else

5 Make notes for an informal letter to a friend who has moved away from your town. Follow the plan below.

Paragraph 1: Start with an appropriate phrase. Apologise for not writing sooner.
Paragraph 2: Give news about yourself.
Paragraph 3: Give news about your friends and/or family.
Paragraph 4: Ask questions about your friend.

Writing tip
In informal letters, we usually use everyday language. We normally use short forms instead of long forms.

6 Read the writing tip. Then write a letter of 120–150 words using your notes from exercise 5. Use phrases from exercises 3 and 4.

Unit 4 • Body and mind

Language Review 3-4

Vocabulary

1 Complete the missing words.
1. My w _ _ k _ _ _ _ h _ _ _ _ are from 9 a.m. to 5 p.m.
2. Harvey has a p _ _ _ -t _ _ _ job in the morning so that he can study in the afternoon.
3. Jasmine e _ _ _ _ £10 an hour as a gardener.
4. Nathan is a l _ b _ _ r _ _ on a building site.
5. There are four people in our advertising t _ _ m.
6. My job is hard work but it's c _ _ l _ _ _ g _ _ _.

Mark /6

2 Match a word in the box with a part of the body.

| heel | lip | nostril | scalp | thigh | thumb |

1. foot _____
2. leg _____
3. mouth _____
4. nose _____
5. head _____
6. hand _____

Mark /6

Grammar

3 Complete the defining relative clauses with *who, whose, where* or *which*.
1. A carpenter is a person _____ makes wooden furniture.
2. A surgery is a place _____ a doctor sees their patients.
3. Labourers are people _____ do manual work.
4. Nannies are people _____ job requires a love of children.
5. Shift work is work _____ hasn't got a fixed timetable.
6. A salary is money _____ is paid monthly directly into your bank account.

Mark /6

4 Combine the two sentences. Use a non-defining relative clause.
1. Lily is studying to be a doctor. Her mother is a nurse.
   Lily, whose mother is a nurse, is studying to be a doctor.
2. My brother works as a lecturer. He also does research into tropical diseases.
   My brother _____
3. My studio is very cheap. I spend most of my time there.
   My studio _____
4. My computer is a laptop. I take it with me everywhere.
   My computer _____
5. My boss spends very little time in the office. His secretary is his wife.
   My boss _____
6. My office is never warm enough. It has a marvellous view of the river.
   My office _____

Mark /5

5 Complete the sentences with the present perfect continuous form of the verbs in brackets.
1. I'm crying because I _____ (watch) a sad film.
2. How long _____ (you / live) in this district?
3. Ryan _____ (not listen) to the teacher so he doesn't know what the homework is.
4. You look awful. _____ (sleep) properly?
5. Hannah _____ (see) Tyler, but nobody knew anything about it.

Mark /5

Everyday English

6 Put the lines (a–e) in the correct order to complete the dialogue.
a Right. What did you do there?
b Because I'm hard-working and reliable.
c I served drinks, and looked after the till.
d I see. And why do you think you're the right person for this job?
e Yes, I have. I used to help my aunt in her café.

Manager Have you worked in a restaurant before?
Boy   ☐
Manager ☐
Boy   ☐
Manager ☐
Boy   ☐
Manager OK, Dylan. Thanks for coming. We'll be in touch soon.

Mark /5

7 Complete the dialogue with the words in the box.

| better | dizzy | flu | temperature | tablets |

Doctor   Good morning. What can I do for you?
Patient Good morning. I've got a headache and I feel ¹_____.
Doctor   How long has this been going on?
Patient For about a week.
Doctor   Can I just take your ²_____?
Patient Of course.
Doctor   I think you've got ³_____.
Patient Oh. Will I get ⁴_____ soon?
Doctor   Take these ⁵_____ and it should clear up soon.

Mark /5

Total /38

EXAM CHALLENGE Workbook pages 94–97

Skills Round-up 1–4

Listening

1 🎧 1.32 Look at the advertisement. Then listen and say which of the three jobs Marek is applying for.

SPORTECH
Health and fitness club

We are currently looking for people to fill these vacancies:
- receptionist
- cleaner
- assistant chef

No experience required

2 🎧 1.32 Listen again. Number the questions in the order that you hear them.

a Have you ever worked in a health and fitness club before?
b What's your address?
c Where are you from?
d Do you think you're good at dealing with people?
e Do you do much exercise?

SPORTECH Health and fitness club
OFFERS

Get fit
Whatever form of exercise you prefer, we have the facilities: a fully-equipped gym, two aerobics studios and a swimming pool. Our trained advisors not only give advice about general fitness, but also design exercise programs for specific needs. Did you know, for example, that gentle exercise with weights is one of the best ways to deal with back pain, neck pain and joint problems?

Unwind
Our salon provides a variety of health and beauty treatments, from haircuts to pedicures. Prepare for your beach holiday by booking five or more sunbed sessions and receive a 10% discount. Or why not try a full body massage for the ultimate in relaxation?

Refresh
Our café is open from 7 a.m. until 11 p.m. Order from our wide range of drinks, meals and snacks, and then relax with friends or watch TV. There is also a quiet area, if you prefer to read the newspaper or just meditate! Children's meals are also available before 6 p.m.

Stay connected
Work out, then log on! Take advantage of two computer terminals and the broadband Internet connection in our café. They are free for all members. The café also offers, for a small fee, wireless Internet facilities for people who prefer to stay connected via their own laptop. Why not enjoy a coffee and a sandwich while you check your e-mails?

Reading

3 Read the text quickly. What kind of text is it?
a a magazine article   c a newspaper report
b a publicity leaflet   d a narrative

4 Choose the best answers.
1 The health club has facilities for swimming, aerobics and
   a tennis.   b martial arts.   c weight training.   d yoga.

2 If you suffer from back pain, it's a good idea to
   a lift heavy weights in the gym.
   b avoid lifting any weights.
   c go swimming regularly.
   d lift light weights in the gym.

3 The salon can help prepare you for a holiday by helping you to get
   a brown.   b thin.   c stronger.   d fitter.

4 In the café, 9 p.m. is too late to
   a watch television.
   b read a newspaper.
   c order snacks.
   d buy special meals for children.

5 You don't need to pay for
   a your coffee when you use the Internet in the café.
   b using the computers in the café if you're a member.
   c getting online wirelessly in the café.
   d any of the Internet facilities in the club.

Writing

5 Write a formal letter to the manager of Sportech applying for one of the jobs in the advertisement in exercise 1. Remember to say:
- which job you are applying for
- what your work experience is (if you have any)
- why you would be a good person for the job
- when you can start work

Speaking

6 Work in pairs. Role-play an interview with your partner for the job that you applied for in exercise 5. Use questions from exercise 2 and your own ideas.

So, your name is …

Yes, that's right.

And which job are you applying for?

The job as a …

5 Our future

A VOCABULARY AND LISTENING
Computing
I can talk about computers and computing.

THIS UNIT INCLUDES
Vocabulary • computing • noun prefixes • compound nouns (1) • verb + noun collocations • making, accepting and declining suggestions
Grammar • zero conditional • speculating and predicting: *will, may, might,* etc. • first conditional • future perfect and future continuous • *will, going to* and present continuous • verbs followed by an infinitive • future time clauses
Speaking • talking about the future • discussing environmental issues • making plans
Writing • an essay: for and against

1 Read what three young people say about computers and how they use them. Who is the most similar to you?

Jenny: 'We've had broadband since January, and it's really changed the way we use our computer. We've bought a webcam, so we can video chat with our friends in the States. I also download a lot more music and videos from the Net because it's faster now, and I burn them onto CDs and DVDs.'

Rob: 'I use a laptop at home. We've got a wireless router in the hall, so it's easy to get online in any room in the house. I've got my own website with photos of myself, my family and my friends. I write a blog (when I remember) so that my friends know all my news. My website also includes lots of links to my other favourite websites.'

Belinda: 'We haven't got a computer at home, but there's an Internet café near my home. I go there two or three times a week and log onto my e-mail account. I also surf the Internet and visit some of my favourite websites. I occasionally download music. The computer that I use hasn't got a CD-writer, but it's easy to copy files onto a flash drive.'

2 Complete the definitions using the words in red in exercise 1.
1 _____ are connections between different web pages or different parts of a web page.
2 _____ is a fast, permanent connection to the Internet.
3 A _____ allows you to _____ and surf the Internet without plugging any wires into your computer.
4 A _____ allows you to send video pictures via the Internet.
5 A _____ is a small, portable computer.
6 A _____ is a diary that you write on the Internet.
7 If your computer has a _____, you can _____ information from your computer onto a CD.
8 The _____ is another word for the Internet.
9 To _____ is to communicate via the Internet with voice and video pictures.
10 To _____ means to copy from the Internet onto your computer.
11 You usually _____ a website by entering your username and password.
12 A _____ is a very small, portable device for storing computer files.

3 Match the two parts of the sentences.
1 If you haven't got broadband,
2 If you click on this link,
3 If you haven't got a DVD-writer,
4 If you type in your password,
5 If you want to know what I've been doing,
6 If you plug this flash drive into the USB port,

a you can't burn DVDs.
b you can copy the files onto your laptop.
c you can log onto this website.
d it takes a long time to download files from the Internet.
e your browser will take you to the Wikipedia website.
f you should read my blog.

•• Grammar Builder 5.1: Zero conditional: p. 114

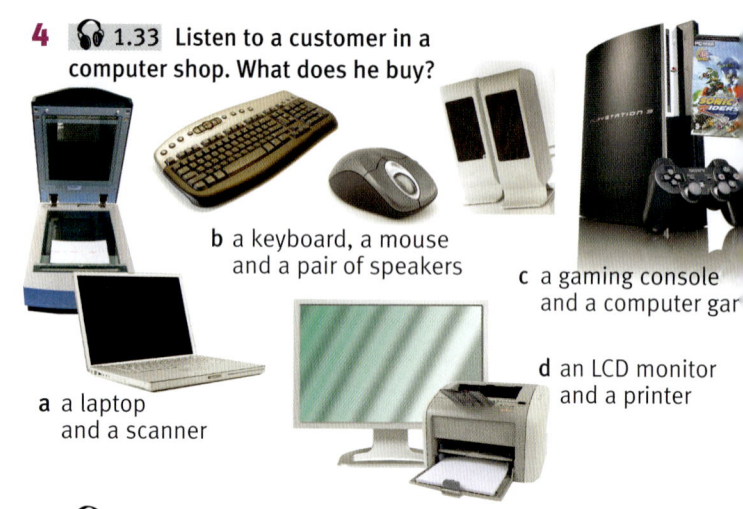

4 🎧 1.33 Listen to a customer in a computer shop. What does he buy?

a a laptop and a scanner
b a keyboard, a mouse and a pair of speakers
c a gaming console and a computer gar[...]
d an LCD monitor and a printer

5 🎧 1.33 Listen again. Complete the descriptions with the numbers in the box and match them to the items in exercise 4.

| 2 | 8 | 20 | 50 | 512 |

1 It's got a ___ gigabyte hard drive.
2 There are ___ multimedia keys.
3 It has ___ buttons, so you can left-click or right-click.
4 It can hold ___ sheets of paper.
5 It's got ___ megabytes of RAM.

6 **SPEAKING** Work in pairs. Ask and answer the questions.
1 How often do you use computer equipment?
2 What do you use it for?
3 How has the way you use a computer changed in the last five years?

•• Vocabulary Builder 5.1: Noun prefixes: p. 132

44 Unit 5 • Our future

5B GRAMMAR
Talking about the future

I can speculate about the future and make predictions.

1 Read the text and look at the photo. What is this man's job? Why is he good at it?

If you try to predict the future of technology, you'll probably get it horribly wrong – like the prediction made by T.J. Watson, the head of IBM, in 1943: 'I think there may be a world market for five computers in total.' Soon, in rich countries, there will be more computers than people.

However, Kazuo Kashio, the president of Casio, is particularly good at predicting the future. 'I can tell immediately which gadgets will sell well and which gadgets won't.'

So what will be the best-selling gadgets ten years from now? Surprisingly, Kazuo believes that watches may be the future – watches with different functions. For example, they could be mobile phones, MP3 players and computers as well. 'It will be the ultimate mobile gadget that you can't drop.' Judging by his success in the past, he might be right!

2 Read the *Learn this!* box. Find an example of these structures in the text: *may*, *might*, *could*, *will*, first conditional.

LEARN THIS! Speculating and predicting

0% ————————————————————→ 100%
won't » might/could » may » will probably » will

1 To talk about **possibility in the future,** we can use *may*, *might* or *could* followed by a base form. *Might* and *could* suggest a weaker possibility than *may*.
He may/might/could/ buy a computer.

2 We use *may not* or *might not* for the negative – we do not use *could not*.

3 To make **predictions,** we can use *will*. When we are not certain, we use *I think* or *probably*.
It will probably rain tomorrow.

3 Look at the numbers in the chart and the key below. Write sentences about Vince's future using *will / won't*, *may*, *might* and *could*.

1 *He'll learn to drive.*

1 = yes   2 = possibility   3 = weaker possibility   4 = no

Will you:	Vince	Your partner
1 learn to drive?	1	
2 get married?	2	
3 have children?	2	
4 have four or more children?	4	
5 move abroad?	3	
6 stay fit?	1	

4 SPEAKING Work in pairs. Ask your partner the questions from exercise 3. Make a note of his or her answers by writing 1–4 in the chart.

Will you learn to drive?

Yes, I think so. / I may. / I might. / No, I don't think so.

LEARN THIS! First conditional

1 We often make predictions with the first conditional.
If you buy a laptop, you'll be able to work anywhere.

2 We can use *may*, *might* or *could* in the main clause.
If you write a blog, you might be famous.

5 🎧 1.34 Read the *Learn this!* box above. Then listen to two young people making predictions about the future of the planet. Who is more optimistic: Martin or Bryony?

6 🎧 1.34 Listen again. Complete Martin and Bryony's predictions using the correct form of the verbs in the box.

| become | change | destroy | find | have | hit | live |
| program | not reduce | use | | | | |

1 If we *don't reduce* carbon emissions, the world's climate *will change*.
2 If petrol _____ very expensive, people _____ their cars less.
3 If we _____ robots to do a lot of menial jobs, everybody _____ more time for hobbies and relaxation.
4 If scientists _____ cures for all major diseases, people _____ much longer.
5 If a huge meteorite _____ the earth, it _____ everything.

Speaking tip

Use these expressions to say that you agree or disagree with a statement:
I think that's true. / I don't think that's true.
I agree / don't agree with (you / him / that opinion).
I believe / don't believe that's right.

7 SPEAKING Read the speaking tip. Say whether you agree or disagree with the predictions in exercise 6. Give reasons.

8 SPEAKING Complete these predictions about the future with your own ideas. Then tell the class. Do they agree?
1 If computers become more intelligent than humans, …
2 If everybody lives past the age of 100, …
3 If the world's climate becomes warmer, …
4 If computer games start to look and feel exactly the same as real life, …

● ● ● Grammar Builder 5.2: Speculating and predicting: p. 114

Unit 5 • Our future   45

5C CULTURE
A greener future

I can understand and react to an article about politics and the environment.

1 Look at the posters for a political party. What issues do you think this party campaigns for? Make a list of your ideas.

2 Read the text. Does it mention any of your ideas from exercise 1?

GOING GREEN

In Britain today, more 18–24-year-olds vote in TV shows like *Pop Idol* than in general elections. All political parties are trying to encourage more young people to get involved in politics. This means talking about the issues that are important to them.

The first political party to make the environment an important issue was The Green Party. The party has existed in the UK for about 30 years. (For the first ten years, it was called the Ecology Party.) The Greens do not have any seats in the House of Commons because in general elections most people vote for the three main parties: Labour, the Conservatives and the Liberal Democrats. However, they have several MEPs (Members of the European Parliament) and many local councillors across Britain. They campaign on many issues, including:

- animal rights: they want to ban scientific experiments on animals and improve conditions for animals on farms
- transport: they want to reduce the amount of traffic and pollution by making buses and trains cheaper, and by encouraging people to walk and cycle more
- green energy: they want to invest in clean, renewable sources of energy – wind farms, wave and solar power
- food and farming: they are against GM (genetically modified) food and the use of chemicals in farming

Twenty years ago, politicians who weren't in the Green Party hardly ever talked about 'green' issues like recycling, renewable energy and climate change. But today, all political parties have 'green' policies. People are realising that the earth is in danger. If we don't change our way of life, the results will be disastrous for our planet.

3 Are the sentences true or false?
1. In Britain, voting in elections is more popular than voting in TV shows like *Pop Idol* for people under 24.
2. The Green Party in the UK used to have a different name.
3. The Green Party has been more successful in local and European elections than in general elections.
4. The Green Party is in favour of scientific experiments on animals if they are really necessary.
5. The Green Party is in favour of people using public transport instead of their cars.
6. The Green Party is the only party in Britain that talks about recycling and renewable energy.

4 Complete the paragraph with the highlighted words in the text in exercise 2. Is the political system similar in your country?

In Britain, there are ¹_____ at least once every five years, when everybody aged 18 or older can ²_____ to decide the next government. A few months before the election, all the main political ³_____ publish a manifesto which describes their most important ⁴_____ and says what they will do if they win. They then ⁵_____ for people's votes by discussing the issues on TV and radio. The candidates who get the most votes win ⁶_____ in the ⁷_____, which is the most important part of the British ⁸_____. (The other part is called the House of Lords.) There are often local elections at the same time, when people choose their local ⁹_____.

5 🎧 1.35 Listen to five teenagers giving their opinions about environmental issues. Match each speaker (1–5) with two opinions.
a We should use solar and wind power to heat our water at home.
b We won't be able to use land-fill sites for much longer.
c We should avoid travelling by plane.
d We should use rockets to send rubbish into space.
e We shouldn't use cars for short journeys.
f There's too much packaging on things we buy.
g The government should ban large, powerful cars.
h We shouldn't go on holiday to distant places.
i We shouldn't replace gadgets and electrical appliances unless they are broken.
j The government should invest in renewable energy.

6 **SPEAKING** Do you agree or disagree with the opinions in exercise 5? Give reasons.

7 **SPEAKING** Work in pairs. Think of three things the local council or the public should do to help the environment where you live. Make notes. Then tell the class your opinions. Do they agree or disagree?

●●○ Vocabulary Builder 5.2: Compound nouns (1): p. 133

46 Unit 5 • Our future

5D GRAMMAR
Future perfect and future continuous

I can talk about actions in the future and when they will happen.

1 Look at the picture. What do you think it is? Read the text and find out.

In twenty years' time, adventurous holiday-makers will have run out of exciting things to do on earth. They will have been everywhere and tried everything. They'll be looking for new adventures. That's why the Maxicom Hotel chain is planning to build a hotel on the moon.

Hotels in space have existed for years in science fiction stories, but Maxicom's plans are not fiction – they're real. By the end of this year, the company will have finished its design for the Lunar Palace Hotel. Soon after that, they will be starting the building work.

2 Read the *Learn this!* box. Underline all the examples of the future perfect and future continuous in the text in exercise 1. Then complete the rules.

LEARN THIS! Future perfect and future continuous

1 We form the future perfect with
   will have + past participle
   This time next week, I'll have done my exams.
2 We form the future continuous with
   will be + *-ing* form
   This time next week, I'll be doing my exams.
3 We use the future _____ to talk about a completed action in the future.
4 We use the future _____ to talk about an action in progress in the future.

3 Look at Maxicom's timetable for the hotel on the moon. Then complete the sentences with the future perfect or future continuous form of the verbs in brackets.

Start to build the hotel	Jan 2015
Look for staff to work at the hotel	Jan–Jul 2017
Start to advertise the hotel	from Aug 2017
Finish building the hotel	Dec 2017
Train staff	Jan–Jul 2018
Welcome first guests for one-month holiday	Aug 2018

1 In July 2015, Maxicom _____ (build) the hotel.
2 In March 2018, they _____ (build) the hotel.
3 In June 2017, they _____ (look) for staff to work in the hotel.
4 In June 2018, they _____ (train) the staff.
5 From August 2017, they _____ (advertise) the hotel.
6 By August 2018, they _____ (train) the staff.
7 In August 2018, the first guests _____ (stay) at the hotel.
8 By November 2018, the first guests _____ (finish) their holiday.

● ● ○ **Grammar Builder 5.3: Future perfect and future continuous: p. 115**

4 Complete the text about Joel's future. Use the future perfect or future continuous form of the verbs in the box.

| do   drive   earn   find   not get married |
| go out   leave   not live   share |

'In five years' time, I ¹_____ school. I ²_____ a computing course and I ³_____ a job in IT. Maybe I ⁴_____ a lot of money in my job. If I am, I ⁵_____ an expensive car! I ⁶_____ with my parents. Perhaps I ⁷_____ a flat with some friends. I hope that I ⁸_____ with the same girlfriend – but we ⁹_____ yet.' *Joel, 17*

5 Think about your own life one year from now. What will you have done? Tick (✓) or cross (✗) the things in the list.

- finish this book ☐
- do some exams ☐
- buy a flat ☐
- get a job ☐
- have a birthday ☐
- leave school ☐
- start university ☐
- earn a lot of money ☐

6 **SPEAKING** Work in pairs. Ask and answer questions about your life in a year's time. Use the list from exercise 5 and your own ideas.

Will you have finished this book in a year's time?

Yes, I will. / No, I won't.

7 **SPEAKING** Work in pairs. Find out what your partner will be doing at:
1 eight o'clock this evening.
2 six o'clock tomorrow morning.
3 nine o'clock tomorrow morning.
4 midday next Saturday.
5 midnight next Saturday.
6 11.59 p.m. on 31 December.

What will you be doing at eight o'clock this evening?

I'll be having dinner.

Unit 5 • Our future 47

5E READING
Visions of the future

I can understand and react to experts' predictions for the future.

1 Look at the pictures which show visions of the future fifty years from now. Describe them.

2 Which one do you think is the most likely to come true?

Fifty Years On

1 Sir David King, scientific adviser to the British Government
If we don't reduce carbon emissions, the earth will become warmer, polar ice will melt and the oceans will rise. Cities like London and New York will disappear under the water. By 2100, Antarctica could be the only continent that is suitable for human life – the rest of the world will be too hot.

2 Francis Collins, geneticist
Fifty years from now, millions of people will live past the age of 100 and remain healthy. This will happen because we'll be able to study each person's genetic code and find the best way to treat and prevent illnesses in that individual. In about fifty years' time, the most important question for our society might not be 'How long can humans live?' but 'How long do we want to live?'

3 J Richard Gott, physicist
During the next fifty years, our earth might suffer a catastrophe. Humans could disappear, just like the dinosaurs and hundreds of other species. The best way to make humans safe from extinction is to start a colony on Mars. This is not a prediction but a hope. Will we be smart enough to do it?

4 Ellen Heber-Katz, biologist
I believe that soon we will be able to repair the human body in the same way that we can replace damaged parts of a car or a washing machine. Five years from now, we will be able to grow new fingers, and, a few years after that, new arms and legs. Within fifty years, replacing your whole body will be normal.

3 Read the reading tip. Then read the texts and match the opinions with experts 1–6. There is one opinion that you do not need.

a ____ hopes that people will go and live on another planet, in case there's a terrible disaster on Earth.
b ____ thinks that computers will find things out without the help of humans.
c ____ predicts that the human race will become extinct.
d ____ predicts that in about 2060 people may be able to determine their own lifespan.
e ____ thinks that the coldest place on Earth might one day have the best climate for humans.
f ____ predicts that medical advances will allow us to grow new limbs.
g ____ thinks that we'll be able to communicate directly with search engines and they'll tell us what we need to know.

4 Match the verbs and nouns to make phrases from the texts.

1 reduce   a a catastrophe
2 treat   b information
3 suffer   c damaged parts
4 start   d important discoveries
5 replace   e carbon emissions
6 provide   f a colony
7 make   g illnesses

5 Peter Norvig, director of research at Google

Today, people all over the world have access to billions of pages of text on the Internet. At the moment, they use search engines to find information, but fifty years from now, people will simply discuss their needs with their computer, and the computer will make suggestions and provide usable information, not just a list of links.

6 Eric Horvitz, principal researcher at Microsoft Research

In fifty years' time, computers will be much more intelligent than today, and this will change people's lives. Computers will help people work, learn, plan and decide. They will help people from different countries to understand each other by automatically translating from one language to another. Intelligent computers will work as scientists, and will start to make important discoveries on their own.

5 Complete the sentences with phrases from exercise 4.

1 You _____ of a machine when it breaks down.
2 They've developed new drugs to _____.
3 The tourist office can _____ about hotels.
4 Computers have helped scientists to _____ about space.
5 We need to use our cars less in order to _____ and stop global warming.
6 Nobody is certain what caused the dinosaurs to _____ and become extinct.
7 In the seventeenth century, a group of pilgrims left England to _____ in North America.

●●○ Vocabulary Builder 5.3: Verb + noun collocations: p. 133

6 **SPEAKING** In your opinion, which expert's prediction is:
1 the most optimistic? Give reasons.
2 the most pessimistic? Give reasons.
3 the most interesting? Give reasons.
4 the most likely to come true? Give reasons.

7 Work in pairs. Make three predictions about the world in fifty years' time. Use the ideas in the box to help you.

buildings   climate   computers   education
entertainment   health   space   transport   work

8 **SPEAKING** Tell the class your predictions. Do they agree or disagree?

Reading tip

When you're looking for specific information in the text, read the first sentence of each paragraph. The first sentence usually shows you what the whole paragraph will be about.

Unit 5 • Our future

5F EVERYDAY ENGLISH
Talking about plans

I can suggest and agree on plans for the weekend.

Kirsty What are your plans for the weekend?
Frank I'm playing tennis on Saturday afternoon.
Kirsty What about Sunday?
Frank I'm going to stay in and do some homework during the day. What about you? Have you got plans?
Kirsty Yes, I have. I'm going to do some shopping on Saturday, and on Sunday, I'm having lunch with my family at a restaurant. Shall we do something on Saturday evening?
Frank I'm afraid I can't. My parents are going out and they've asked me to babysit.
Kirsty Well, what about Sunday evening?
Frank Sure. What do you fancy doing?
Kirsty Why don't we go to the cinema?
Frank That's a good idea. I'll find out what's on.
Kirsty OK. Let's speak again on Sunday morning.
Frank Fine. I'll call you.

1 🎧 1.36 Read and listen to the dialogue. What are Kirsty and Frank planning to do this weekend? Write K (Kirsty) and F (Frank) next to the activities in the box.

do some homework ☐	go to the cinema ☐
do some shopping ☐	play computer games ☐
write some e-mails ☐	read ☐
play tennis ☐	watch a DVD ☐
visit relatives ☐	have lunch at a restaurant ☐

2 Read the *Learn this!* box and underline all the examples of the tenses in the dialogue.

> **LEARN THIS!**
> **will, going to and present continuous**
> 1 We use **will** for things we decide to do as we are speaking (instant decisions, offers, promises).
> 2 We use **going to** for things we have already decided to do (intentions).
> 3 We use the **present continuous** for things we have already agreed to do, usually with somebody else (arrangements).

>> Grammar Builder 5.4: *will, going to* and present continuous: p. 116

3 **SPEAKING** Work in pairs. Practise reading the dialogue in exercise 1 replacing the words in red with your own ideas.

4 🎧 1.37 Listen to two dialogues. What does each pair arrange to do on Sunday evening?
1 Michelle and Damien: _____
2 Paula and Richard: _____

5 🎧 1.37 Read the *Learn this!* box below. Listen again and tick the phrases that the speakers use: four for making suggestions, two for accepting suggestions and two for declining suggestions.

> **LEARN THIS!**
> **Making suggestions**
> Shall we … ?   Why don't we / you … ?   Let's …
> Do you fancy (+ *-ing* form)?   Maybe we / you could …
> **Accepting suggestions**
> Great idea.   That's a good idea.   Sure.
> **Declining suggestions**
> I'm afraid I can't.   I don't really fancy (+ *-ing* form).
> Thanks, but I've already got plans for …
> It's kind of you to ask, but …

6 **SPEAKING** Work in pairs. Practise making suggestions and reacting to them using phrases from the *Learn this!* box above. Use activities from the box in exercise 1 and your own ideas.

> Why don't we watch a DVD?
>> That's a good idea.

7 **SPEAKING** Work in pairs. Prepare a dialogue using the chart below. Use phrases from exercise 5.

A
Ask what B's plans are for the weekend.

B
Say what your plans are for Saturday. Suggest doing something on Sunday afternoon.

Decline B's suggestion. Give a reason. Make a suggestion for Sunday evening.

Accept A's suggestion.

Offer to find out more information (e.g. times, prices, etc.).

Agree. Promise to call A at a specified time on Sunday.

8 **SPEAKING** Act out your dialogue to the class.

50 Unit 5 • Our future

5G WRITING
An essay: for and against

I can write an essay presenting my opinion for or against a statement.

1 Read the task below and the essay. Does the writer generally agree or disagree with the statement in the task? In which paragraph is the writer's opinion clearly stated?

> 'Twenty years from now, the world will be a better place to live in.' **Do you agree or disagree with the statement? Give reasons.**

> **1** The modern world is changing faster than at any time in history. This is creating problems for our planet, but it is also creating new and exciting opportunities. Twenty years from now, which will make the most difference to our lives – the problems or the opportunities? That is the key question.
>
> **2** Many people are pessimistic about the future of our planet. They believe that entire regions will be uninhabitable because of global warming. Others argue that the world will become more and more polluted, until it is no longer a safe or healthy place to live. It is true that global warming and pollution have both increased rapidly during the past twenty years. If they increase at the same rate during the next twenty years, the situation will become disastrous.
>
> **3** On the other hand, there are many reasons to be optimistic about the future. During the next twenty years, there will be important advances in medicine and technology. Our lives will be healthier and more enjoyable because doctors will be able to cure most illnesses. What is more, I believe that scientists will find ways to slow down or even prevent global warming.
>
> **4** In conclusion, I believe that life will be better twenty years from now. Although there are serious problems facing the world, I don't think that the situation will get out of control. I believe science will advance quickly enough to find solutions.

2 Choose the paragraph plan that matches the essay in exercise 1.

  a 1 An introduction to the main issues.
       2 Evidence to support the writer's own opinion.
       3 Evidence to support the opposite side of the argument from the writer's opinion.
       4 A summary of the writer's opinion.

  b 1 A summary of the writer's opinion.
       2 An introduction to the main issues.
       3 Evidence to support the opposite side of the argument from the writer's opinion.
       4 Evidence to support the writer's own opinion.

  c 1 An introduction to the main issues.
       2 Evidence to support the opposite side of the argument from the writer's opinion.
       3 Evidence to support the writer's own opinion.
       4 A summary of the writer's opinion.

Look out!

I think + *won't* does not sound natural in English. It's better to use *I don't think* + *will*.
~~I think I won't pass my exams.~~ ✗
I don't think I'll pass my exams. ✓

3 Read the *Look out!* box. Find an example of *I don't think* + *will* in the essay in exercise 1.

4 Write sentences expressing your own ideas of the future in fifty years. Use *I think* or *I don't think* + *will*.

  1 robots / replace factory workers
  2 doctors / be able to cure most diseases
  3 new diseases / appear
  4 ordinary people / be much richer
  5 computers / be much cheaper
  6 global warming / cause serious problems
  7 scientists / invent new forms of transport
  8 children / spend a lot of time playing outside
  9 most people / live much longer

5 Read the task below and think about your own opinions. Use ideas from exercise 4 to help you.

> 'Fifty years from now, life will be much easier and healthier for ordinary people than it is today.' **Do you agree or disagree with the statement? Give reasons**.

6 Copy the paragraph plan you chose in exercise 2 into your notebook. Then add your ideas from exercise 5.

Writing tip

Remember that we normally use the present simple in future time clauses beginning *when*.

When I reach my sixties, people will retire much later. People will have to find greener alternatives to cars when fossil fuels run out.

●● Grammar Builder 5.5: Future time clauses: p. 116

7 Read the writing tip. Then write an essay of 200–250 words following your plan from exercise 6.

Unit 5 • Our future   51

Get ready for your EXAM 5

1 **Get ready to READ** Look at the sports in the box. How old do you think they are? Underline the ones that you think were known in ancient Egypt.

> boxing   cricket   curling   hockey   horse riding
> javelin   rugby   swimming   wrestling   yoga

2 Read the text in the exam task quickly. What sports from exercise 1 are mentioned in the text?

3 Do the Reading exam task.

READING exam task

Six sentences have been removed from the text. Choose from sentences A–G the one that best fits each gap. There is one sentence that you don't need.

SPORTS IN ANCIENT EGYPT

Egypt has been called the cradle of human civilisation, and museums are full of fascinating and beautiful artefacts taken from the burial chambers of the pharaohs. ¹☐ People led normal lives and enjoyed many of the same things that we still enjoy today. For example, physical fitness was almost a national obsession. From about 3,000 BC up until the Roman occupation, Egypt was a land of people training and strengthening their bodies. ²☐ The murals depict both men and women of all social classes participating in sports. The oldest shows a pharaoh who lived in about 3,000 BC, which is over 5,000 years ago. We can see him participating in a running competition. ³☐ Athletics, wrestling and other games were also very popular among children. In fact, it would probably be easier to list the sports not practised in Egypt than mention all those we know were popular.

Although many people associate Egypt with sand and deserts, it is a land whose existence revolves around its river – the Nile. ⁴☐ They used most of the strokes we know today. Wrestling, boxing and other types of combat sport were also commonly practised. Yoga, which is not usually connected with Egypt, was popular as well. ⁵☐

The idea of sport for leisure was widespread but the Egyptians also enthusiastically organised championships and held competitions. ⁶☐ In order to make sure decisions were made fairly, without national bias, the judges were also from various countries. Naturally, the competitions attracted plenty of participants as well as spectators.

A It is therefore hardly surprising that swimming was a particular favourite of the ancient Egyptians.

B Some of these were on an international scale, with participants from neighbouring countries.

C Hatshepsut, a pharaoh queen of the 18th dynasty, seemed to enjoy the same sport and other rulers were equally fit and active.

D But there was more to life in ancient Egypt than building pyramids and mummifying bodies.

E And the famous murals, the pictures which decorated their tombs and temples, are still there to tell us the story of these activities.

F That is why we know so much about ancient Egyptian sports and the clothes that were generally worn while participating in them.

G Another activity not usually associated with the ancient Egyptians is horse riding, which was keenly pursued once horses had been introduced to Egypt in 1650 BC.

4 Do the Use of English exam task.

USE OF ENGLISH exam task

Complete the text with the correct form of the words given.

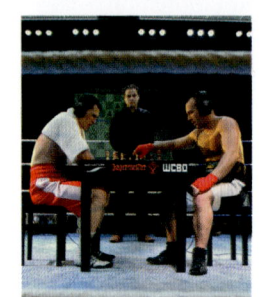

Chess-boxing

Most people would regard chess and boxing as so different that they are almost opposites: one relies on physical ¹_____ (STRONG), courage and aggression, the other on mental ²_____ (CONCENTRATE), planning and tactics. But despite (or perhaps because of) these ³_____ (DIFFERENT), a new sport has been invented which combines the two: chess-boxing. In a chess-boxing match, the two ⁴_____ (COMPETE) take part in alternating rounds of chess and boxing. The contest starts with a round of chess, followed by a round of boxing, followed by another round of chess, and so on, up to a maximum of eleven rounds: six of chess and five of boxing. The rounds of chess are a minute ⁵_____ (LONG) than the rounds of boxing.

You achieve victory in a chess-boxing match by ⁶_____ (WIN) either the chess or the boxing. In the chess rounds, you can win by checkmate, or by your opponent running out of time on the clock. In the boxing, you can win by a knock-out or by the referee's ⁷_____ (DECIDE). If there is no winner at chess or boxing, the ⁸_____ (PLAY) with the black chess pieces wins.

Chess-boxing is a minority sport, but it is growing ⁹_____ (STEADY). The first world championship was held in Berlin in 2007 and was won by a 37-year-old German policeman ¹⁰_____ (NAME) Frank Stoldt thanks to a checkmate in the chess in round seven.

5 **Get ready to SPEAK** Work in pairs. Read the task in exercise 6 and think of three arguments in favour of the statement and three against it. Then compare your ideas with the class.

6 Do the Speaking exam task.

SPEAKING exam task

Do you agree or disagree with this statement? Give reasons.

Professional sportswomen should earn as much money as professional sportsmen.

Get ready for your EXAM 6

1 **Get ready to LISTEN** Look at the picture. What do you think this is? Use *may*, *might* or *could*.

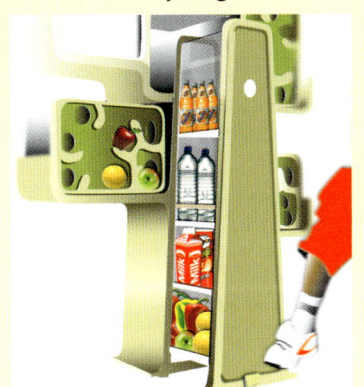

> This might be a toy from the future.

> Oh, I'm not sure. It could be a piece of art.

2 Work in pairs. Choose two household appliances from the box below. How do you think they will change in the future?

| coffee maker   cooker   iron   kettle   oven   refrigerator |
| toaster   vacuum cleaner   washing machine |

3 🎧 1.38 Do the Listening exam task.

LISTENING exam task

Listen to three young people talking about a special fridge. Match the opinions 1–8 to the speakers.

	Which speaker	Anna	Jon	Mark
1	thinks the fridge will use too much electricity?			
2	has a bad memory?			
3	thinks cleaning the fridge might be difficult?			
4	likes the way the fridge opens?			
5	believes the fridge could find many buyers?			
6	likes the fact the fridge is so unusual?			
7	doesn't find the fridge pretty?			
8	believes the fridge could be educational?			

4 **Get ready to SPEAK** Work in pairs. Look at the list of workplaces below and, for each one, decide:
 a whether you are likely find robots or other hi-tech machines there.
 b what the robots or hi-tech machines might do.

  a small farm   a large factory
  a TV studio   a hospital
  a café   a school
  an artist's studio   a small hotel

5 Work in pairs. Discuss which of these tasks robots or machines:
 a can do now.
 b will probably be able to do in the near future.

 1 fly an aircraft
 2 perform surgery in a hospital
 3 teach students in a classroom
 4 make computers in a factory
 5 go on missions into space
 6 drive a taxi
 7 perform music on stage
 8 serve customers in a shop
 9 give help and advice to people who are depressed
 10 take part in the Olympic Games

What other tasks will robots be able to do in the near future, in your opinion?

6 Do the Speaking exam task.

SPEAKING exam task

Compare and contrast the two photos. Answer the questions.

 1 What is being made in each photo?
 2 What are the advantages and disadvantages of making things by hand?
 3 What are the advantages and disadvantages of using robots to make things?
 4 Is there anything which could not be made by a robot, in your opinion?

6 Telling tales

THIS UNIT INCLUDES
Vocabulary • house and garden • compound nouns (2) • phrasal verbs
Grammar • *must have, might have, can't have* • reported speech (statements)
• *say* and *tell* • reported speech (questions) • verbs with two objects
Speaking • deciding who committed a crime • role-playing a TV interview
• negotiating and compromising
Writing • a formal letter: making a reservation

A VOCABULARY AND LISTENING
Murder in the library

I can decide who committed a crime.

1 Find these things in the pictures. What other objects can you identify?

> **House and garden** armchair   balcony   basin
> bookcase   carpet   chandelier   chest of drawers
> cooker   cupboard   curtains   dining table   drainpipe
> fireplace   flowerbed   hedge   lawn   mirror
> path   rug   sink   sofa   stepladder   stool
> vase   wardrobe

2 🎧 2.01 Millionaire Lord Snodbury has been murdered. Listen to the interviews with Inspector Fox who is investigating the murder. Match the people with the descriptions.

1 Martha is
2 Harold is
3 Lord Algernon is
4 Lady Snodbury is

a the gardener.
b Lord Snodbury's wife.
c Lord Snodbury's son and heir.
d the cook.

3 🎧 2.01 Listen again. Complete the Inspector's notes from the interviews.

> **Lord Snodbury's murder**
> Time: exactly 6 p.m.   Place: the library
> Witness statements:
> Martha 'was preparing ^{1}_____ in the ^{2}_____ at 6 p.m.'
> Says Lord Snodbury is 'mean and ^{3}_____'.
> Harold 'was cutting ^{4}_____ in the ^{5}_____ at 6 p.m.'
> Had argued with Lord Snodbury about ^{6}_____. Received
> £^{7}_____ from Lord Algernon.
> Lord Algernon 'was ^{8}_____ in his ^{9}_____ at 6 p.m.
> Went to library ^{10}_____ minutes later.' Had argued with
> Lord Snodbury about his ^{11}_____ to Emma Jones.
> Lady Snodbury 'was arranging ^{12}_____ in the ^{13}_____
> at 6 p.m. Heard gunshot and went to the ^{14}_____. Lord
> Algernon arrived there ^{15}_____ minutes later.'

4 Match the sentences (1–3) with the meanings (a–c).
1 Martha must have murdered Lord Snodbury.
2 Martha might have murdered Lord Snodbury.
3 Martha can't have murdered Lord Snodbury.

a It's impossible that Martha murdered Lord Snodbury.
b It seems certain that Martha murdered Lord Snodbury.
c It's possible that Martha murdered Lord Snodbury.

> **Grammar Builder 6.1:** *must have, might have, can't have*: p.116

5 **SPEAKING** Work in pairs. Who do you think murdered Lord Snodbury? Discuss the evidence in the interviews and the pictures.

> It can't have been _____ because ...
> It might have been _____ because ...
> It must have been _____ because ...

6 🎧 2.02 Vote for who you think killed Lord Snodbury. Listen to Inspector Fox's conclusion. Were you correct?

> **Vocabulary Builder 6.1:** House and garden: p.133

54   Unit 6 • Telling tales

6B GRAMMAR
Reported speech (statements)

I can report what other people have said.

1 Read the text. Where did the diamonds originally come from?
  a San Francisco   b a secret location   c London

The Great Diamond Hoax

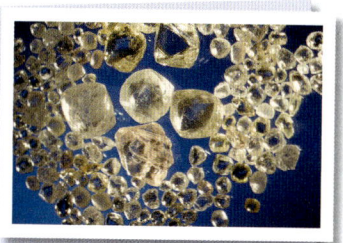

One night in 1871, two men called Philip Arnold and John Slack arrived at the San Francisco office of a rich businessman called George Roberts and said that they had come to discuss important business with him. They were carrying a small, leather bag and Arnold told Roberts that it contained diamonds. They said that they had found the diamonds in a secret location the week before and that they were looking for businessmen to invest in the mine. An expert examined the diamonds and confirmed that they were genuine, so Roberts told the men that he was happy to invest there and then. News of the new mine spread quickly and in the following weeks, lots of businessmen gave thousands of dollars to Arnold and Slack. When some of the investors wanted to visit the secret location, Arnold and Slack said they would take them there the next day. Arnold told them that they could dig for diamonds themselves, and when they did, they soon found some. But it was all a hoax. In fact, Arnold and Slack had bought the diamonds in London for $35,000, returned to the USA and buried them in the earth. The diamonds were real but the mine was fake. Arnold and Slack disappeared with $660,000 of investors' money.

2 Read the quotations below of what was said. Underline the parts of the text in exercise 1 that match them.
  1 'We've come to discuss important business with you.'
  2 'It contains diamonds.'
  3 'We found the diamonds in a secret location last week.'
  4 'We're looking for businessmen to invest in the mine.'
  5 'I'm happy to invest here and now.'
  6 'We'll take you there tomorrow.'
  7 'You can dig for the diamonds yourselves.'

3 Compare the quotations in exercise 2 with the parts of the text that you underlined. Complete the table with the correct tenses and words.

Direct speech	Reported speech
1 present simple	past simple
2 _____	past continuous
3 past simple	_____
4 _____	past perfect
5 can	_____
6 _____	would

4 Read point 1 in the *Learn this!* box. Find examples of pronouns that change when you change from direct to reported speech in exercises 1 and 2.

LEARN THIS!
When you change direct to reported speech
1 the pronouns often change: *I, you, we, they, myself, yourself,* etc.
2 time expressions often change: *today, tomorrow, yesterday, last month,* etc.

5 Read point 2 in the *Learn this!* box. Match the time expressions (1–5) to the time expressions (a–e).

Direct speech	Reported speech
1 today	a the next week
2 tonight	b the month before
3 next week	c that day
4 yesterday	d that night
5 last month	e the day before

6 Look again at exercises 1 and 2. Find three other time expressions that change.

Grammar Builder 6.2: Reported speech (statements): p. 117

Look out!
say and *tell*
tell somebody (something)
He told me his news. NOT He said me his news.

say something (to somebody)
He said hello to his friend.

7 Read the *Look out!* box. How many examples of *say* and *tell* are in the text in exercise 1?

8 Complete the sentences with *said* or *told*. Then rewrite the direct speech as reported speech.
  1 'I don't believe your story,' Jack said to his sister.
     Jack said to his sister that he didn't believe her story.
  2 'I've spent all my money,' his mother _____ .
  3 'We'll be in London tomorrow,' she _____ her friend.
  4 'I arrived yesterday,' _____ Mary.
  5 'You always spoil my fun!' Jack _____ his sister.
  6 'I'm not listening to you,' Suzie _____ her dad.
  7 'We can't see you until next week,' they _____ me.

9 **SPEAKING** Think of something that somebody told you which you didn't believe. Why didn't you believe it? Tell the class.

> My brother once told me that he'd seen a wolf in our garden, but I didn't believe him because he's always making things up. He probably saw a dog.

Unit 6 • Telling tales   55

6C CULTURE
Myth or reality?

I can talk about myths.

1 Look at the photos in the text. What can you see?

2 Read the text, ignoring the gaps. Answer the questions with your own ideas and opinions.
1. Why do you think so many people have reported sightings of a monster?
2. Why do you think Wilson produced a fake photo?
3. Why do you think Spurling waited 60 years before admitting that the photo was a hoax?

3 Match the sentences to the gaps in the text (1–4). There is one sentence that you do not need.
a. Wilson said that his photo showed the monster.
b. In fact, scientists are still looking, using boats, submarines and cameras.
c. There have been many reports of a strange creature in Loch Ness since the sixth century.
d. But Wilson always claimed that his photo was genuine.
e. Plesiosaurs had long necks and small heads, and they lived in deep water.

4 Describe the photo. Where is the creature? What do you think it might be?

The Loch Ness Monster

Loch Ness is a beautiful lake in the highlands of Scotland. It's a popular place for tourists, partly because of the beautiful scenery, but also because it is traditionally the home of Nessie, the Loch Ness Monster. ¹ ☐ However, in spite of the number of sightings, there wasn't any real evidence until 1934 when an English surgeon called Wilson took a famous photograph. ² ☐ The black and white photo clearly showed a creature with a long neck and a small head, and some experts said that it might be a Plesiosaur, a creature from the time of the dinosaurs. ³ ☐ However, other people believed that the photo was a fake. They said that the Loch was only 10,000 years old, much too recent for a Plesiosaur. For nearly 60 years, people asked themselves if the photo was genuine or fake. Then, in 1993, the truth came out: a film director called Wetherell had arranged the photo as a hoax. He had asked a man called Ian Spurling if he could make a model of the monster. Sixty years later, when he was 90 years old, Spurling admitted that the 'monster' was in fact a toy submarine!

Although Wilson's photo was fake, there have been lots of other reports of a monster in the lake since. Many people still believe that something strange lives there. ⁴ ☐ And you don't need to visit Loch Ness to look for the monster. You can visit www.lochness.co.uk and look for Nessie on the live webcam!

5 🎧 2.03 Listen to the programme about the mysterious creature, Sasquatch. How many sightings does it describe?

6 🎧 2.03 Listen again. Are the sentences true or false?
1. The earliest stories of Sasquatch come from Native Americans who lived in the North West.
2. In 1884, some men captured a creature that they named 'Jacko'. It was like a human but taller and stronger.
3. They didn't take 'Jacko' back to London because the creature didn't want to leave its home.
4. Albert Ostman claimed that he spent six days camping in the mountains.
5. Albert Ostman told his story 33 years later.
6. In 1988, a boy saw Sasquatch while he was fishing.
7. Sasquatch is white with a pink face.

7 Work in pairs. Imagine that one of you has seen a Sasquatch. Decide:
- what you were doing when you saw it
- what it looked like
- what it did
- how you reacted when you saw it

8 **SPEAKING** Work in pairs. Role-play a dialogue using your notes from exercise 7. One of you is the witness, the other is a TV news reporter.

> I understand that you recently saw a creature that you believe to be a Sasquatch.

> That's right.

> Could you tell me what you were doing at the time?

> Well, I was …

56 Unit 6 • Telling tales

6D GRAMMAR
Reported speech (questions)

I can report questions which other people have asked.

1 Describe the picture. Why do you think the old man is there? What might they be talking about?

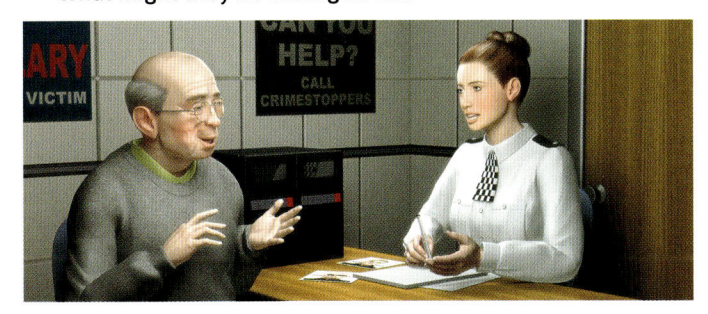

2 🎧 **2.04** Complete the interview with the questions. Then listen and check.

> Can you describe him?
> Are you sure?
> What did you see?
> Why are you smiling, Inspector?
> Do you recognise any of these men?
> How many men did you see?
> Will you have a look at these photos?
> Have you had a cup of tea?

Police Inspector	Good morning, Mr Brown. Come in. ¹_____
Mr Brown	Yes, I have, thank you.
PI	I'd like to ask you a few questions. First, ²_____
Mr Brown	I saw the men running out of the post office.
PI	³_____
Mr Brown	Two. One of them was carrying a gun.
PI	⁴_____
Mr Brown	He was quite tall. He had long dark hair and he was wearing jeans and a leather jacket.
PI	⁵_____
Mr Brown	Yes, of course.
PI	⁶_____
Mr Brown	Um, let me see … Yes, that's him!
PI	⁷_____
Mr Brown	Yes, absolutely certain. ⁸_____
PI	Because we arrested him this morning!

3 Mr Brown went home and told his wife about the interview. This is what he said. Underline all the reported questions.

> 'First, the inspector asked me if I'd had a cup of tea, which was very kind. But I'd just had one. Anyway, then she asked me what I'd seen, so I told her about the man. And she asked me if I could describe him. Well, I could, of course. Then she asked me if I would have a look at some photos and asked me if I recognised any of the men in them. And I did! It was the man with the gun! She asked me if I was sure. But I'd recognise him anywhere. The inspector had a big grin on her face, so I asked her why she was smiling. She told me they had arrested the man that morning!'

4 Compare the questions in the dialogue with the reported questions in exercise 3. Then choose the correct words in the *Learn this!* box to complete the rules.

> **LEARN THIS!**
> **Reported questions**
> In reported questions
> 1 the reporting verb is *ask* / *say* / *tell*.
> 2 the tense changes *are* / *aren't* are the same as for reported statements. (See page 55 if necessary.)
> 3 the subject comes *before* / *after* the verb.
> 4 we *use* / *don't use* *do* or *did*.
> 5 we use *if* / *that* when we report yes/no questions.

●● Grammar Builder 6.3: Reported speech (questions): p. 118

5 Read the dialogue. Then complete the text.

Rob	Can I go out tonight?
Mum	Where are you planning to go?
Rob	I want to see the new Brad Pitt film.
Mum	Have you got much homework?
Rob	No, I haven't. The teacher didn't give us any.
Mum	OK. Do you want to eat before you go?
Rob	Yes, please. Is there any pasta?

Rob asked ¹_____ that night.
His mum asked him ²_____.
Rob told ³_____ film. Then she ⁴_____ homework. He said he didn't.
He added that the teacher ⁵_____.
His mum agreed that he could go out and asked him ⁶_____. Rob said he did and asked ⁷_____.

6 Write down six questions to ask your partner. Use a different tense or verb from the box in each question.

> present simple   present continuous   past simple
> present perfect   can   will

What kind of music do you like?

7 **SPEAKING** Play a class game in two teams.
• One pair from team 1 asks and answers a question from exercise 6.

> What kind of music do you like?
> I like dance music.

• One person from team 2 has to remember and report the question and answer.

> Nick asked Fiona what kind of music she liked.
> Fiona said that she liked dance music.

Unit 6 • Telling tales   57

6 E READING
Was he who he said he was?

I can understand an account of a famous nineteenth-century legal case.

'I'm your long-lost son!'

A Over 150 years ago, a rich woman in England called Lady Tichborne put advertisements in newspapers around the world. They announced that she was looking for news about her son, Sir Roger Tichborne, who had been on a ship called *The Bella* travelling back from South America in 1854. *The Bella* had sunk, and all passengers were presumed drowned, but Lady Tichborne refused to believe that Roger had died.

B Eleven years after the accident Lady Tichborne received a letter from a lawyer in Sydney, Australia. The lawyer explained that he was representing a man called Arthur Orton. Orton had told the lawyer that he was Lady Tichborne's son. Overjoyed, Lady Tichborne asked an old family servant who was now living in Sydney to visit Orton and corroborate his story. The servant remembered a slim, dark-haired young man, but found Orton to be fat with light brown hair. However, Orton could remember so many details about the family that he soon convinced the servant that he was Sir Roger.

C So, Orton met Lady Tichborne in Paris. She was French and had taught Roger to speak the language fluently. When she saw Orton she was so happy to have her precious son back, even though he looked rather different and couldn't speak a word of French. Lady Tichborne promised Orton that he would receive £1,000 a year. Once Lady Tichborne had accepted him, many other friends and family members did the same. However, several members of the family were unhappy. They alleged that the man was an impostor, but Lady Tichborne ignored them.

D When Lady Tichborne died, Orton wanted to claim all of the family land and money from Lady Tichborne's younger son, Henry. The family

Roger Tichborne (above) and Arthur Orton (right)

The trial of Arthur Orton

58 Unit 6 • Telling tales

hired lawyers to investigate him, and in 1874 there was a famous trial that lasted 188 days. Over 100 witnesses claimed that Orton was Sir Roger. However, the lawyers proved that Orton had been born in London, the son of a butcher. The jury found him guilty and he was sentenced to ten years in prison. Many people who had supported him refused to believe the truth and started a protest in the streets of London. However, when he left prison in 1884 everyone had forgotten him. In 1885, Orton confessed that he had been an impostor all along, but later he claimed he was innocent. He died in poverty in 1898, and his coffin still bears the name Sir Roger Tichborne!

1 Read the text quickly. Match four of the topics with the paragraphs (A–D).
1 The case comes to court
2 Sir Roger Tichborne – lost at sea?
3 A meeting in Europe
4 The impostor's early life
5 News from Australia

2 Choose the best answers.
1 Lady Tichborne put advertisements in newspapers because
   a she wanted to contact her son on *The Bella*.
   b she didn't believe that *The Bella* had sunk.
   c she thought that her son was still alive.
   d her son hadn't written to her for a long time.
2 The Australian lawyer contacted Lady Tichborne because
   a he was her son.
   b Arthur Orton had told him that he was Sir Roger.
   c he saw one of the newspaper advertisements.
   d Arthur Orton wanted to return to England.
3 When a former family servant met Orton in Australia
   a he was sure that Orton was Lady Tichborne's son because Orton could remember a lot of things about the family.
   b he didn't think that Orton was Lady Tichborne's son because he was fatter and his hair was a different colour.
   c he wasn't sure if Orton was Lady Tichborne's son.
   d he didn't think he was Lady Tichborne's son, but he told her that he was convinced.

4 Lady Tichborne
   a taught Orton to speak French when he arrived in Paris.
   b had taught Sir Roger to speak French.
   c could speak French, but Sir Roger hadn't learnt the language.
   d was so happy because Orton could speak French.
5 Lady Tichborne believed Orton was her son
   a and so did her family and friends.
   b but her family ignored Orton.
   c but none of her family believed Orton.
   d but some members of her family thought she was wrong.
6 At the trial
   a Orton admitted he wasn't Sir Roger.
   b the jury believed Orton's story.
   c Orton was found guilty.
   d 100 witnesses gave evidence.
7 After Orton came out of prison
   a nobody remembered him and he died fourteen years later, a poor man.
   b everyone said that he was an impostor.
   c people protested in the streets of London.
   d he always insisted that he was Sir Roger.

3 Read the *Learn this!* box. Find three examples of the noun *family* used like an adjective in the text. Does it come before or after the noun?

> **LEARN THIS!**
> **Compound nouns: nouns functioning as adjectives**
> We can use a noun like an adjective to define another noun.
> a **ham** sandwich   an **egg** sandwich
> a **football** team   a **volleyball** team
> a **wine** glass   a **beer** glass

●●● Vocabulary Builder 6.2: Compound nouns (2): p. 134

4 Complete the text about Orton's trial. Use the words in the box.

| guilty innocent jury lawyers prison prove |
| sentenced trial witnesses |

At his ¹_____ in London, the ²_____ tried to ³_____ that Orton was an impostor. Orton claimed that he was ⁴_____ , and many ⁵_____ corroborated his story. However, the ⁶_____ found him ⁷_____ and he was ⁸_____ to ten years in ⁹_____ .

5 **SPEAKING** Work in pairs. Tell your partner three things about your past – two true and one imaginary. Don't say which one is not true. Can your partner guess?

Unit 6 • Telling tales **59**

6F EVERYDAY ENGLISH
Deciding what to do

I can negotiate and compromise.

William What shall we do tonight? Do you fancy going out?
Jessica Mmm. Not really. I'm not in the mood. I think I'd rather stay in and watch TV.
William But there's nothing worth watching on the telly tonight. Let's go and see a film.
Jessica But I don't want to go out. I'm tired. We could get a DVD instead.
William Maybe, but I still think it would be nice to go out.
Jessica Why don't I cook you a meal?
William That sounds nice. What will you cook?
Jessica I'll do your favourite – steak and chips.
William OK, you've persuaded me. I'll go and fetch a DVD.
Jessica And I'll start cooking!

1 🎧 2.05 Cover the dialogue. Listen and answer the questions.
1 What does Jessica want to do at first?
2 What does William want to do at first?
3 What do they finally agree to do?

2 Read the dialogue and check your answers.

3 Look at the coloured phrases in the dialogue. Match them with the functions in the box.

compromising or agreeing   objecting   persuading suggesting

green _____   red _____
blue _____   orange _____

Intransitive phrasal verbs
Some phrasal verbs are intransitive. They do not take a direct object and you cannot separate the verb and the preposition.
carry on   wake up   break down   get up
I asked him to stop, but he carried on walking.

4 Read the *Learn this!* box. Then find two more intransitive phrasal verbs of this kind in the dialogue.

● ● Vocabulary Builder 6.3: Intransitive phrasal verbs: p. 134

5 🎧 2.06 Listen. Complete the sentences with the correct names.
First dialogue: Tanya and Peter
1 _____ wants to go for a walk.
2 _____ doesn't want to go on a bike ride.
3 _____ suggests going swimming.
4 _____ doesn't really want to walk to the pool.
5 _____ offers to buy ice creams for both of them.
Second dialogue: Ann and David
6 _____ suggests going to the cinema.
7 _____ hasn't got much money.
8 _____ doesn't like badminton.
9 _____ suggests chess.
10 _____ suggests playing cards.

6 🎧 2.06 Listen again. Complete the sentences.
First dialogue: Tanya and Peter
1 ___ ___ ___ go out for a walk?
2 ___ ___ ___ fancy it. It's too hot.
3 ___ ___ a bike ride, then?
4 Oh, ___ on!
5 OK, you've ___ ___ ___ it.
Second dialogue: Ann and David
6 ___ ___ ___ to the cinema.
7 You'll ___ ___ when you get there.
8 ___ ___ a game of badminton?
9 I'm ___ ___ badminton.
10 OK. ___ not?

7 🎧 2.07 **PRONUNCIATION** Listen, check and repeat. Copy the intonation.

8 Match the sentences in exercise 6 with the four functions in exercise 3.

9 **SPEAKING** Work in pairs. Use phrases from exercise 6 and the dialogue in exercise 1.
Student A: Make a suggestion. Use the activities below or your own ideas.
Student B: Object to it. Give a reason for objecting.
1 go for a walk
2 go out for something to eat
3 play cards
4 do some homework together
5 play computer games
6 listen to music

> Do you fancy going for a walk?
> Not really. It's too cold out.

10 **SPEAKING** Work in pairs. Prepare a dialogue like the one in exercise 1. Each of you should suggest something to do, make objections and then agree on a compromise.

11 **SPEAKING** Act out your dialogue to the class.

6G WRITING

A formal letter: making a reservation

I can write a letter making a reservation.

19-21 August

MURDER MYSTERY WEEKEND

people, 6 twin rooms same floor?

The murderer is one of your group. It could be **YOU**!

Stay in our beautiful country house hotel near the historic city of York. On arrival, we will give you a character to play and a costume to wear.

Come as an individual or come as a group (minimum ten people) and have a murder mystery weekend just with your friends.

Phone 08716 7287 for more information.

Spoke to Ms Weatherby, who will send directions. (Can she send by e-mail?) Needs £600 deposit. How much is total?

we need to send sizes

1 Read the advertisement. What do you think happens at a 'Murder Mystery Weekend'? Would you enjoy it?

2 Read the notes that Tyler added to the advertisement. Then read his letter. What information does he forget to include?

Dear Ms Weatherby

Further to our recent telephone conversation, I am writing to confirm that I wish to make a reservation for the Murder Mystery Weekend from 19 to 21 August.

There will be twelve people in our party and we will require six twin rooms in total. I would be very grateful if you could give us rooms on the same floor.

On the telephone, you mentioned that you would send me directions by post. Would it be possible to e-mail me the directions instead so that I can forward them to everyone in our group?

I am enclosing a cheque for £600 as a deposit. Please could you confirm the total amount due? I assume that the balance will be payable at the end of the weekend. Would you mind sending me a receipt for the deposit?

I look forward to hearing from you in due course.

Yours sincerely

Tyler Hamlyn

Mr T Hamlyn

3 **Find the phrases in the letter.**

1 A phrase for referring back to a telephone conversation.
2 A more formal way of saying 'I want to …'.
3 A phrase meaning 'a room with two beds'.
4 Four different ways of making polite requests:
   a ______ ______ ______ grateful ______ ______ ______ … .
   b ______ ______ ______ possible ______ …?
   c Please ______ ______ …?
   d Would ______ ______ …?
5 A phrase that anticipates a reply to the letter.
6 The phrase that comes immediately before the sender's signature.

LEARN THIS!

Verbs with two objects

1 Some verbs can be followed by both an indirect and a direct object.
   My cousin wrote ***me a letter.***
   John bought ***his girlfriend a CD.***
2 The indirect object comes first and is usually a person. The direct object is usually a thing.
3 If we want the direct object to come first, we must put *to* or *for* before the indirect object.
   My cousin wrote a letter ***to me.***
   John bought a CD ***for his girlfriend.***

4 **Read the *Learn this!* box. Find three verbs with two objects in the letter.**

5 **Rewrite the sentences. Replace the phrase with *to* or *for* with an indirect object after the verb.**

1 Can you do a favour for me?
2 Would you mind showing your pictures to us?
3 She read her poem to the class.
4 He cooked dinner for his friends.
5 I'm going to tell that story to my brother.
6 They didn't offer any food to their guests.

Grammar Builder 6.4: Verbs with two objects: p. 119

6 **Plan a formal letter to Ms Weatherby making a reservation. Include this information:**

- the dates of your stay and the number of guests/rooms
- correct some information you gave on the phone, e.g. one friend is a vegetarian (and the hotel needs to know this)
- request a brochure or leaflet, if the hotel has one
- make an additional request or instruction

7 **Write a formal letter making a reservation of 120–150 words. Use your notes from exercise 6.**

LANGUAGE REVIEW 5–6

Vocabulary

1 Complete the text with the words in the box.

> blog   flash drive   laptop   web cam   website
> wireless router

Brad has got all the latest computer technology. When he wants to video chat with his friends he uses the ¹_____ on his main computer. He's got a ²_____ which he takes to work, but he can go online in any room in his house because of the ³_____ he has in the living room. He's designed his own ⁴_____ where he posts his photos and writes his thoughts on his ⁵_____. He saves all his files on a ⁶_____ which he keeps in the drawer of his desk.

Mark /6

2 Complete the words to make objects in the house.

1 a _ _ c _ _ _ _ r   4 b _ _ k _ _ s _
2 c _ _ b _ _ r _   5 m _ _ r _ _
3 c _ _ p _ _   6 w _ _ d _ _ b _

Mark /6

Grammar

3 Correct the sentences.
1 I think I won't get married until I'm 30.
2 Reece might to buy a flat if he earns enough money.
3 If Erin will pass her driving test, she'll buy a car.
4 Toby could not go to university because he doesn't like studying.
5 Isabelle goes to university if she passes her exams.

Mark /5

4 Complete Kai's life plan with the future continuous or the future perfect form of the verbs in brackets.

I ¹_____ (finish) university by the time I'm 22 and then I'll get a job. By the time I'm 30 I ²_____ (save) enough money to buy my own flat. In ten years time I ³_____ (go out) with one of my colleagues and by the time I'm 35 we ⁴_____ (get married). We'll have two beautiful children, and they ⁵_____ (grow up) by the time I retire. I think life is going to be good to me.

Mark /5

5 Rewrite the direct speech as reported speech.
1 'I didn't finish the report yesterday,' said Rebecca.
   Rebecca said _____.
2 'I'm having problems with my computer,' she said.
   She said _____.
3 'I haven't been able to log onto the Internet this week,' she told Ben.
   She told _____.
4 'I'll look at it for you some time today,' said Ben.
   Ben told _____.
5 'If you can mend my computer, I'll cook you dinner,' said Rebecca.
   Rebecca told Ben _____.
6 'That sounds fine by me,' said Ben.
   Ben said _____.

Mark /6

Everyday English

6 Put the lines (a–e) in the correct order to complete the dialogue.
a I haven't got anything planned either. Shall we go out on Saturday night?
b I don't really fancy dancing. Shall we go out for dinner?
c Great idea. Maybe we could try that new Italian?
d OK. Let's go dancing.
e Nothing special. How about you?

Boy   What are you doing this weekend?
Girl   ☐
Boy   ☐
Girl   ☐
Boy   ☐
Girl   ☐
Boy   Why not? Shall I book a table?

Mark /5

7 Put the words in the correct order.
1 really / tennis / playing / in / for / not / mood / the / I'm
   _____
2 on / worth / TV / watching / There's / nothing
   _____
3 really / to / centres / into / I'm / going / shopping / not
   _____
4 there / enjoy / You'll / you / it / get / when
   _____
5 talked / out / dinner / me / You've / going / into / for
   _____

Mark /5

Total /38

EXAM CHALLENGE Workbook pages 94–97

62 Language Review 5–6

Skills Round-up 1–6

Speaking

1 Work in pairs. Talk about your plans for the weekend. Use phrases from the box to help you.

> What are your plans for …? What about you?
> What are you up to on …?

Reading

2 Read the descriptions of four flats (A–D). If you had to live in one of them, which would you choose, and why?

A Two-bedroom flat, furnished

Above a shop, very close to the city centre. The accommodation consists of one double bedroom and one single bedroom, a bathroom (with bath, no shower), and a living room with kitchen area. Modern furniture and brand new cooker and fridge. (No washing machine.)
Available from 1 November
Monthly rent: £750   Deposit: £750

B One-bedroom flat, unfurnished

Basement flat in a quiet, residential area. Accommodation comprises one large bedroom, a small study, a living room and a separate kitchen equipped with cooker, fridge and washing machine. There is a bathroom with a bath and a shower.
Available from 15 August
Monthly rent: £700   Deposit: £1,400

C Studio flat, furnished

Unusually spacious, ground floor studio flat for rent. Combined living room/bedroom measures 5 x 6 metres. Separate kitchen with electric cooker, fridge and microwave (no washing machine). Shower room and separate WC. Rent includes broadband connection.
Available from 1 December
Monthly rent: £600   Deposit: £1,000

D One-bedroom flat, furnished

A beautiful flat on the sixth floor of a tower block, with stunning views over the city. The accommodation consists of a bedroom with single bed and wardrobe, a living room, a bathroom, and a kitchen with cooker, fridge and microwave (no washing machine). Rent includes heating but excludes electricity. Satellite TV included in rent.
Available immediately
Monthly rent: £550   Deposit: £750

3 Match the sentences with the flats (A–D). There is one sentence that you do not need.
1 This flat is ready to move into now.
2 You don't have to pay extra to use the Internet in this flat.
3 You can do your laundry in this flat.
4 The deposit for this flat is less than a month's rent.
5 There are beds for three people in this flat.

Listening

4 🎧 2.08 Which flat from exercise 2 does Marek go to see?

5 🎧 2.08 Listen again. Answer the questions.
1 Is the flat above or below the level of the pavement?
2 Is the main room bigger or smaller than Marek imagined?
3 What surprises Marek about the kitchen?
4 What does Marek think of the shower room and WC?
5 How many other flats has Marek arranged to see?

Writing

6 Write a questionnaire with six questions to find out as much as possible about your partner's house or flat. Use the ideas in the box to help you.

> house or flat?   which floor?   number of bedrooms?
> near or far from the town centre?   large living room?
> modern or old-fashioned furniture?   satellite TV?
> broadband Internet?   washing machine?

7 True love?

THIS UNIT INCLUDES
Vocabulary • dating and relationships • time expressions • three-part phrasal verbs
Grammar • comparative and superlative adjectives and adverbs
• second conditional • *I wish, If only, I'd rather* • question tags • *in, at* and *on* with time expressions
Speaking • telling the story of a relationship • making conversation
Writing • an informal letter: reply to an invitation

A VOCABULARY AND LISTENING
Relationships

I can talk about dating and relationships.

1 Work in pairs. Put the phrases in the box into the order that they might happen in a relationship.

Dating and relationships	
chat somebody up	ask somebody out
fall in love (with somebody)	fancy somebody
get back together (with somebody)	fall out (with somebody)
get engaged (to somebody)	get divorced
get on well (with somebody)	get married (to somebody)
make up	go out (with somebody)
	split up (with somebody)

2 Complete the story with *in, on, out, up, with* or nothing.

Zak and Lily met at a party in 1994. Zak fancied ¹___ Lily the moment he saw her. He started to chat her ²___ and they got ³___ really well. Lily thought Zak was cute, but she was already going ⁴___ ___ somebody. Zak and Lily didn't see each other for a few months. Then Zak heard from a friend that Lily had split up ⁵___ her boyfriend. Zak phoned Lily the same day – he didn't want to give her time to get back together ⁶___ her boyfriend! He asked her ⁷___ . She said yes, and Zak and Lily went ⁸___ for three months. They fell ⁹___ love. It wasn't an easy relationship – they were always falling ¹⁰___ and then making ¹¹___ again – but they stayed together. After about six months, they got engaged ¹²___, and a year after that, they got married ¹³___. More than ten years later, many of their friends have got divorced ¹⁴___ but Zak and Lily are still together.

3 🎧 2.09 Listen. What is happening in each scene? Use expressions from exercise 1.

Scene 1	They're getting engaged.
Scene 2	
Scene 3	
Scene 4	
Scene 5	

4 Look at the story of Harry and Daisy's relationship. Label each picture with a phrase or phrases from exercise 1.

1. *Do you come here often?* — one day in July
2. *Would you like to go to* — two days later
3. for six months
4. a week later
5. *Sorry!* — the next day
6. on 14 February

Speaking tip

When you're preparing for a speaking task, make a note of the words and expressions that you can use in your answers.

5 Read the speaking tip. Then answer the questions about the pictures.

Picture 1: Where were they? What were they doing?
Picture 3: Where were they?
Picture 4: What did Daisy do when she was angry?
Picture 6: What did Harry give Daisy?

6 **SPEAKING** Tell the story of Harry and Daisy's relationship. Use the pictures, your notes from exercise 5 and the time expressions in the box to help you.

Time expressions	after a (few days) after that
before finally first for (two months) in the end (two years) later the moment … the same day	

• • Vocabulary Builder 7.1: Three-part phrasal verbs: p.134

64 Unit 7 • True love?

7B GRAMMAR Comparison

I can make comparisons.

1 Look at the photo. What do you think is happening?

Speed dating

Modern life is becoming ¹_____ (fast) and ²_____ (busy), but at the same time, people are becoming ³_____ (isolated). These days, people in their twenties and thirties are finding it ⁴_____ (difficult) to socialise and meet potential partners because they work harder and have ⁵_____ (small) social circles. They can go to bars and clubs, but for many, speed dating is a ⁶_____ (good) option because it allows them to meet a lot of people more quickly, and in a less stressful environment. This is how it works: an equal number of men and women meet at a café, get into pairs, and chat for three minutes; when a bell rings, you move round to the next person and chat for another three minutes; after three more minutes you move round again, and so on. At the end of the evening, you make a list of the people that you got on with the best and found the ⁷_____ (attractive) – or the least unattractive! Then you give your list to the organisers, and if the people on it feel the same way about you, the organisers give you each other's contact details. It may not be ⁸_____ (romantic) as a traditional date, but for many, it's the ⁹_____ (easy) and ¹⁰_____ (sensible) choice.

2 Complete the text with the comparative or superlative form of the adjectives in brackets.

3 🎧 2.10 Listen and check your answers to exercise 2. Do you think speed dating sounds fun? Give reasons.

4 Read the *Learn this!* box. Then match the words in red in the text with the explanations (1–5).
1 a comparative form of an adjective with *less*.
2 a superlative form of an adjective with *least*.
3 a comparative form of an adverb with *more*.
4 a comparative form of an adverb with *-er*.
5 a superlative form of an irregular adverb.

> **LEARN THIS!**
> **Comparative and superlative adverbs**
> We usually form comparative and superlative adverbs with *more* and *most*. However, we add *-er* to some adverbs.
> *Please drive more slowly! Mum drives faster than dad.*
> **less and least**
> *Less* is the opposite of *more*, *least* is the opposite of *most*. We can use them with adjectives and adverbs.
> *Who finished the exercise least quickly?*

5 🎧 2.11 Listen to five people talking about their experiences of speed dating. Match the sentences (a–e) with the speakers (1–5).
a It was difficult at first but later I could chat more easily. ☐
b It's the least enjoyable experience I've ever had. ☐
c It was less enjoyable than I expected. ☐
d Time passed most quickly when I was talking to people I liked. ☐
e It was less stressful than chatting somebody up in a bar. ☐

6 Read the *Learn this!* box. Then find examples of points 1 and 2 in exercise 5.

> **LEARN THIS!**
> **Comparison**
> 1 We can make comparisons with simple nouns (*She's more confident than her brother.*) and also with clauses (*She's less talkative than she used to be.*).
> 2 We often use a superlative with the present perfect and *ever*. *He's the shyest person I've ever met.*

7 Read sentence A. Then complete sentence B so that it means the same. Include the word in brackets.
1 A London isn't as crowded as Tokyo.
   B London _____ Tokyo. (less)
2 A I've never met anyone nicer than Tom.
   B Tom _____ met. (the)
3 A Kieran has got a louder voice than Phoebe.
   B Kieran talks _____ Phoebe. (more)
4 A This is the easiest question.
   B This is _____ question. (difficult)
5 A Roger is a faster worker than Dan.
   B Roger _____ Dan. (quickly)

8 **SPEAKING** Work in pairs. Ask and answer questions with *most* or *least* and the present perfect with *ever*. Use the prompts below and your own ideas.
1 stressful exam / take   4 sensible person / meet
2 isolated place / visit   5 good choice / make
3 romantic film / see   6 long book / read

> What's the most/least stressful exam you've ever taken?
>> Our science exam last month.

● ● ● **Grammar Builder 7.1: Comparison: p. 119**

Unit 7 • True love? 65

7C CULTURE W B Yeats

I can understand a poem.

1 How many poets can you name:
a from your own country?
b from other countries?

2 🎧 **2.12** Listen to a radio documentary about the life of W B Yeats, a famous poet. Which of these things does the speaker talk about?

growing up   relationships   school   travel   writing

3 🎧 **2.12** Listen again and choose the correct answers.
1 Where did Yeats spend his childhood?
  a In Ireland.
  b In Ireland and England.
  c In England.
2 Where did he first hear Irish folk tales?
  a At home.   b In Dublin.   c At school.
3 Maud Gonne was
  a an English nationalist.
  b a terrorist.   c an Irish nationalist.
4 Yeats asked Maud Gonne to marry him
  a twice.   b three times.   c four times.
5 Which of Yeats' works are more romantic?
  a His early poems.
  b His later poems.   c His plays.
6 When did Yeats die?
  a In 1923.   b In 1939.   c In 1948.

4 Try to complete this famous poem by Yeats with the nouns in the box. Remember that poems often rhyme.

bars   beauty   book   eyes   face   fire   mountains
sleep   sorrows   stars

5 🎧 **2.13** Listen and check your answers to exercise 4. Is it a romantic poem or a political poem?

6 Match each verse of the poem (1–3) with a summary (a–c).
a Remember that there were lots of people who loved you for your looks, but that I loved you for yourself. I especially loved you when you looked sad.
b As you bend down near the fire, say quietly to yourself how you lost my love. But though I was very sad, my love for you didn't die.
c When you are an old woman, falling asleep by the fire, read the book which contains this poem and think about how beautiful you were when you were young.

7 **SPEAKING** Think of a famous poet from your own country. How much do you know about their life and works? Can you think of any similarities with W B Yeats?

> They both wrote works with a political message.

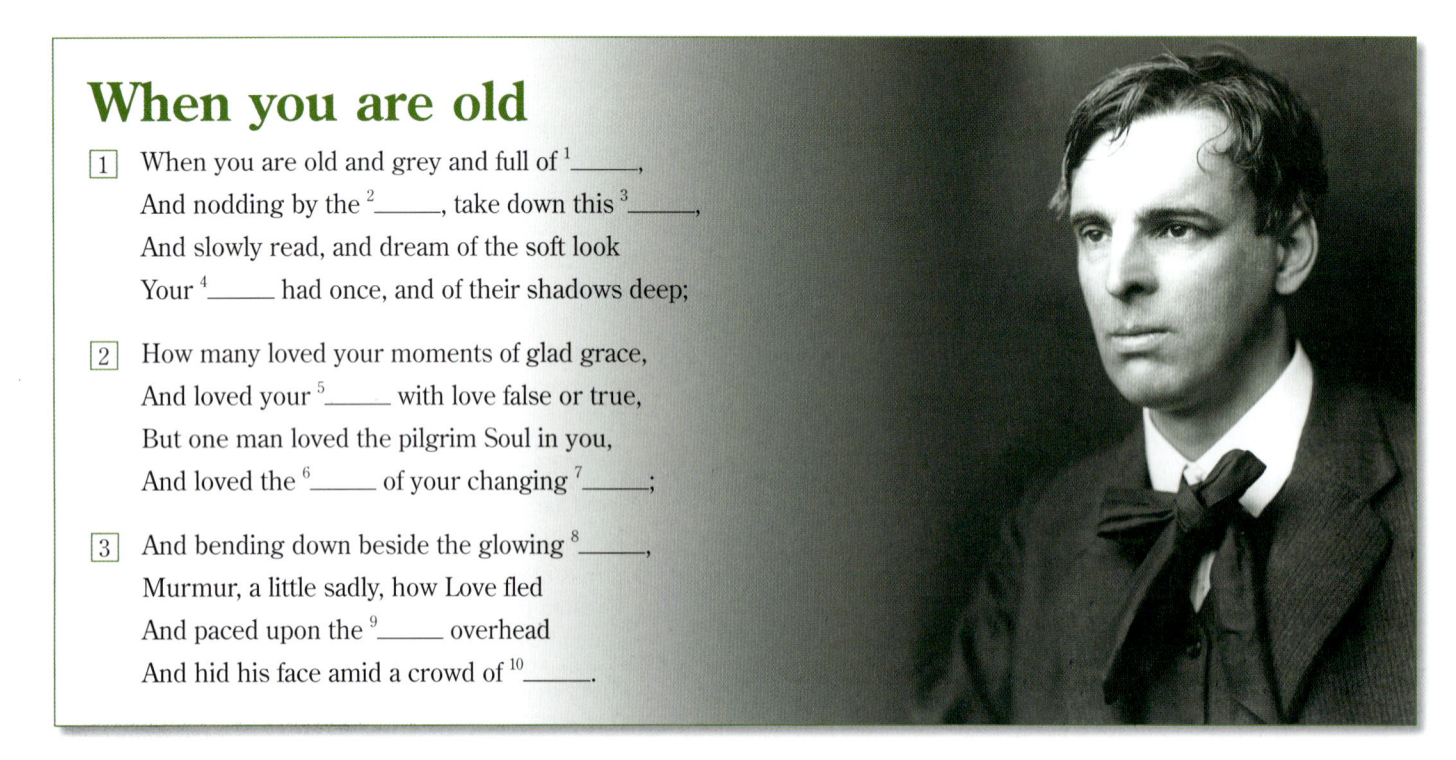

When you are old

[1] When you are old and grey and full of ¹_____,
And nodding by the ²_____, take down this ³_____,
And slowly read, and dream of the soft look
Your ⁴_____ had once, and of their shadows deep;

[2] How many loved your moments of glad grace,
And loved your ⁵_____ with love false or true,
But one man loved the pilgrim Soul in you,
And loved the ⁶_____ of your changing ⁷_____;

[3] And bending down beside the glowing ⁸_____,
Murmur, a little sadly, how Love fled
And paced upon the ⁹_____ overhead
And hid his face amid a crowd of ¹⁰_____.

66   Unit 7 • True love?

7D GRAMMAR
Talking about imaginary situations

I can talk about imaginary situations and things I would like to change.

1 🎧 **2.14** Listen to the conversation and choose the correct verb forms. Decide whether Max and Jade are:
   a getting on well.   b falling out.   c making up.

Jade   I wish we ¹**can / could** afford a holiday this year. These beaches look amazing!
Max   Yes. If only we ²**have / had** €3,000!
Jade   If I ³**am / was** rich, ⁴**we'd spend / we spent** every winter together on a tropical island.
Max   Really? I'd rather go skiing in the Alps. Lying on a beach is boring.
Jade   Max! It ⁵**wouldn't be / wasn't** boring if you ⁶**are / were** with me. I wish ⁷**you'd be / you were** more romantic sometimes!
Max   Well anyway, we can't afford it. If you ⁸**didn't / wouldn't** buy so many clothes, ⁹**we'd have / we had** more money for holidays.
Jade   But I like clothes! Would you rather I ¹⁰**wear / wore** a tracksuit all the time, like you?
Max   What's wrong with my tracksuits?!

2 Read and complete the *Learn this!* box. How many examples of the second conditional are in the dialogue?

> **LEARN THIS!**
> **Second conditional**
> We use the **second conditional** to talk about an imaginary situation or event and its result. We use the _____ simple for the situation or event and _____ + base form for the result.

3 Complete the sentences with your own ideas.
   1 If I had €3,000 for a holiday, …
   2 If I had €1,000 for some new outfits, …
   3 If I could live anywhere in the world, …
   4 If I spoke perfect English, …
   5 If I fancied my friend's boyfriend/girlfriend, …
   6 If I lived on a tropical island, …
   7 If I had a holiday home in the Alps, …
   8 If I fell out with my best friend, …

● ● **Grammar Builder 7.2:** Second conditional: p. 120

4 Read the *Learn this!* box. Underline an example of each expression in the dialogue in exercise 1.

> **LEARN THIS!**
> **I wish, If only, I'd rather**
> 1 We use *I wish …* or *If only …* with the past simple to say that we really want a situation to be different.
>   *I wish it was the weekend. If only I had a car.*
> 2 We use *I wish …* or *If only …* with *would* + base form to say that we really want somebody's (or something's) behaviour to be different.
>   *I wish you wouldn't shout. I wish this pen would work.*
> 3 We use *I'd rather* with a base form to express a preference.
>   'Do you want a pizza?' 'I'd rather have a sandwich.'
> 4 We use *I'd rather* with the past simple to say that we really want somebody's (or something's) behaviour to be different. *I'd rather you didn't keep interrupting.*

5 Complete the sentences with *I wish* (or *If only*) and *I'd rather*.
   1 I can't afford that jacket. _____ it was cheaper!
   2 I don't like living in a flat. _____ live in a house.
   3 I'd like to know how Jackie is. _____ she would phone.
   4 I'm getting fat. _____ do some exercise than go on a diet.
   5 You can wear jeans if you want, but _____ you wore something more formal.
   6 _____ my brother wouldn't borrow my bike.

6 How many sentences can you make using this chart?

I wish	she'd do better in her exams.
If only	she had a job.
I'd rather	I didn't have to work.
If she worked harder,	stay in bed.
She'd have more money if	we lived in the USA.
	our parents wouldn't worry.

7 **SPEAKING** Work in pairs. Student A: Make comments with *I wish …* and the ideas in the box or your own ideas. Student B: Reply using *I'd rather …* and your own ideas. Student A: Say how life would be different.

> I / live near the sea   I / be 21 years old
> I / have a new mobile phone   lessons / be longer
> it / be Christmas   I / can play the piano   I / own a Ferrari

> I wish I lived near the sea.

> Really? I'd rather live in the mountains.

> But if I lived near the sea, I could go to the beach every day in the summer.

● ● **Grammar Builder 7.3:** *I wish, If only, I'd rather*: p. 121

Unit 7 • True love?   **67**

E READING
Internet relationships

I can understand and react to a website article about Internet relationships.

1 SPEAKING Discuss the questions with the class.
1. Can you fall in love with somebody without meeting them face to face?
2. In what ways can online relationships be dangerous?
3. Do you know anybody who has started a relationship online?

Reading tip
Find out what kind of text you're going to read and what type of information you may expect to find in it. This will help you understand the text better.

2 Read the reading tip. Then look quickly through the text and decide what type of text it is.
- a a newspaper report
- b an online article
- c an informal letter
- d a literary review

3 Read the text. Does the writer think Internet relationships have more advantages or disadvantages?

4 Are the sentences true or false? Correct the false sentences.
1. The writer's family are worried that she has too many friends.
2. A lot of people read the writer's articles online.
3. The writer's online friends get angry with her if she is late.
4. The writer thinks online relationships are less stressful than friends in the 'real' world.
5. The writer hardly ever interacts with people in the 'real' world.
6. The writer knows some of her online friends better than she knows her neighbours.
7. The writer thinks it is difficult to care about somebody you've never met face to face.
8. The writer thinks the Internet allows you to get to know people more deeply.

5 Complete the definitions with the words and phrases from the text in the box.

| an obligation   close to your heart   fulfilling   interrupt |
| judge   nothing in common   running in circles |

1. If something is _____, it is very important to you.
2. If something is _____, you have to do it.
3. If you are _____, you are too busy to think.
4. If something is _____, it is very satisfying.
5. If you have _____ with somebody, you do not share any interests or opinions.
6. If you _____ somebody, you speak while they are speaking.
7. If you _____ somebody, you decide what somebody is like, whether you like them, etc.

Are Online Relation...
by Linda Johnson

Well, this is a topic that is close to my heart. My family and friends are always worrying about me because more and more of my life exists online. They keep telling me I should get out more. They say I need a life. I tell them I HAVE a life, it's just different from theirs!

What do they have that I don't? Well, let's explore that question.

They have lots of visitors to their homes. But fewer than I do. Every time I write an article for my website, I'm talking to thousands of people. (The difference is, I don't have to clean my house after my visitors have left!)

They have relationships that require a lot of time and effort. Not me. I have many more friends than they do, but mine don't interrupt me when I'm talking. Mine don't care what I look like. Mine don't judge me by anything other than how I treat them. And mine don't fall out with me if I'm late.

They have obligations that keep them running in circles ... this appointment, that date, this arrangement, that party. Not me. I just sit at my computer with a hot cup of coffee and relax.

I agree that we all need some kind of human interaction and we can't do all our communicating through a keyboard. I have a job that requires that I get out of the house and interact in the 'real' world. But is this the most fulfilling part of my life? Not at all. Most of my most fulfilling experiences recently have been with people I know through the Internet.

For example, I work regularly with a team of computer experts who write articles for this website. I've never even seen most of these people, but they feel like true friends to me: friends that live all over the world, friends that I wouldn't know if it weren't for the Internet. True, I would love to meet them in real life. But, even if I don't, these people remain very real and dear to me. Because I really KNOW them. I certainly know them better than the guy who lives next door to me and with whom I have nothing in common.

So, my answer to the question 'Are Internet relationships real?' is a resounding YES, YES, YES. And don't let your families and 'real' friends convince you differently. Just because you can't 'see' someone, doesn't mean you can't care about them. The Internet allows you the opportunity to know someone for who they are and not for how they look or how they dress. In some ways, the people you know on the Internet are more real than the ones you pass on the street.

Unit 7 • True love?

6 SPEAKING Read the comments about Internet relationships. Is each one an advantage or disadvantage?
1 Nobody can judge you by the clothes you wear.
2 You can say things that you'd be too shy to say face to face.
3 You can't be sure if the other person is telling the truth about their sex, age or appearance.
4 You can 'meet' your friend without leaving the house.
5 You can have friends all over the world.
6 You can't see each other's faces when you're chatting online.

7 Complete the song with the base form or past simple of the verbs in the box.

| ask   be   care   care   dance   hide   hold   hold |
| laugh   love   run   save   see   stand   touch |

8 🎧 2.15 Listen to the song and check your answers to exercise 7.

9 Choose the best ending for the summary of the song.
I love you a lot, but ...
a you don't love me.
b I don't know how to tell you my feelings.
c you're with somebody else.
d how much do you love me?
e we're a long way apart from each other.

10 SPEAKING Work in pairs. Think of songs (in English or your own language) which match the other summaries in exercise 9. Compare your answers with the class.

Hero

▾ Would you ¹_____ if I ²_____ you to dance?
  Would you ³_____ and never look back?
  Would you cry if you ⁴_____ me crying?
  And would you ⁵_____ my soul tonight?

▾ Would you tremble if I ⁶_____ your lips?
  Would you ⁷_____ ?
  Oh please tell me this.
  Now would you die for the one you ⁸_____ ?
  Hold me in your arms tonight.

[chorus]

▾ I can be your hero, baby.
  I can kiss away the pain.
  I will ⁹_____ by you forever.
  You can take my breath away.

▾ Would you swear that you'll always ¹⁰_____ mine?
  Or would you lie?
  Would you run and ¹¹_____ ?
  Am I in too deep?
  Have I lost my mind?
  I don't ¹²_____ ...
  You're here tonight.

[chorus]

▾ Oh, I just want to ¹³_____ you.
  I just want to ¹⁴_____ you.
  Oh yeah. Am I in too deep?
  Have I lost my mind?
  Well, I don't ¹⁵_____ ...
  You're here tonight.

[chorus x2]

Unit 7 • True love?   69

F EVERYDAY ENGLISH
Making conversation

I can introduce myself to someone and find out more about them.

Connor	Excuse me. You're Ben Wilson's sister, aren't you?
Tanya	Yes, I am. My name's Tanya.
Connor	Pleased to meet you, Tanya. I'm Connor.
Tanya	Hi Connor. How do you know Ben?
Connor	We sometimes play volleyball together.
Tanya	Oh, right. Are you really into sport?
Connor	Yes, I am. What about you? Have you got any hobbies?
Tanya	Not really. I like watching TV – and DVDs.
Connor	What kind of films do you like?
Tanya	Anything, really. Comedies, thrillers, horror films.
Connor	I like films too. There are some good films on at the cinema now, aren't there?
Tanya	Yes, I think so.
Connor	Maybe we could go to the cinema some time.
Tanya	Yes, good idea.
Connor	Anyway, I'd better get back to my friends. Nice talking to you.
Tanya	And you. See you around.

1 🎧 2.16 Read and listen to the dialogue. Answer the questions.
1. What is the social connection between Connor and Tanya?
2. What hobby do they share?
3. Why does Connor end the conversation?

2 Read the *Learn this!* box. Find two question tags in the dialogue in exercise 1.

> **LEARN THIS!**
> **Question tags**
> 1 We use question tags when we want somebody to confirm what we are saying. A statement with a question tag often sounds more polite than a direct question or a plain statement.
> *You live near the station, don't you?*
> 2 We use auxiliary verbs (*do*, *have*, *would*, etc.) or the verb *be* in question tags. When the main verb is affirmative the question tag is negative, and vice versa.
> *You passed your exams, didn't you?*
> *You weren't at Jake's party, were you?*

● ● ● **Grammar Builder 7.4: Question tags: p.121**

3 Add question tags to the statements.
1. I've met your friend before.
   I've met your friend before, haven't I?
2. You came to my party.
3. You're the girl who works in the supermarket.
4. You used to be at my school.
5. You were at the concert last weekend.

4 🎧 2.17 Listen to three dialogues. Which pair get on best?
1 Ben and Sue   2 Ed and Jo   3 Mat and Zoe

5 🎧 2.17 Listen again. Complete the sentences from the dialogues. They aren't in the order that you hear them!
1. So _____ me more about your band.
2. I saw you at Rebecca's party, _____ I?
3. Well, I'm _____ I'll see you around.
4. I'm sure we'll _____ into each other again.
5. We've met _____ before, haven't we?
6. What _____ do you like doing at weekends?
7. You were at the gig last week, _____ you?
8. _____, it's time I got back to work.

6 Put the phrases in red in exercise 5 into the correct groups (a–c). Then find one or two more phrases for each group in the dialogue in exercise 1.
a Phrases for initiating a conversation
b Phrases for sustaining a conversation
c Phrases for ending a conversation

7 Work in pairs. Invent two characters and decide:
1. where they are meeting.
2. what the social connection is between them (a friend of a friend, a classmate's brother, etc.).
3. what hobbies they each have.

8 **SPEAKING** Work in pairs. Prepare a dialogue using your notes from exercise 7 and the chart below. Remember to use phrases from exercise 6.

A
- Initiate the conversation.
- Introduce yourself.
- Reply. Ask about B's hobbies.
- Reply.
- Accept or decline.

B
- Reply. Introduce yourself.
- Ask about A's hobbies.
- Reply. Sustain the conversation.
- Make a suggestion or invitation.
- End the conversation.

9 **SPEAKING** Act out your dialogue to the class.

7G WRITING
An informal letter: reply to an invitation

I can write a letter replying to an invitation.

1 Complete the invitations with two of the special occasions from the box.

21st birthday	christening	Christmas	confirmation
engagement	Halloween	May Day	New Year's Eve
Valentine's Day	wedding		

Dear Colin
We're having a ¹_____ party on Saturday, 14 February and would be delighted if you could join us. The party starts at 8.30. There will be food, so please don't eat before you come!
Hope you can make it.
Steve

Dear Megan
Please come to my fancy dress ⁴_____ party on Saturday, 31 October, from 8.00 until late at 97 Morton Lane. There will be a prize for the scariest costume, so you'd better start thinking about your outfit now!
Hope to see you there. Please bring a bottle.
Love
Hannah

2 Read the letter below. Which invitation in exercise 1 does the writer reply to? Complete the first and last lines with the names.

Dear _____
I hope you are well. Thank you so much for your invitation. It sounds like it's going to be a great party, and I wish I could come, but I'm afraid I won't be able to make it. I'm going on holiday with my family the next morning. Our flight leaves at seven o'clock in the morning, so I'll need to get a really early night! We're going to Egypt for some winter sun – I'm really looking forward to it!
I'm sorry I haven't been in touch recently. This year at school is really hard. We have exams almost every week, and I don't go out much even at the weekend. I wish weekends were longer! If I had more free time, I'd be able to see all my friends. Are you working hard too?
I'll give you a call when I'm back from holiday. Maybe we could go to the cinema one evening, or a music venue – there are usually some good gigs in the winter. I'll need something to cheer me up!
Anyway, that's all from me. Thanks again for the invitation and sorry I won't be there. Please take plenty of photos – I'd love to see them. I'm sure there will be some great outfits. Do you remember Lucy's witch costume from last year?
Love _____

3 In which paragraph of the letter does the writer:
1 suggest meeting up?
2 decline the invitation?
3 mention a previous party?
4 give a reason for not going to the party?
5 talk about school?
6 make a request?

4 Underline all the examples of *in*, *at* and *on* with time expressions in the texts in exercises 1 and 2. Then choose the correct prepositions in the *Learn this!* box.

LEARN THIS!

in, *at* and *on* with time
1 We use *in* / *at* / *on* with
  a clock times (seven o'clock, 8.30, etc.)
  b festivals and holidays (Christmas, Easter, etc.)
  c *the weekend*, *night*
2 We use *in* / *at* / *on* with
  a parts of the day (the morning, the afternoon, etc.)
  b seasons (summer, winter, etc.)
  c months (January, February, etc.)
  d years (2005, 1492, etc.)
3 We use *in* / *at* / *on* with
  a days of the week (Monday, Tuesday, etc.)
  b dates (12 May, 1 April, etc.)

5 Complete the sentences with *in*, *at* or *on*.
1 Americans often have a family party ___ Thanksgiving, which is ___ November.
2 His last party started ___ nine o'clock ___ the evening ___ Saturday and finished ___ midday ___ Sunday!
3 ___ the weekend, we usually have lunch ___ two o'clock ___ the afternoon.
4 They last went to a party ___ Christmas ___ 2001.
5 She was born ___ 14 September 1973 and got married ___ July 2001. She got divorced ___ 2004.

● ● Grammar Builder 7.5: *in*, *at* and *on* with time: p. 122

6 Imagine that you have received the other invitation from exercise 1. Write an informal letter to the sender using the following plan:

Dear _____

Paragraph 1: Decline the invitation and explain why you will not be able to make it.

Paragraph 2: Say what you have been doing recently.

Paragraph 3: Suggest meeting up after the party. Include ideas for an activity.

Paragraph 4: Finish by returning to the topic of the party.

Love _____

Unit 7 • True love? 71

Get ready for your EXAM 7

1 **Get ready to LISTEN** Describe the photos. Do you know what kind of game this is? What health benefits is it supposed to have for the player?

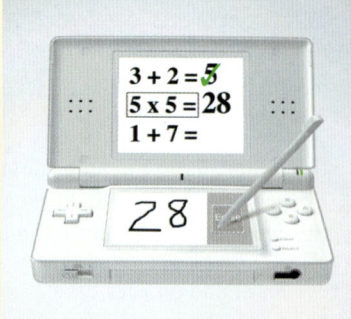

2 🎧 2.18 Do the Listening exam task.

LISTENING exam task

Listen to part of a radio programme. Complete each sentence with one word only.
1 Scientists have often argued that computer games can have a negative effect on people's _____ .
2 An addiction to computer games often means that young people spend less time doing _____ .
3 The makers of this new kind of game claim that the brain needs _____ , just like the body.
4 The games include a lot of different _____ .
5 The makers claim that the games can permanently improve your concentration and _____ .
6 The games are advertised by well-known _____ .
7 Most research into the games' effectiveness is paid for by the _____ .
8 Even if the games do not improve your brain, they at least allow you to have _____ .

3 Read the definition. Why do you think some people are worried about GM food?

> **genetically modified** adj. (*abbr.* **GM**) (of a plant, etc.) having had its genetic structure changed artificially, so that it will produce more fruit or not be affected by disease: *genetically modified foods* (= made from plants that have been changed in this way)

4 Do the Use of English exam task.

USE OF ENGLISH exam task

Complete gaps 1–10 in the text with a suitable word. There is an example (0).

Can GM food be good for your health?

It looks just ⁰*like* an ordinary carrot, it tastes the ¹_____ too, but the 'supercarrot' is in fact the result of years of scientific work. And the scientists who developed it claim that it is much healthier ²_____ a normal carrot because it has been genetically modified to contain high levels of calcium. Calcium is a necessary part of a healthy diet and is mostly found in high-fat foods ³_____ cheese. Supercarrots offer the chance to get plenty of calcium without eating too ⁴_____ fat.

GM (genetically modified) food is a controversial topic, and many people claim that ⁵_____ is unnatural and even dangerous. Environmental groups often campaign against GM foods and ⁶_____ scientists who are developing them. But it ⁷_____ worth remembering that GM food could perhaps bring major health benefits. In addition ⁸_____ 'supercarrots', scientists are also working on a new kind of potato which makes much healthier chips and crisps. This could cause a big reduction in rates of obesity and heart disease.

Probably the most significant new GM food is 'golden rice', ⁹_____ contains a lot of Vitamin A. At present, more than a million people, mostly women and children, die every year in poorer regions of Africa and South East Asia, and 500,000 go blind, because they do not get enough vitamin A. ¹⁰_____ farmers in these regions grew 'golden rice' instead of ordinary rice, the effect on people's health would be dramatic.

5 Look at the pictures in the exam task below. Match the adjectives in the box with one or both of them.

> challenging   elegant   exhausting   heavy   muscular
> painful   relaxed   supple   strong   sweaty

6 Do the Speaking exam task.

SPEAKING exam task

Compare and contrast the two photos. Answer the questions.  
1 What would be the health benefits of each activity, in your opinion?
2 What kind of person would be best suited to each activity, in your opinion?
3 Overall, which activity would be better for your health, do you think?
4 Which activity would you personally enjoy more? Give reasons.

Get ready for your EXAM 8

1 **Get ready to READ** Who are these people in the photos? What do you know about them? Use the words in the box.

| fall in love | get divorced | get married | have children |

2 Match the couples. Which of them are fictional?

1 Bonnie   a Antony
2 Cleopatra   b Clyde
3 John Lennon   c Courtney Love
4 Kurt Cobain   d Josephine
5 Napoleon Bonaparte e Juliet
6 Romeo   f Yoko Ono

3 Do the Reading exam task.

READING exam task

Read the texts. Match the famous couples (A–C) to the questions 1–7. There is only one correct answer for each question.

A Victoria and Albert

In 1837 the 18-year-old Princess Victoria became the Queen of England. Three years later she married Albert, her first cousin from Germany, who was also 21. She was a cheerful girl and he was an honest, intelligent man, and throughout their marriage they were deeply in love. As Victoria was the queen, Albert was not officially a king, but they were both highly respected and Victoria relied on Albert's advice, especially regarding diplomatic matters. Yet his main devotion was to their family and their nine children. Albert died 40 years before Victoria, and devastated by the loss of her beloved prince, she never wore anything but black from then on.

B Edward VIII and Wallis Simpson

In 1930, Edward, the heir to the British throne, met Wallis Simpson, a married American woman a little younger than himself. Six years later he became King of England, and after she divorced her second husband later that year, they were free to marry. The problem was that his family and royal officials did not want to accept her as the Queen of England because she was divorced. And so, in order to make her his wife, Edward abdicated. It was a controversial love affair and Mrs Simpson was never liked by her husband's family. They spent most of their lives abroad, where they both died – Edward in 1972 and his wife in 1986.

C Tristan and Isolde

There are many versions of this myth but all agree on the essential details of this story of star-crossed lovers. Tristan was a knight sent to bring Isolde to his king, who she was supposed to marry. But before they reached the king's court, Tristan and Isolde fell in love. The lovers had an affair but in the end separated. She married the king and he another girl. Yet, when he was dying from a poisoned wound, Tristan sent for Isolde. However, Tristan's wife lied to him telling him that Isolde wasn't coming. This news killed him. When Isolde arrived and found him dead, she died of a broken heart.

Which love story

1 involves two people from different continents?
2 involves a woman who found her husband's advice very valuable?
3 involves both people dying around the same time?
4 concerns fictional characters?
5 talks about a woman who had more than one husband?
6 involves people of the same age?
7 did not end in marriage?

4 **Get ready to SPEAK** Which place in the box would you choose for a first date with somebody you did not know very well? Why?

| café | disco | museum | park |

5 Work in pairs. What forms of evening entertainment are usually available in a big city? Which would you find most enjoyable? Think about different types of:

| clubs | music | dance | sport | theatre |

6 Do the Speaking exam task.

SPEAKING exam task

Work in pairs. Imagine you are going out for the evening. Look at the adverts from a magazine and agree where you would like to go.

MUSIC

❶ The Killjoys
Heavy metal band
Live gig starts 8.30 p.m. at the Town Hall
Tickets: £10 in advance, £12 on the door

❷ DJ Sheriff
Club night at The Venue 9 p.m. – 2 a.m.
Dance and hip-hop tracks from the 90s until now
Entrance £5 before 11 p.m., £10 after 11 p.m.

❸ Bartók String Quartets
Performed by the Belgravia Quartet
Concert starts 7.30 p.m. at the Chamber Music Rooms
Tickets: £15 and £20 (students £5)

SPORT

❹ The Bulls vs The Nicks
Touring basketball legends from the NBA in the US
Match starts 7 p.m. at the Blair Arena
Tickets from £8–£35

DANCE

❺ 'Street Life'
Contemporary dance performance
Original soundtrack
Performance starts 7.30 p.m. at the Modern Arts Theatre
Tickets £8

8 Travel

THIS UNIT INCLUDES
Vocabulary • travel and transport • travel and transport adjectives • holidays, trips and excursions • tourism and travel • verbs + prepositions
Grammar • the passive • indefinite pronouns: *some-, any-, no-* • indirect questions • introductory *it*
Speaking • discussing different modes of travel • planning an ideal holiday • exchanging information
Writing • a postcard

A VOCABULARY AND LISTENING
Getting from A to B

I can talk about travel.

1 Look at the photos. What is happening? What are the people thinking and feeling?

2 🎧 2.19 Read and listen to Melanie's story. Match the photos with paragraphs (A–C).

A Our plane **landed** at Heathrow Airport.¹ ☐ We had been away for months and were now returning home for Mum's birthday. We went through **passport control**, and collected our **rucksacks**. After **backpacking** round the world, this was the easy part – or so we thought. We were pushing our **trolleys** through **customs**, when a customs officer stopped us ² ☐ and spent ages searching through our **luggage**. He must have thought that we were carrying drugs.

B We needed to get to London to catch the last train to Cambridge. We went down to the Underground, bought a ticket ³ ☐ and found out which train to get. The **platform** was unbelievably crowded, but we managed to push our way onto the train. Halfway through the journey the train suddenly stopped. Then a voice announced that there was a problem with the **track** and we would have to get off. ⁴ ☐

C We climbed down from the **carriage** and were directed outside. ⁵ ☐ We decided to get a taxi to the station instead. A **cab** pulled up and we got in gratefully. ⁶ ☐ It drove quickly through the streets but then came to a sudden halt. Not again! There was a terrible **traffic jam**. The taxi driver suggested that it would be quicker to walk. ⁷ ☐ We got out and started running to the station. We got to the train just as the guard was blowing his whistle, and jumped on. It was the wrong train! ⁸ ☐ We ended up having to **change** at Stevenage ⁹ ☐ and didn't get home until 1.30 a.m.

3 Complete the definitions with the correct form of the words in red in exercise 2.

1 To _____ means to get off one train and onto another.
2 A _____ is a bag that you carry on your back.
3 A _____ is where you stand when you are waiting for a train at the station.
4 A _____ is a long line of cars that isn't moving.
5 To _____ means to come down from the sky onto the ground.
6 _____ means all the suitcases and bags that you take with you on a journey.
7 A _____ is a section of a train for passengers.
8 _____ is the place where they can check your bags for illegal goods as you enter a country.
9 _____ is the place where they check your travel documents as you leave or enter a country.
10 _____ means travelling around with your bag on your back, usually staying at cheap places.
11 A _____ is a cart with wheels for carrying heavy bags.
12 A _____ is the set of metal rails that a train runs along.
13 _____ is another word for taxi.

4 🎧 2.20 Listen to eight announcements and dialogues. Write the number of the announcement or dialogue in the box at the point in the story when you think it happened. There is one box that you do not need.

●● Vocabulary Builder 8.1: Travel and transport: p.135

5 SPEAKING Work in pairs. Brainstorm the advantages and disadvantages of travelling by bicycle, car, train, bus, plane and ship. Use the adjectives in the box to help you.

Useful adjectives cheap – expensive
comfortable – uncomfortable fast – slow
dangerous – safe reliable – unreliable
relaxing – stressful convenient – inconvenient

> Travelling by bus is slower than travelling by train.

> That's true, but travelling by bus is cheaper.

> When you travel by train, you can see more on the journey.

6 SPEAKING Discuss your ideas with the class.

8B GRAMMAR
The passive

I can identify and use different forms of the passive.

1 Read the text and answer the questions.
1 Where was the first car built?
2 Who was the first person to travel more than 100 kilometres in a car?
3 In which country were cars first produced in large numbers in factories?

The first motor car was built by Karl Benz in Germany in 1885. The first petrol engine had been designed some years earlier, but Benz was the first to fit it successfully in a vehicle that he could mass-produce. On 5 August 1888, his wife Bertha drove the car for 106 kilometres, proving that the car could travel long distances. Today, Bertha Benz's famous drive is celebrated as a national holiday every year in Germany. However, it was in America that cars were first produced in large numbers in factories. Henry Ford founded the Ford Motor Company in 1903, and since then over a billion cars have been manufactured by companies all over the world. Now, over a hundred years later, over 63 million cars are built every year. Many environmentalists believe we should replace cars with greener means of transport, but motor companies are confident that cleaner engines will be developed.

2 Complete the table with the examples of the passive in blue in the text.

The passive	
present simple	
past simple	
present perfect	
past perfect	
future with *will*	

3 When we use the passive, which word do we use if we want to say who (or what) performed the action? Find two examples in the text.

> Grammar Builder 8.1: The passive: p.122

4 Make the sentences passive. Use *by* where necessary.
1 Karl Benz built the first motor car in 1885.
   The first motor car was built by Karl Benz in 1885.
2 Engineering works have caused a lot of delays.
3 They'll probably search your bags at customs.
4 The guard had already directed us to platform 4.
5 A lot of commuters use this train.
6 They've recently increased the price of rail tickets.
7 Somebody left this bag on the plane.

5 Complete the text with the passive form of the verbs in brackets. Add *by* where necessary.

> 'For some years I have been afflicted with the belief that flight is possible to man.'
> Wilbur Wright

Today, 17 December 1903 ¹_____ (remember) as the day when the first powered flight ²_____ (make) two brothers, Wilbur and Orville Wright. The plane ³_____ (make) of wood and ⁴_____ (power) a small petrol engine. It ⁵_____ (control) the pilot who pulled strings that changed the angle of the wings. By the time the aircraft took to the air, the engine and propeller ⁶_____ (test) thoroughly in their workshop. The flights ⁷_____ (witness) five people and a photograph ⁸_____ (take) of the first flight. The events ⁹_____ (report) in the press on the next day and the brothers became celebrities overnight. Since that day, flying ¹⁰_____ (become) an everyday form of transport, but it all began with the ingenuity of the Wright brothers.

6 SPEAKING Complete the sentences. Use a passive form of the verbs in brackets. Then, in pairs, decide on the correct answers.
1 The train _____ (invent) in Britain in
   a 1729.   b 1829.   c 1929.
2 In 2000 the Channel Tunnel _____ (open) between
   a England and France.   b England and Ireland.
   c England and Wales.
3 The Trans-Siberian Railway _____ (finish) in
   a 1866.   b 1916.   c 1966.
4 The first motorway in the world _____ (build) between the two cities of
   a Cologne and Bonn in Germany.
   b New York and Washington in the USA.
   c London and Edinburgh in the UK.
5 Dacia cars _____ (make) in
   a Hungary.   b Italy.   c Romania.

7 🎧 2.21 Listen and check your answers to exercise 6.

Unit 8 • Travel   75

8C CULTURE
Tourism and travel

I can understand a magazine article about changing holiday habits.

The British on holiday

In the nineteenth century, railways were built from the big industrial cities like Leeds and Manchester to seaside towns like Blackpool and Scarborough. For the first time, ordinary working people could visit the seaside. They used to take day-trips on
5 Sundays and special days like Easter. Traditionally, people sat in deckchairs on the beach, swam in the sea, and ate fish and chips. Children could watch *Punch and Judy* puppet shows, build sandcastles and ride donkeys on the beach.

In the 1950s, the first package holidays were launched. Throughout
10 the 60s and 70s, the British increasingly began to abandon the traditional seaside holiday in favour of sunshine and warmer seas in countries like Spain and Greece. Caravan and camping holidays also became popular in the 60s and 70s as car ownership increased.

15 In the 1990s, budget airlines like easyJet slashed the cost of air tickets to many European destinations. Long-haul flights also came down in price, so holidays to exotic destinations in Australia and Asia became affordable to ordinary families. A growing number of people began to book their own flights and accommodation and, as
20 a result, the package holiday market declined.

The holiday habits of the British are continuing to change. Increasing levels of affluence mean that, for many families, a second foreign holiday – often a winter skiing holiday – is possible. City breaks are also growing in popularity, and not only to nearby
25 destinations – Las Vegas, Dubai and Cape Town are all favourites for long weekends. And independent travel is becoming more and more popular as the Internet allows holidaymakers to find the best deals online.

Top 10 holiday destinations for UK holiday-makers

1 Spain 25%	6 Greece 5%
2 France 20%	7 Germany 4%
3 USA 7%	8 The Netherlands 3.5%
4 Eire 7%	9 Portugal 3.5%
5 Italy 6%	10 Belgium 3%

1 Describe the photos. What are the people doing? Where do you think they might be?

2 Read the text. Are the sentences true or false?
1. In the nineteenth century, new railways made it possible for working people to go to the coast.
2. In the nineteenth century, people used to have long holidays at the seaside.
3. Traditionally, water sports were the most popular holiday activity.
4. A lot of British people bought cars between 1960 and 1979.
5. As package holidays became more popular, seaside holidays in Britain became less popular.
6. In the 1990s, short flights were cheap, but long flights were still very expensive.
7. Short holidays in distant places are becoming more popular.
8. Most Britons have their holidays outside Europe.

3 Read the list of trips and excursions. Which ones are mentioned in the text?

Holidays, trips and excursions   activity holiday   camping holiday   caravan holiday   city break   coach tour   cruise   day-trip   excursion   package holiday   round-the-world trip   safari

4 Explain the phrases from the text in your own words.
1. seaside towns
2. budget airlines
3. slashed the cost
4. long-haul flights
5. exotic destinations
6. long weekends
7. the best deals

● ● ○ **Vocabulary Builder 8.2: Tourism and travel: p.135**

5 🎧 2.22 Listen to people talking about holidays. Which countries do they mention?

6 🎧 2.22 Listen again. Match the opinions with the people: Tony, Karen, Dan and Jill, and Chris.
1. _____ discovered a new type of holiday and now go away every year in the winter.
2. _____ doesn't like his/her home city in warm weather, but wouldn't like to be in the countryside in the winter.
3. _____ got fed up with family holidays abroad and now goes on activity holidays.
4. _____ travels around and goes to a variety of places.

7 **SPEAKING** Work in pairs. Discuss the questions.
1. What are popular holiday destinations in your country? Why do people go to these places?
2. Do people from your country go on holiday abroad? What destinations are popular?

Unit 8 • Travel

8D GRAMMAR
Indefinite pronouns: *some-*, *any-*, *no-*

I can use different pronouns.

1 Read the text. Are the sentences true or false?
1 Sharon gave the young woman a lift to a pub.
2 Sharon didn't notice anything unusual about the woman.
3 The young woman disappeared inside the pub.
4 Sharon showed the woman's lipstick to the barman.

It was about 10 o'clock on a cold winter's night and Sharon Walters was driving home. Suddenly, she saw **somebody** standing at the side of the road, trying to hitch a ride. It was a young woman, about 20 years old, with a pale face and old-fashioned clothes. Sharon stopped the car, and said to the girl, 'Can I give you a lift **somewhere**?'

'Yes, I'm meeting **somebody** in a pub up the road.'

'OK. Jump in,' said Sharon. There wasn't **anything** unusual about the girl except for her old-fashioned clothes. When they arrived at the pub, the girl thanked Sharon, got out of the car and went into the pub. Suddenly, Sharon noticed that the girl had left **something** in the car – it was her lipstick. She went into the pub but she couldn't find the woman **anywhere**. 'Did you see **anybody** come into the pub a couple of minutes ago?' she asked the barman. 'Nobody's come in here for the past fifteen minutes,' he replied, 'except you.'

'But I've just given her a lift here. She left her lipstick in the car.' Sharon put her hand in her pocket to take out the lipstick, but there was **nothing** there.

'Was she wearing old-fashioned clothes?' asked the barman.

'Yes. So you did see her!'

'I didn't see **anybody**, but I know this: a young woman was killed in a road accident near here about 30 years ago. She was on her way to this pub to meet her boyfriend … Ask **anybody** round here – they all know about her.'

2 Look at the examples of indefinite pronouns in red in the text. Complete the table.

Indefinite pronouns		
somebody /someone	anybody/anyone	¹_____ /no-one
something	²_____	³_____
⁴_____	⁵_____	nowhere

3 Study the examples of indefinite pronouns in red in the text. Then complete the rules with *affirmative*, *negative* and *interrogative* in the *Learn this!* box.

> **LEARN THIS!**
> 1 We use pronouns with *some-* in _____ sentences and in offers and requests.
> 2 We use pronouns with *any-* in _____ and _____ sentences.
> 3 We can also use pronouns with *any-* in affirmative sentences when we mean *it doesn't matter who/what/where …* .
> 4 We use pronouns with *no-* with _____ verbs as the meaning is already negative.

4 Choose the correct words.
1 It's dark. I can't see **anything** / **something**.
2 There was **no-one** / **anyone** else on the train.
3 He's smiling. He must be thinking about **anything** / **something** funny.
4 'I can't find my ticket. It's **somewhere** / **nowhere** to be seen.' 'It must be **anywhere** / **somewhere**.'
5 You can get online **anywhere** / **nowhere** in the airport.
6 Does **anybody** / **nobody** mind if I smoke?
7 I'm really hungry. I've had **anything** / **nothing** to eat.

●● Grammar Builder 8.2: Indefinite pronouns: p. 123

5 Complete the dialogue with indefinite pronouns.
Joe I'm going out to get ¹_____ to eat. There's ²_____ in the fridge.
Tina Who are you going with?
Joe ³_____ . I'm going on my own.
Tina Where are you going?
Joe I don't know. ⁴_____ . It doesn't matter.
Tina You're behaving very strangely. Is ⁵_____ wrong?
Joe No, I just don't want to talk to ⁶_____ right now.

6 Complete the questions with indefinite pronouns.
1 If you could visit _____ in the world, where would you go?
2 Do you think the world would be better or worse if _____ ever travelled by plane?
3 Would you prefer to live _____ very hot or _____ very cold?
4 Do you think _____ will ever travel backwards or forwards in time?

7 **SPEAKING** Work in pairs. Ask and answer the questions in exercise 6. Give reasons for your answers.

Unit 8 • Travel

8E READING
Trip of a lifetime

I can understand a description of a holiday.

Big Cat Diary

I've always dreamed of seeing a leopard face to face ever since I watched a BBC wildlife documentary about them. I like the fact that they're so independent. The females are the boss, basically — they hunt alone, and they're stealthy
5 and strong. The markings are beautiful. The South Luangwa Valley in Zambia has one leopard for every kilometre, and you can do night drives there, which adds to your chances of seeing them. I think the fact they are nocturnal and hard to find makes it more exciting. Dad doesn't agree. He's already
10 worrying about not seeing one, but that's just my dad.

Mfuwe international airport is the smallest I have ever seen. There is a tiny shop selling postcards and that's it. We pay for our postcards and climb into a jeep which takes us to Nkwali, trundling past mud huts and groups of children
15 wearing school uniform or carrying farm tools – sometimes both. Finally, we arrive at the camp – six huts and a bar built round a tree. Our hut has lizard wallpaper – except it's not wallpaper, it's just lizards. I go to sleep and dream about leopards.

20 On the first game drive, Rocky is our guide. Straight away, we're driving across a plain full of impala and baboons. Now comes the big moment of the first night. We hear something in the trees, and suddenly we are right in the middle of a lion hunt. In the dark! We listen to the baboons' alarm calls, and
25 when Rocky switches on the light, we see two lionesses on either side, and one tearing after an impala. They miss the kill, but even so, my heart is thumping.

The next morning, we go on a drive and spot baboons crossing the road. Suddenly, a trunk appears from the bush
30 and three elephants, including a baby, stroll across right in front of us.

That's how it is on the drives: a new creature every time. We get giraffes, then a crocodile, then a buffalo. But my favourite morning is the walking safari. We set off across the plain with
35 an armed guard. Rocky tells us The Golden Rule: 'Never run ... unless I say so. And if I say get up the tree, get up the tree.'

The next morning, two other guests boast about having seen a leopard and her cub. We look at pictures on their digital camera. I'm really cross, because there probably won't be
40 another sighting for ages, and tonight is our last night here. But I'm still hoping for a lucky break.

This time, we're out with Zebron, but after just a few minutes, our jeep gets stuck on a muddy trail. It takes ages to dig us out, and my heart is sinking. Then it starts pouring. We sit in
45 the dark while my dad complains about the rain. And then, suddenly, two impala hurtle from the bushes.

Moments later, the leopardess springs out behind us. We all sit in absolute silence and stare at her. Leopards are much stronger than lions, and she looks incredibly powerful. After
50 giving us a long show, she darts back into the bush. Awesome. We're soaked through, but I don't care about that. Mum and I sing and dance as we head for camp: 'We saw a
55 leopard, we got a picture ... .'

78 Unit 8 • Travel

1 Describe the photos. Answer the questions.
1 What animals can you see?
2 What are the people doing?
3 What kind of holiday is it?
4 Would you like to go on this kind of holiday? Why?/Why not?

2 Read the text quickly. Are the verbs in the past, present or future? Complete the reading tip.

> **Reading tip**
> We sometimes use _____ tenses to tell a story. This makes the story sound more exciting and immediate.

3 Read the text. Put the events in the correct order.
- [ ] Daisy got very close to some elephants.
- [ ] The jeep got stuck in the mud.
- [ ] Daisy saw baboons.
- [ ] The plane landed in Mfuwe.
- [ ] Daisy saw some lions.
- [ ] Two other guests saw a leopardess and her cub.
- [ ] Daisy saw a leopard.
- [ ] They travelled by jeep to their camp.

4 Choose the best answers.
1 Daisy first got interested in leopards
  a when she had a dream about them.
  b when she saw a TV programme about them.
  c because they live alone.
  d because she once saw one face to face.
2 South Luangwa valley is a good place to look for leopards because
  a there are a lot of leopards there and you can look for them at night.
  b there are more leopards there than anywhere else in Africa.
  c it's easy to find leopards at night.
  d it's exciting looking for leopards at night.
3 Daisy's hut at the camp is
  a built around the tree.
  b full of lizards.
  c covered in strange wallpaper.
  d made of mud.
4 Their first excursion is
  a exciting because they see lions hunting.
  b frightening because it is very dark.
  c exciting because the baboons make a lot of noise.
  d sad because they see lions killing an impala.
5 Rocky's Golden Rule for the walking safari basically means
  a never run if an animal is chasing you.
  b if an animal chases you, climb a tree.
  c don't climb a tree unless I tell you to.
  d always do exactly what I say.

6 How does Daisy feel when she hears that two other guests have seen leopards?
  a She feels sad because she wasn't with them.
  b She feels angry because it means she probably won't see any leopards herself.
  c She feels pleased that somebody has seen leopards.
  d She feels hopeful because it means that there are leopards in the area.
7 When Daisy finally sees a leopard, it
  a stays nearby for a while and then disappears suddenly.
  b runs quickly behind them and disappears into the bush.
  c walks close to them, but leaves before they can take a photo.
  d stays close until somebody shouts, then it runs away.

5 Match the movement verbs highlighted in the text with the definitions below.
1 to walk slowly and calmly
2 to move very quickly (3 verbs)
3 to move slowly on wheels
4 to jump

> **LEARN THIS!**
> **Verbs + prepositions**
> 1 Some verbs are often followed by certain prepositions.
>   Let's listen **to** some music. She smiled **at** her mother.
> 2 In questions, we often put the preposition at the end.
>   What are you waiting **for**?

6 Read the *Learn this!* box. Then find the verbs in the box in the text and underline them and the prepositions which follow them. Which verb appears twice, with two different prepositions? How are the meanings different?

> dream   worry   pay   arrive   listen   boast   look
> hope   complain   stare   care   head

7 **SPEAKING** Work in pairs. Complete the questions with the correct prepositions. Then ask and answer the questions.
1 Before the holiday, what does Daisy's dad worry ____?
2 Before leaving the airport, what do they pay ____?
3 Just before seeing the lions, what do they listen ____?
4 What do two other guests boast ____?
5 On the last night, what does Daisy's dad complain ____?
6 After seeing the leopardess, where do they head ____?

●● Vocabulary Builder 8.3: Verbs + prepositions: p. 135

8 **SPEAKING** Work in pairs. Plan your ideal holiday. Make notes about:
1 What kind of holiday would it be? (see page 76, exercise 3)
2 Where would you like to go?
3 How would you get there?
4 What type of accommodation would you stay in?
5 What would you do on holiday?

9 **SPEAKING** Present your ideas to the class.

Unit 8 • Travel   79

8F EVERYDAY ENGLISH
At the airport: exchanging information

I can ask for information politely.

Immigration officer Good morning, sir.
Jack Wilson Good morning.
Officer May I see your passport, please?
Jack Yes, certainly.
Officer Thank you. ¹_____ which flight you arrived on, Mr Wilson?
Jack Yes. The British Airways flight from Heathrow.
Officer I see. ²_____ how long you'll be staying in the United States, sir?
Jack Three weeks.
Officer You have a return flight, don't you?
Jack Yes, I do – on 14 July. Would you like to see the ticket?
Officer No, that's OK. ³_____ what the purpose of your visit is?
Jack Yes, I'm visiting relatives. My uncle lives here.
Officer ⁴_____ where you'll be staying, sir?
Jack At his house in Boston.
Officer ⁵_____ if you'll be visiting any other cities during your stay?
Jack We'll probably be travelling round a bit. I'd like to see New York.
Officer OK. Thank you, Mr Wilson. Enjoy your stay.

1 🎧 **2.23** Listen and complete the dialogue with the phrases in the box.

> Can you tell me … Could you tell me … Do you know …
> May I ask … Would you mind telling me …

2 Match these direct questions with the indirect questions in the dialogue.

> Will you be visiting any other cities during your stay?
> Which flight did you arrive on?
> Where will you be staying?
> What is the purpose of your visit?
> How long will you be staying in the United States?

3 Compare the indirect questions in the dialogue with the direct questions in exercise 2. Choose the correct words to complete the rules in the *Learn this!* box.

LEARN THIS! Indirect questions
1 If there is not a question word (*who*, *when*, etc.) we use *if / how*.
2 The word order and verb forms in an indirect question are the same as in a **direct question / statement**.

●● Grammar Builder 8.3: Indirect questions: p. 123

4 🎧 **2.24** Listen. Where are the people? Write the number of the dialogue next to the place where it happens.

check-in desk ☐ airport information desk ☐
tourist information desk ☐

5 🎧 **2.24** Put the words in the correct order. Then listen again and check. Which are indirect questions?
1 you / me / Can / where / I / should / in / tell / check / ?
2 know / which / Do / are / flying / airline / you / with / you / ?
3 you / Have / if / the / on / time / any / idea / flight / is / ?
4 if / wonder / could / you / help / me / I / ?
5 how / many / Could / nights / you'll / be / you / tell / me / staying / ?
6 please / I / have / your / and / passport / May / ticket / ?
7 you / me / if / you / check / in / Can / have / any / bags / tell to / ?
8 have / I / a / please / window / seat / Could / ?

Speaking tip
We sometimes use indirect questions when we want to sound more polite.

6 Read the speaking tip. Then make the questions into indirect questions.
1 Where's the nearest post office?
2 Do the buses run all night?
3 How old are you?
4 What's your friend's name?
5 Are you from the Czech Republic?
6 Why are you here?

7 **SPEAKING** Work in pairs. Prepare a dialogue for the situation below. Use indirect questions to make the questions more polite.

A passenger is at the information desk and wants to know
• the best way to get into town.
• how far it is.
• how much the journey will cost.
• where to buy a ticket.

The information clerk answers all the questions and wants to know
• how quickly the passenger needs to get into town.
• if the passenger needs information about hotels.

8 **SPEAKING** Act out your dialogue to the class.

Unit 8 • Travel

8G WRITING A postcard

I can write a postcard about a disastrous holiday.

Dear Patricia
We've been in Malaga for three days now, and we're having a terrible time. The holiday started really badly – the plane was delayed and *it* was nearly 1 a.m. when we arrived at the hotel. The restaurant had closed, so *it* was a good job we still had some sandwiches from the journey. The next day we set off early for the beach. *It* said in the holiday brochure that *it* was only 100 metres from the hotel to the beach – which is true, but there's a motorway in between! The hotel itself is OK – but they gave us a room right above the disco, so *it* was impossible to get to sleep. They've given us another room but *it* isn't much better. *It* probably isn't worth complaining again, though.
It's time to go down for dinner now. Let's hope *it*'s better than lunch.
See you soon.
Love, Hilary and Daniel xxx

1 Read the postcards quickly. Which postcard does the photo go with?

2 Answer the questions.
1 What was the first thing that went wrong for Hilary and Daniel?
2 What did they have to eat when they finally arrived?
3 Why are they unhappy with the room they are in now?
4 What was the hardest part of Simon and Jackie's journey?
5 Why did Simon have to go to the police station?
6 Why does Simon have to pack his bag?

3 What is the first piece of information in both postcards? What is the last piece of information?

4 Read the *Learn this!* box. Then look at the highlighted examples of *it* in the postcards and say which are introductory *it* and which are normal pronouns.

Dear Sam,
I'm in Scotland, but I wish I wasn't. *It*'s Thursday now, and *it*'s been raining since we arrived on Monday. *It*'s really cold, too. Still, *it*'s no use moaning – we can't do anything about the weather. The journey up here was OK, but *it* took ages to find the hotel. Then yesterday I lost my wallet – *it* had all my money and cards inside – and had to go to the police station. *It*'s unusual for Jackie to complain, but even she's had enough and wants to go home.
I'd better pack my bag now. We're going to Fort William first thing tomorrow.
Love, Simon

LEARN THIS! Introductory *it*

1 We often use *it* in sentences referring to time, weather, temperature and distance.
   It's eight o'clock. It's Tuesday. It took an hour to do this exercise. It's raining. It's 20°C. It's 100 km from Paris.
2 We can use *it* when we want to avoid starting a sentence with an infinitive, *-ing* form or clause, which often sounds unnatural or very formal.
   It's nice being with you. (= Being with you is nice.)
   It's hard to explain my feelings. (=To explain my feelings is hard.)
   It's a shame that he missed the party. (That he missed the party is a shame.)
   It doesn't matter what you wear. (= What you wear doesn't matter.)

→ Grammar Builder 8.4: Introductory *it*: p. 124

5 Imagine you are having an awful time on holiday. Choose four of the problems below (or invent your own) and make notes about them.

- a disastrous journey here
- the airline lost our luggage
- the weather is terrible
- the hotel room is cold and damp
- the people are unfriendly
- the food is terrible
- the hotel isn't finished
- I got food-poisoning
- somebody stole something
- the view from the window is terrible
- the car broke down
- it's three kilometres to the nearest beach
- there was nobody at the airport to meet us
- the beach isn't sandy, it's rocky

6 Write a postcard to a friend about your holiday.

Unit 8 • Travel   81

Language Review 7-8

Vocabulary

1 Complete the text with the words in the box.

> asked   chatting   fallen   fell   going   made

'Have you heard the news? Noah has ¹_____ Scarlett out and she said no. Alice spent most of last night ²_____ Mason up before he told her he was already ³_____ out with Maisie. Daisy and Harvey ⁴_____ out last week but since then they have ⁵_____ up. And finally, I have ⁶_____ in love at last!'

Mark /6

2 Complete the missing words.

1 She had a lot of luggage, so she went to find a t _ _ _ l _ _ .
2 They waited on the p _ _ _ f _ _ _ for the train.
3 The train was delayed because a tree had fallen onto the t _ _ c _ .
4 They were late for Sam's wedding because they got stuck in a t _ _ f _ _ _ j _ _ .
5 Rosie's going backpacking, so she needs to buy a new r _ _ _ s _ _ _ .
6 It took a long time going through c _ _ t _ _ _ because they stopped us to search our bags.

Mark /6

Grammar

3 Complete the sentences with the past simple form or *would* + base form of the verbs in brackets.

1 If Aaron _____ (drive) more slowly, he _____ (not have) so many accidents.
2 I wish I _____ (can) go speed dating.
3 I'd rather Simon _____ (chat) me up than James.
4 If only my boyfriend _____ (give) me roses instead of CDs for once!
5 If Freya _____ (be) more confident, she _____ (have) more friends.
6 I wish I _____ (not have) so much homework.

Mark /6

4 Rewrite the sentences using the passive.

1 People speak Portuguese in Portugal and Brazil.
   _____
2 Someone stole my luggage while I was waiting for the train.
   _____
3 The airline has cancelled our flight so we're waiting for the next one.
   _____
4 They had closed the motorway so the coaches weren't running.
   _____
5 They'll transfer all passengers to another airport.
   _____

Mark /5

5 Complete the sentences with the words in the box.

> anything   anywhere   nothing   somebody   something

1 Would you like _____ to help you with your bags?
2 Have you got _____ to declare?
3 Would you like _____ to drink, Madam?
4 There wasn't _____ to change money in the departure lounge.
5 I got bored during the flight as I had _____ to read.

Mark /5

Everyday English

6 Put the lines (a–e) in the correct order to complete the dialogue.

a That's right. Lucy Knight. Pleased to meet you.
b Yes, you're Jordan's brother, Luke, aren't you?
c He's going out with my best friend, Hannah.
d Oh, now I remember. You're Hannah's friend Lucy, aren't you?
e Yes, I am. How do you know Jordan?

Luke We've met before, haven't we?
Lucy ☐
Luke ☐
Lucy ☐
Luke ☐
Lucy ☐
Luke Pleased to meet you, Lucy.

Mark /5

7 Complete the indirect questions with the words in the box.

> idea   know   mind   tell   wonder

1 Can you _____ me where the toilets are, please?
2 Do you _____ where I can change some money?
3 Would you _____ telling me why my flight is delayed?
4 Have you any _____ what time the next train leaves?
5 I _____ if you could tell me how much a single ticket to London costs?

Mark /5

Total /38

EXAM CHALLENGE Workbook pages 94–97

Skills Round-up 1–8

Reading

1 Read the text quickly. In which of the places could you see:
- a monkeys?
- b jewels?
- c the distant past?
- d toy trains?

Places to visit in Edinburgh

Edinburgh Castle The castle is the top attraction not only in Edinburgh, but in Scotland, and you do not need to be a history fanatic to enjoy it. See the crown jewels of Scotland and the 'Stone of Destiny', on which generations of Scottish and British kings and queens have been crowned. There are also reminders scratched on the walls of the dungeons from the days when the castle was a prison for the Frenchmen who were captured during the Napoleonic wars.

Edinburgh Zoo Edinburgh Zoo, which is situated only ten minutes from the city centre, is another of Scotland's top tourist attractions. The zoo is particularly noted for its large collection of penguins, who parade in front of the visitors at feeding time. There are over 1,000 other animals there, including polar bears, monkeys and tigers.

Museum of Childhood A magical world of dolls, toys, teddy bears, games, puzzles, train sets, models and loads of other items from all over the world to keep children amused. It has been described as the 'noisiest museum in the world' and, when it opened in 1955, was believed to be the first museum in the world to specialise in the history of childhood. And admission is free!

Dynamic Earth One of Edinburgh's newest attractions, Dynamic Earth has a virtual reality 'time machine' that takes you from the formation of the universe through 4,500 million years of planet Earth. You will be shaken by earthquakes, feel the cold of the ice ages and see tropical rainstorms. Travel to the depths of the oceans and fly high above towering glaciers and mountains. You will see, hear, feel and smell the planet as it was millions of years ago, and how it might be in the future.

2 Are the sentences true or false?
1. More people visit Edinburgh Castle than any other attraction in Scotland.
2. Edinburgh Castle used to be a prison.
3. Edinburgh Zoo is located in the city centre.
4. Edinburgh has the only museum in the world which specialises in the history of childhood.
5. Dynamic Earth allows visitors to experience different times and places using virtual reality.

Speaking

3 Work in pairs. Role-play a dialogue between Marek and somebody who works at the tourist information office in Edinburgh. Marek wants to know:
- what the most popular attraction is in Edinburgh
- how far the zoo is from the city centre
- how much it costs to get into the Museum of Childhood
- what you can see at Dynamic Earth

Listening

4 🎧 2.25 Listen. What unusual coincidence happens to Marek during his trip to Edinburgh?

5 🎧 2.25 Listen again. Number four of these scenes in the order that you hear them. There are two scenes that you do not need.
- a at Edinburgh Castle ☐
- b on the train ☐
- c in the Princes Street Gardens ☐
- d at the hotel ☐
- e in a restaurant ☐
- f at the railway station ☐

Writing

6 Imagine you are Marek. Write a postcard from Edinburgh to Sarah. Include this information:
- where you are staying
- what the weather is like
- what you have done
- your general opinion of Edinburgh

Skills Round-up 1–8 83

9 Spend, spend, spend!

THIS UNIT INCLUDES ●●●●●
Vocabulary • money and payment • prepositions and noun phrases
• small and large numbers
Grammar • *have something done* • reflexive pronouns
• third conditional • clauses expressing purpose
Speaking • discussing advertising in schools
• arguing your case
Writing • a formal letter: asking for information

A VOCABULARY AND LISTENING
Money and finance

I can talk about money and people's attitudes to it.

'This planet has – or rather had – a problem, which was this: most of the people living on it were unhappy for pretty much of the time. Many solutions were suggested for this problem, but most of these were largely concerned with the movements of small green pieces of paper, which is odd because on the whole it wasn't the small green pieces of paper that were unhappy.' —*Douglas Adams*

1 Read the quotation from a science fiction novel. Which planet do you think it is describing? What are the 'small green pieces of paper'? What does the author think about them?

2 Complete the text with the words in the box.

| Money and payment | cash | cash machine | cheque | coins |
| credit card | currency | debit card | notes | PIN number |

In the past, when people needed ¹_____, they used to go into their local bank and write out a ²_____. Now, you can go to a ³_____ at any time of the day or night, type in your ⁴_____ and get £100 in brand new £20 ⁵_____. (Of course, if you need £1 ⁶_____, you still need to go to the bank.) But who uses real money anyway these days? Most of the time, we pay by ⁷_____ or ⁸_____. It's certainly the easiest way to pay when you're abroad and unfamiliar with the ⁹_____.

3 🎧 2.26 Listen to five people talking about money. Match the speakers (1–5) with the sentences. There is one sentence that you do not need.

1 He/She wants to borrow some money. ☐
2 He/She has wasted money. ☐
3 He/She doesn't like to be in debt. ☐
4 He/She is saving money for a present. ☐
5 He/She has bought a bargain in the sale. ☐
6 He/She was overcharged for something. ☐

4 🎧 2.26 Listen again. Complete the sentences with the correct prepositions. There is one sentence that does not need a preposition. Then listen again and check.

| for | for | from | off | in | in | into | on | on |

1 I've been saving up for ages _____ a new pair of trainers.
2 I don't like to borrow money _____ my family.
3 I went up to the till to pay _____ it.
4 It was £4.99 and I paid _____ cash.
5 The problem is, I've just spent all my savings _____ a new bike, so I'm really broke.
6 He said I shouldn't waste money _____ computer games.
7 I'm paying £2 a week _____ my savings account.
8 They were £20, but as they were _____ the sale I got £5 _____.

5 **SPEAKING** Work in pairs. Ask and answer the questions.

1 Have you ever bought something that was a waste of money? What?
2 Have you ever saved up to buy something? What?
3 Have you ever lent somebody money? How much?
4 Have you ever borrowed money from somebody? How much? What for?
5 Is there something that you'd like to buy, but can't afford? What?
6 Do you always pay for things in cash?
7 Have you ever been overcharged for something?

●● Vocabulary Builder 9.1: Money and payment: p. 135

6 **SPEAKING** Try to explain the meaning of these quotations. Do you agree with them?

> Money can't buy you happiness.

> A bank is a place that will lend you money if you can prove that you don't need it.

> Those who believe money can do anything will often do anything for money.

●● Vocabulary Builder 9.2: Prepositions + noun phrases: p. 136

84 Unit 9 • Spend, spend, spend!

9B GRAMMAR
have something done

I can use the structure 'have something done'.

1 Compare the two photos of Ashlee Simpson below. What has changed about her appearance?

2 **SPEAKING** Read the text. Why do you think Ashlee Simpson changed her appearance?

Makeover
Ashlee Simpson: before and after

Pop star Jessica Simpson has always looked like the perfect all-American girl: blonde and beautiful. When her younger sister, Ashlee, became a pop star too, she looked much more like the 'girl next door'. But then suddenly, she changed her image. She had her hair dyed blonde – and, some people agree, she has spent thousands of dollars on having her face changed too. She had her nose altered; she had her teeth whitened, and she looks as though she's had her chin reduced too. Some people think Ashlee looks better now, but others think it is sad that she wanted to change her appearance.

3 Read the *Learn this!* box. Underline examples of the structure *have something done* in the text.

LEARN THIS!

have something done
1 You can use the structure *have* + object + past participle to say that you arranged for somebody to do something for you. (You didn't do it yourself.)
I had my hair cut yesterday.
2 You can also use the structure for unpleasant things that have happened to you.
I had my car stolen last week.
He had his arm injured in an accident.

4 Complete the dialogue using the past simple form of *have something done*.

Jasmine Hi, Courtney. You look great!
Courtney Thanks. I went to a beauty parlour yesterday and ¹_____ (my hair / cut).
Jasmine ²_____ (it / dye) too?
Courtney No, I did that myself at home. It's cheaper. But I ³_____ (my nails / paint). Look! And I ⁴_____ (my make-up / do).
Jasmine Very nice.
Courtney You look different too.
Jasmine Yes, I ⁵_____ (my teeth / whiten) last week. They used to be really yellow!
Courtney Did it cost a lot?
Jasmine Actually, yes. Especially because I ⁶_____ (my bag / steal) while I was there!

●● Grammar Builder 9.1: *have something done*: p. 124

5 Read the *Learn this!* box. Find an example of a reflexive pronoun in exercise 4. Is it use 1 or use 2? What are the other reflexive pronouns?

LEARN THIS!

Reflexive pronouns
1 We use a reflexive pronoun when the object of a verb is the same as the subject.
*He cut **himself** while he was shaving.*
2 We can use a reflexive pronoun to add emphasis.
*They painted the house **themselves**, without any help.*

●● Grammar Builder 9.2: Reflexive pronouns: p. 125

6 Rewrite the sentences using *have something done*. Write a negative sentence using a reflexive pronoun as well.

1 Somebody did her make-up.
   She had her make-up done. She didn't do it herself.
2 Somebody removed her tattoo.
3 Somebody repaired our car.
4 Somebody examined his teeth.
5 Somebody tested my eyes.
6 Somebody cleaned their car.
7 Somebody decorated your house.
8 Somebody washed your backs.

7 **SPEAKING** Work in pairs. Find out if these things have ever happened to your partner. Use *Have you ever had …?*

> Have you ever had your hearing checked?

> Yes, I have. / No, I haven't. / Pardon?

1 hearing / check
2 hair / dye
3 home / burgle
4 picture / paint
5 mobile phone / steal
6 future / tell

Unit 9 • Spend, spend, spend! 85

9C CULTURE
Advertising in schools

I can discuss opinions about advertising in schools.

1 Which of these things can you find in your school?
1. vending machines
2. advertisements
3. textbooks with the logos of large companies (e.g. Nike, Coca-Cola) on the cover
4. equipment supplied by large companies (e.g. supermarkets)

2 Read the text. Which things from exercise 1 does it mention?

Young minds for sale

[1] For advertisers, there are three good reasons to target schoolchildren. Firstly, they have money to spend – and the amount of money is growing. In the USA, teenagers between 12 and 17 are now spending about $190 billion a year. Secondly, they have 'pester power': if they want something, they repeatedly ask their parents to buy it. Thirdly, they are tomorrow's adult consumers, and may stay loyal to the brands they bought as children.

[2] There are financial advantages for schools who allow advertising. For example, most secondary schools in Britain have vending machines which are provided by large food and drink companies. Schools usually earn between £10,000 and £15,000 a year from these. This income can then be spent on books and equipment.

[3] Some companies supply books and other equipment directly to schools. In the past thirteen years, the giant supermarket firm, Tesco, has provided more than 50,000 computers and 500,000 pieces of computer equipment to thousands of schools, in exchange for vouchers which the students and their parents collect when they shop at Tesco. Another company, Be Sport Ltd, supplies free sports kits to schools which have the names of sponsors on the shirts and shorts. These kits would normally cost £400 per team.

[4] However, many people are unhappy about the growing influence of big business in education. Schools should encourage free-thinking – the opposite goal of advertising, which tries to influence our thoughts in a particular direction. They argue that vending machines promote unhealthy food and drink at a time when obesity in young people is a serious problem in Britain. When Cadbury's, who make chocolate in the UK, offered to supply free sports equipment to schools in return for vouchers, there was a big protest. It was pointed out that pupils would have to purchase 5,440 bars of chocolate in order to get a free volleyball set!

3 Answer the questions.
1. How much do US teenagers spend a year?
2. What is 'pester power'?
3. How do schools benefit from having vending machines?
4. How many computers has Tesco supplied to British schools?
5. How much do Be Sport Ltd charge for sports kits?
6. Why are some people against all advertising in schools?
7. Why are some people against vending machines?
8. What was the problem with Cadbury's plan to provide sports equipment to schools?

4 Find and underline these words in the text.
Paragraph 1: consumers, brands
Paragraph 2: income
Paragraph 3: supply, firm, vouchers, sponsors
Paragraph 4: promote, purchase

5 Match the definitions with the words in exercise 4.
1. money that you earn
2. pieces of paper that you exchange for goods
3. buy
4. people who buy things
5. companies who pay to have their logo on something
6. company or business
7. products made by a particular company
8. to give somebody something that they need
9. make something more attractive

6 🎧 2.27 Listen to five people talking about advertising in schools. Match the opinions with the speakers (1–5).
a Some advertising in schools is OK, but not too much. ☐
b Advertising in schools wouldn't be necessary if schools got more money from the government. ☐
c Vending machines don't have any effect on what students buy. ☐
d For companies, advertising is more important than education. ☐
e Sponsorship is a good idea because everybody benefits from it. ☐

7 **SPEAKING** Say whether you agree or disagree with the opinions in exercise 6. Give reasons.

I agree / don't agree that … because …

It's fair / It isn't fair to say that … because …

I think / I don't think it's true to say that … because …

●● Vocabulary Builder 9.3: Small and large numbers: p.136

86 Unit 9 • Spend, spend, spend!

9D GRAMMAR
Third conditional

I can talk about an imaginary event in the past and its consequences.

1 🎧 **2.28** Listen and complete the dialogue.

Amy Have you got any dollars?
Tyler No, I haven't. You said that you were going to get them.
Amy If I'd had more time in the airport, I ¹____ have changed some money.
Tyler Why do you always leave everything to the last minute?
Amy Well, we ²____ have arrived at the airport late if you ³____ made a mistake with the train times!
Tyler Look, it doesn't matter whose fault it is. We need some currency.
Amy There's a cash machine over there. We can use our credit card to get some dollars.
Tyler Good idea. Where's the green bag?
Amy It's on the kitchen table at home. I didn't bring it.
Tyler It's got my wallet in it with all my cards.
Amy If I'd ⁴____ that, I would have brought it. But you didn't tell me.
Tyler I put it on the table. I wouldn't have put it there if I ⁵____ wanted you to bring it!
Amy So, we're in New York with no currency and no plastic. What are we going to do?

2 Answer the questions about the dialogue.
1 Did Amy and Tyler have a lot of time in the airport?
2 Who made a mistake with the train times?
3 Did Amy bring Tyler's green bag?
4 Why did Tyler put his green bag on the table?

3 Read the *Learn this!* box. How many examples of the third conditional are there in exercise 1?

> **LEARN THIS!**
> **Third conditional**
> 1 We use the third conditional to talk about the imaginary result of things that did not happen.
>   *If I'd left home earlier, I wouldn't have arrived late.*
> 2 We often use it to express criticism or regret.
>   *I wouldn't have got angry if you'd told the truth!*
> 3 We form the third conditional with *if* + past perfect, *would have* + past participle
> 4 We can also put the *if* clause in the second part of the sentence.
>   *I'd have cooked more food if I'd known you were so hungry.*
> 5 We often use short forms in third conditional sentences. The short form of both *had* and *would* is *'d*. *If I'd had enough money, I'd have bought it.*

4 🎧 **2.29** Complete the third conditional sentences with the correct form of the verbs in brackets. Use short forms. Then listen and check.
1 If she *hadn't become* (not become) a singer, she'd have been an actress.
2 If they hadn't accepted credit cards, we ____ (pay) in cash.
3 We ____ (win) if we'd played better.
4 If that picture ____ (be) for sale, I'd have bought it.
5 She ____ (not fail) her exams if she ____ (work) a bit harder.
6 I ____ (not eat) that sandwich if I ____ (see) you drop it on the floor.
7 She ____ (not leave) it if you ____ (not be) rude to her.
8 You ____ (be able) to afford the jacket if you ____ (not spend) all your money on CDs.

5 🎧 **2.29** **PRONUNCIATION** Listen again and repeat the sentences in exercise 4. How is the word *have* pronounced?

6 Rewrite the sentences as third conditional sentences.
1 We couldn't pay for dinner because you didn't bring your credit card.
   We could have paid for dinner if you'd brought your credit card.
2 We didn't go skiing because it didn't snow.
3 I didn't invite you to my party because I didn't have your number.
4 She didn't buy you a present because she didn't know it was your birthday.
5 I didn't make pizza because I didn't have any flour.
6 They didn't go to the beach because it wasn't sunny.

7 **SPEAKING** Work in pairs. Find out what your partner would have done if he or she:
1 had seen a robbery on the way to school this morning.
2 hadn't come to school today.
3 had woken up an hour later than usual this morning.
4 hadn't brought any books to the class.
5 had felt really hungry on the way to school this morning.

> What would you have done if you'd seen a robbery on the way to school this morning?

> I'd have taken a photo with my mobile and then I'd have called the police.

●● Grammar Builder 9.3: Third conditional: p. 125

Unit 9 • Spend, spend, spend! 87

9E READING
Giving it all away

I can understand a newspaper article about a millionaire.

1 SPEAKING Imagine you had €1 million and had to give it away to people that you didn't know personally. Who would you give it to, and why?

2 Read the text. How did Percy Ross decide who to give money to?

3 Match the sentences (a–f) with the gaps (1–5) in the text. There is one sentence that you do not need.
- a Nobody knows exactly how much this was.
- b He would have given it all away.
- c Surely, nobody in their right mind would do that.
- d If Ross thought they genuinely needed and deserved the money, he gave it to them.
- e Then disaster struck and he lost all his money.
- f His parents would have bought him one if they had been able to afford it, but they were too poor.

Reading tip
When you need to find specific information (like, for example, times or prices) in a text, you do not have to read every word. It's easier to find numbers quickly just by looking through.

Thanks a MILLION

Imagine you'd bought a lottery ticket and won $30 million. What would you do with the money? Would you give it all away? ¹☐ But in fact, there have been several examples over the years of millionaires who gave away all their money to help others. One of the most famous was Percy Ross.

Ross was born in 1916 in Michigan. His parents had come to the USA from Latvia and Russia and the family were poor. But Percy soon showed a talent for business and made a fortune in the fur trade and auction business. ²☐ But he soon made a fortune again – this time by manufacturing plastic bags. In 1969, he sold his plastic bag company for millions of dollars.

Ross started giving away his fortune in 1977: he gave $50,000 to 50 Vietnamese refugees so that they could make a new home in the USA. Then he held a Christmas party for 1,050 poor children in the American town of Minneapolis. Ross remembered that, when he was a child, he really wanted a bike. ³☐ Ross bought a bike for every one of the 1,050 children at the party.

After these first experiences of giving money away, Ross decided to do it on a regular basis. He started a newspaper column called 'Thanks a Million', and later a radio show, in order to give away his money. Readers and listeners wrote in and asked for money. ⁴☐ He received about 40,000 requests every month and sent cheques to about 150 every week. His gifts included money for poor families to help with their shopping bills and $16,500 in silver coins for children at a parade.

It took years, but Ross finally succeeded in giving away his entire fortune. He published his last newspaper column on 19 September 1999. 'I've achieved my goal,' he wrote. 'I've given it all away.' ⁵☐ 'I never tell anybody,' he said. 'It's not a question of how much one gives. Would I be a better person if I gave away $2 million than if I gave $1 million?' However, people estimate that he gave away around $30 million. And did he have any regrets? On the contrary. 'If I'd had twice as much,' he said, 'I still would have given it all away. For every person I helped, there were 400 to 500 I couldn't help.'

Percy Ross died in 2001 at the age of 85.

88 Unit 9 • Spend, spend, spend!

4 Read the reading tip. Then explain the significance of these dates and numbers in the life of Percy Ross.

1 1916
2 1969
3 50,000
4 1,050
5 40,000
6 16,500
7 1999
8 30 million

5 Are the sentences true or false? Correct the false ones.
1 Percy Ross is the only millionaire who has given away all his money.
2 Ross's parents were born in the USA.
3 Ross's first business was a company that made plastic bags.
4 Ross gave money to some people who had come to the USA to start a new life.
5 Ross gave bikes to poor children because his parents hadn't been able to give him a bike.
6 Ross started his newspaper column and radio show at the same time.
7 Ross did not send money to everybody who asked for it.
8 After giving away all his money, Ross wished that he hadn't done it.

6 Look at the highlighted phrases in the text. Complete the *Learn this!* box.

> **LEARN THIS!**
> **Clauses expressing purpose**
> 1 We can use an infinitive to explain the purpose of an action.
>   *He went to the Alps to go skiing.*
> 2 We can also use these phrases
>   ___ ___ *to* + base form
>   ___ *that* + subject + verb (usually a modal verb, e.g. *could*)

7 Match the two parts of the sentences and join them with one of the expressions from exercise 6.
1 Ben saved for years and years in _____
2 I asked for a receipt _____
3 He does a lot of housework _____
4 She borrowed £30 _____
5 He took his debit card with him _____

a he could get money from the cash machine.
b I could take the jeans back if they didn't fit.
c earn some pocket money.
d buy a new car.
e she could buy a new MP3 player.

8 🎧 2.30 Read and listen to the song. Find phrases which mean:
1 you looked after me
2 the best years of my life
3 I would die (to have you back again)
4 the part of me that can't forget
5 you don't show how important someone is to you

9 SPEAKING Do you think the song is happy or sad? Give reasons for your opinion.

10 SPEAKING Imagine that you had to give away everything you own. Which three objects would you be saddest to lose?

Everything I Own

You sheltered me from harm,
Kept me warm, kept me warm.
You gave my life to me,
Set me free, set me free.
5 The finest years I ever knew
Were all the years I had with you.

  [Chorus]
  I would give anything I own,
  Give up my life, my heart, my home.
  I would give everything I own,
10 Just to have you back again.

You taught me how to love,
What it's of, what it's of
You never said too much,
But still you showed the way,
15 And I knew from watching you.
Nobody else could ever know
The part of me that can't let go.

  [Chorus]

Is there someone you know,
You're loving them so,
20 But taking them all for granted.
You may lose them one day,
Someone takes them away,
And they don't hear the words you long to say.

  [Chorus]

Just to touch you once again.

Unit 9 • Spend, spend, spend! **89**

9F EVERYDAY ENGLISH
Arguing your case

I can argue a point.

Sophie It's ten o'clock in the evening. We need somewhere to stay.
Lydia I think we should stay in that youth hostel. It's right opposite!
Sophie Really? I'm not sure that's a good idea.
Lydia Why not?
Sophie Youth hostels aren't always very clean. Personally, I'd rather we found a campsite. We've got a tent. We should use it.
Lydia True, but it's late, and there aren't any campsites in the centre of town. I really think we'd be better off staying in the youth hostel.
Sophie I'm not convinced. A campsite would be cheaper, and we could get a bus there.
Lydia Well, if that's what you really want to do, then OK.
Sophie Great! Let's find a bus stop.

1 🎧 2.31 Sophie and Lydia are backpacking. Read and listen to their conversation and answer the questions.
  1 What do they disagree about?
  2 Who gets her own way in the end?

2 Who uses these facts and opinions to argue their case? Write *Sophie* or *Lydia*.
  1 The youth hostel is very near. _____
  2 Youth hostels are sometimes dirty. _____
  3 They've got a tent with them. _____
  4 The campsites are all out of town. _____
  5 Campsites are cheaper than youth hostels. _____
  6 There are buses to the campsites. _____

3 🎧 2.32 Listen to three conversations. Match the speakers with the disagreements.
  1 Lily and Cameron disagree about
  2 James and Chloe disagree about
  3 Leo and Millie disagree about

  a what to buy their dad for his birthday.
  b what food to prepare for a party.
  c whether to have a vending machine in the school.

4 🎧 2.32 Listen again. Who gets their own way in each disagreement?

5 Put the expressions from the dialogues into the correct group: A, B, C or D.
  1 I suppose you could be right.
  2 Oh, I don't agree.
  3 I take your point, but on the other hand, …
  4 Are you sure about that?
  5 I see what you mean, but …
  6 OK, whatever you want. I don't feel strongly about it.
  7 I still think I'm right.
  8 Do you really think so?

A	Doubting a suggestion
1	
2	
B	**Giving an alternative suggestion**
1	
2	
C	**Conceding the argument**
1	
2	
D	**Refusing to concede**
1	
2	

6 Find phrases in exercise 1 to add to the groups in exercise 5.

7 SPEAKING Work in pairs. Choose one of the ideas below and think of suggestions and alternative suggestions. Include reasons.
  • where to go on holiday
  • what to watch on television
  • who to invite to a party
  • which computer to buy

8 SPEAKING Work in pairs. Prepare a dialogue like the one in exercise 1. Include your ideas from exercise 7 and expressions from exercise 5.

9 SPEAKING Act out your dialogue to the class.

90 Unit 9 • Spend, spend, spend!

9G WRITING
A formal letter: asking for information

I can write a letter to a company asking for information.

1 Read the letter. What two things does Clare need to buy?

Dear Sir or Madam,

I am writing to enquire about the range of tents that I recently saw advertised in *Let's Go Camping* magazine.

I am planning a camping holiday this summer in Scotland. As you know, it can be quite wet and windy there, even in summer, so could you please tell me whether the Backpacker or the Campout range would be more suitable?

I am going with two friends, and we are planning to take quite a lot of equipment. Do you know if the three-berth tents have plenty of storage space?

I would be grateful if you could also let me know what colours the tents are available in, and how long it will take to deliver.

Finally, could you also tell me if you sell sleeping bags?

I look forward to hearing from you.

Yours faithfully

Clare Baines

Clare Baines

---

2 Look at the advertisement. In which paragraphs of the letter does Clare ask about the things that she has noted?

OK for wet and windy Scottish weather?
sleeping bags?

THE GREAT OUTDOORS

We specialise in budget tents and camping equipment.

Backpacker tents. Prices start at £75.

Campout tents – light-weight tents at affordable prices. From £55.

All tents available in two-, three- or four-berth sizes.

Limited colours.

Delivery free in the UK

big enough for three with lots of luggage? *how long?* *which colours?*

3 How does Clare start and end the letter? How would she start and end it if she knew the name of the person she was writing to?

> **Writing tip**
> - At the start of your letter, give your reason for writing.
> - Use indirect questions to make them more polite.
>   *How much is a two-berth tent?* ✗
>   *Could you tell me how much a two-berth tent is/would be?* ✓

4 Read the writing tip and find four indirect questions in Clare's letter.

5 Imagine you are going on a cycling holiday and you need to buy a bicycle. Look at the advertisement and the notes that you have made. Answer the questions:
1. Will you be cycling only on roads?
2. Why do you need panniers?
3. What other equipment do you need?

OK for riding on rough terrain – which bike? *taking lots of luggage – fit panniers?*

Discount Bikes

The UK's leading discount bike outlet.
Great bikes for the summer holidays.

Easyride Touring bikes. **From £175**
Adventurer bikes. **From £199**
Available in most sizes. We also stock bike accessories.
Free postage and packing on orders over £200.

cost for bikes under £200? *large frames available?* *lights and locks?*

6 Now write a letter to Discount Bikes asking for more information. Use the writing guide below.
- Start and end the letter correctly.
- Use indirect questions.
- In the first paragraph, say where you saw the advertisement and why you are writing.
- In the second paragraph, explain what you need the bike for and ask your most important question.
- Put your remaining questions into two or three paragraphs, with the most important questions first.

Unit 9 • Spend, spend, spend!

Get ready for your EXAM 9

1 **Get ready to READ** Look at the photo of a floating hotel. Which adjectives from the box could be used to describe it.

close to nature   exciting   inexpensive   luxurious
movable   simple   spacious   unconventional

2 Do the Reading exam task.

READING exam task

Read the text. Choose the best option: A, B, C or D.

Friendlier FOOTPRINTS

Providing five-star luxury in the middle of a treasured wilderness without damaging the environment might not be easy, but it is far from impossible. The King Pacific Lodge in British Columbia's Great Bear Rainforest proves that if enough care and attention is taken, the task is within the reach of any tourist provider.

Unlike many other hotel building projects no trees were cut down and no land was wasted in order to build it. The Lodge does not have a permanent location but sits on a floating barge towed into the sea bay in May, where it anchors till September. Those wishing to stay in one of its seventeen rooms must access it by boat or seaplane. Each guest staying at the Lodge is charged 3% conservation tax, but is rewarded by the chance to sight whales and bears. And since these are the main attractions of the area and of the Lodge, the management is well aware that in order to stay in business they must leave the area untouched.

In 2000, the Lodge management signed an agreement with the native Gitga'at people by whom they were later adopted. Together they work for the benefit of the area. The Lodge recognises the native tribe as the owners of the land, pays the tribe for the use of their land and even supports the native youth and employs the tribe's people. They, in turn, teach the newcomers about the local culture.

The King Pacific Lodge is one of a growing number of tourism companies that go beyond purely minimising their environmental impact to win the approval of the local community where they establish their business. These companies use eco-friendly solutions to problems, and are careful to restrict their use of resources and protect threatened species. Realising how destructive tourism can be, they want to avoid the love-it-to-death effect of tourism and leave a lighter environmental footprint.

1 According to the text, luxury hotels
   A usually have a positive effect on their environment.
   B are more eco-friendly when they are difficult to reach.
   C do not harm the environment if they are carefully designed.
   D are impossible to find in the middle of a wilderness.
2 The King Pacific Lodge
   A is situated far away from an important wilderness.
   B has been created after careful consideration.
   C is less luxurious than might be expected.
   D is based on a good example.
3 What is true about the Lodge?
   A It is located in an area without any trees.
   B It can be moved from place to place.
   C Guests have to pay extra for the flight to get there.
   D Guests can take part in conservation programmes.
4 The Lodge management
   A cooperate with the native people.
   B bought the land for a lot of money.
   C do not care about the local culture.
   D are difficult to cooperate with.
5 Some of the native people
   A did not want to sell their land.
   B go to school to learn about the local culture.
   C work from a very early age.
   D earn money at the Lodge.
6 According to the text, the tourist industry
   A ignores the importance of eco-friendly tourism.
   B will always be a threat to the environment.
   C can limit the damage it does to the environment.
   D is in conflict with the local communities.

3 Do the Speaking exam task.

SPEAKING exam task

Work in pairs. Imagine that you are planning a holiday at the King Pacific Lodge. Using information from the reading text and your imagination, agree on:

1 when you will visit the hotel,
2 how you will travel there,
3 how long you plan to stay there,
4 two activities from the list below that you would like to do there together.

ocean fishing   hiking   helicopter trips
kayaking   wildlife tours   whale watching

Get ready for your EXAM 10

1 `Get ready to LISTEN` Match words from the two columns to make phrases connected with money.

1 cash	a account
2 debit	b card
3 hard	c currency
4 PIN	d machine
5 pocket	e money
6 savings	f number

2 🎧 2.33 Do the Listening exam task.

LISTENING exam task

Listen to five speakers talking about money. Match statements A–F to speakers 1–5. There is one statement you do not need to use.

A You should teach children how to save money for things they really desire.
B You should buy children whatever they want, if you can afford it.
C You should set a good example to your children regarding money.
D You should only give children pocket money if they help around the house.
E You should give children control of their own money as soon as possible.
F You should protect children from having to think about money at all.

Speaker 1		Speaker 2		Speaker 3	
Speaker 4		Speaker 5			

3 Do the Use of English exam task.

USE OF ENGLISH exam task

Choose the best word (A–D) to complete each gap.

A 21st century epidemic

While medical scientists are always on the lookout for new and deadly forms of the influenza virus, a few psychologists ¹_____ started to talk and write about the dangers of a completely different kind of epidemic: affluenza. The word itself is a mixture of 'influenza' and 'affluent', ²_____ means 'wealthy or rich'. It describes an unhealthy obsession with money and material possessions.

British psychologist Oliver James, ³_____ has written two books on the subject, defines affluenza as 'placing a high value on money, possessions, appearances and fame'. He believes that the condition is more common in English-speaking countries ⁴_____ in other parts of the world. The reason for this, according to James, is that the USA, Britain, Australia, New Zealand and Canada are more obsessed with making money than other nations. This leads to stress and ⁵_____. In support of his theory, James points ⁶_____ that people in English-speaking countries are twice as likely to suffer mental health problems as people who live in mainland Europe.

Perhaps the most worrying aspect of affluenza is that it is starting to affect people at younger and younger ages. Teenagers, and ⁷_____ young children, make constant demands for possessions, and become genuinely unhappy if they do not have these things ⁸_____ for them. Some experts blame advertising in schools; ⁹_____ think that Hollywood and TV shows are the cause. The only cure seems to be for parents to spend time ¹⁰_____ their children the value of other things in life, like friendship, charity and laughter.

1	A will have	B have	C had	D were
2	A who	B that	C where	D which
3	A who	B that	C where	D which
4	A that	B as	C for	D than
5	A unhappy	B unhappily	C unhappier	D unhappiness
6	A up	B to	C towards	D out
7	A even	B every	C enough	D each
8	A to buy	B buying	C buy	D bought
9	A another	B others	C each other	D otherwise
10	A teaching	B taught	C to teach	D teach

4 Do the Speaking exam task.

SPEAKING exam task

Compare and contrast the two photos. Answer the questions.

1 What do you think the woman is paying for? What makes you think this?
2 What do you think the man is paying for? What makes you think this?
3 What are the advantages and disadvantages of using a credit card?
4 What would be the advantages of disadvantages of only using cash to buy things?

10 Inspiration

THIS UNIT INCLUDES
Vocabulary • visual and performing arts • artists and artistic activities • compound nouns (3)
Grammar • participle clauses • determiners: *all, each, every, few, little*, etc. • *so* and *such* • nominal subject clauses
Speaking • talking about the arts • describing a picture • discussion about graffiti • evaluating an experience
Writing • a discursive essay

A VOCABULARY AND LISTENING
Art and artists

I can talk about different types of art.

1 Label the photos with words and phrases from the box. Check the meaning of all these words in the Wordlist in the Workbook.

> **Visual and performing arts**   an abstract painting
> buskers   a gig   graffiti   an installation   juggling
> performance art   a portrait   a sculpture
> a stage musical   a recital   a still life

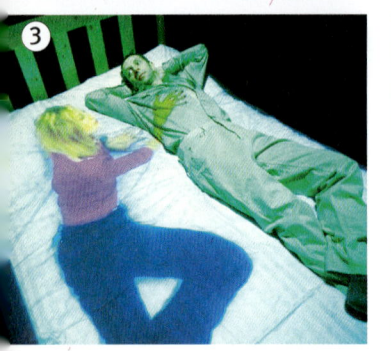

2 Match the works of art and performances from the box in exercise 1 with one or more of the places where you could see or hear them.

a   an art gallery   c   a concert hall   e   outdoors
b   a theatre   d   a club

3 Work in pairs. What other types of works of art or performances can you see or hear at the places in exercise 2?

art gallery: photographs, vases …

4 🎧 3.01 Read the sentences and, if necessary, check the meaning of the words in red in the Wordlist on page 143. Then listen. What is happening? Match the sentences to the dialogues (1–7).

a   An actress is changing into her costume. ☐
b   Two opera singers are rehearsing a scene. ☐
c   An artist is talking to his model. ☐
d   A dancer is practising some steps. ☐
e   Two stage hands are moving some scenery. ☐
f   A conductor is talking to his orchestra. ☐
g   A technician is testing the sound and lighting. ☐

5 🎧 3.01 Listen again. Complete the sentences from the conversations with the words and phrases in the box.

> aria   audience   director   drum kit   lines   melody
> mikes   oil painting   script   sketch   violins

1   It isn't a _____, it's an _____.
2   I'm going to have a word with the _____.
3   And I sing my _____.
4   Where's my _____? I need to practise my _____.
5   Can you test the _____ on the _____?
6   Remember that the _____ have the _____.
7   Look straight at the _____.

6 **SPEAKING** Work in pairs. Discuss the questions. Give reasons for your answers.

1   Which musical instrument would you most like to be able to play?
2   Which of the arts in exercise 1 do you think needs the most skill, and which the least?
3   Which of the arts in exercise 1 would you most like to be really good at?

●● Vocabulary Builder 10.1: Artists and artistic activities: p.1

94   Unit 10 • Inspiration

B GRAMMAR
Participle clauses

I can correctly use participle clauses.

1 Look at the picture. Who painted it? Read the first sentence of the text and check.

2 Read the text. Find two mistakes in the description of the painting.

This picture, **painted** by the French artist Georges Seurat between 1884 and 1886, is called *Sunday afternoon on the island of La Grande Jatte*. It shows Parisians **relaxing** beside a lake on a cloudy afternoon. The young men and women, **wearing** their best Sunday clothes, appear as graceful as the speedboats **reflected** in the water.
This large picture, **measuring** approximately 200 cm by 300 cm, is made up of thousands of tiny dots of colour. Seurat believed that this form of painting, now **known** as *pointillism*, would make the colours more brilliant. *La Grande Jatte*, permanently **displayed** in Chicago, is Seurat's most famous work. There is even a stage musical **based** on the picture, **composed** in 1984 by Stephen Sondheim.

3 Read the *Learn this!* box. In which of the examples does the participle clause replace a non-defining relative clause?

> **LEARN THIS!**
> **Participle clauses**
> 1 We can use participle clauses to give more information about a noun. They can be described as shortened relative clauses (defining or non-defining).
> There's a man **reading a book**. (=who is reading a book)
> 2 They contain either a present participle (*-ing* form) or past participle (*-ed*).
> 3 Clauses with a present participle replace an **active** verb. The verb they replace can be in any tense.
> He lived in a flat **belonging to his father**.
> (=which belonged to)
> 4 Clauses with a past participle replace a **passive** verb. The verb they replace can be in any tense.
> The final episode, **shown on TV tomorrow**, will be watched by millions. (=which will be shown on TV tomorrow)

4 Underline all the participle clauses in the text in exercise 2. Answer the questions for each clause.
  1 Does it replace a defining or non-defining relative clause?
  2 Does it begin and end with a comma?

5 Rewrite the participle clauses in the text as relative clauses.
This picture, which was painted by the French artist Georges Seurat ...

●● Grammar Builder 10.1: Participle clauses: p. 126

6 Complete the description of *La Grande Jatte* with the present and past participle form of the verbs in the box.

| accompany hold leave lie lose smoke |
| startle wear |

In the foreground, there's a woman on the right ¹_____ a black top and a grey skirt and ²_____ a black parasol. On the left, there's a man in casual clothes ³_____ on the grass ⁴_____ a pipe, and in the centre, there are two black dogs and a monkey. One of the dogs is eating some food ⁵_____ on the ground. The smaller dog, ⁶_____ by the monkey, is running away. In the middle of the picture, there's a tall woman ⁷_____ by a small girl in a white dress. Several people, ⁸_____ in thought, are gazing across the water.

7 **SPEAKING** Find the people and things (1–7) in the picture below and describe them. Use present participle clauses and the verbs in the box to help you.

| cook drink kiss hold lie ride smile talk |
| watch wear |

1 the man on the left with a beard
2 the woman in the centre of the picture
3 the men with black hats
4 the woman in the foreground
5 the bald man
6 the man in the top right-hand corner of the picture
7 the two women on the right.

Unit 10 • Inspiration   95

10 C CULTURE Is it art?

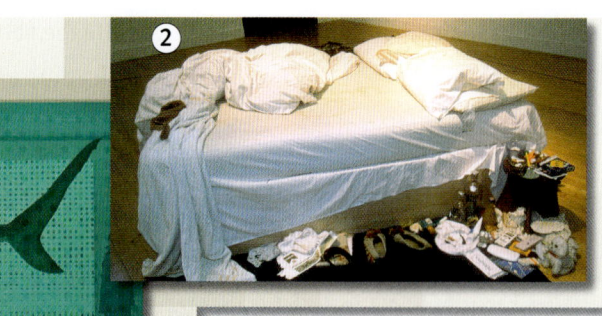

I can discuss works of art that I like and dislike.

Britart

1 Young British Artists (or Britart) are a group of conceptual artists, painters, photographers and sculptors based in London who became famous in the 1990s for their 'shock tactics' – their use of strange materials and unusual subject matter.

2 Their first exhibition, called Freeze, was organised in 1988 by Damien Hirst, a leading member of Britart who at that time was still a student at art college. The exhibition was seen by a keen art collector, Charles Saatchi, who bought one of Hirst's earliest installations: a glass case containing real flies and maggots feeding off a rotting cow's head. Saatchi became an important supporter of Britart.

3 In 1997, a major exhibition called Sensation, held in the Royal Academy in London and seen by over 300,000 people, brought Britart to the attention of a wide audience. Damien Hirst exhibited a dead shark floating in a tank. Tracey Emin, another famous artist, exhibited a tent which she had decorated with the names of all the boyfriends she'd ever had. (Her most famous work, though, is *My Bed*, which is actually her real-life, and rather messy, bed standing in the middle of an art gallery!) Although the exhibition was a huge success, there were many public complaints in the media, as a lot of the artwork was considered offensive or in bad taste.

4 Since then, Britart has continued to dominate the British art scene, and it has provoked endless 'Is this art?' discussions. People still can't agree, and although the artists have their supporters, they still receive a lot of criticism. However, their exhibitions are always well attended. It will be interesting to see how long they can continue to challenge our ideas of what art really is. Or will it all start to look normal?

1 Describe what you can see in the photos.

2 Read the text quickly. Which of the three works of art is not mentioned in the text?

3 Match four of the headings with paragraphs (1–4).
 a Success and scandal
 b Who are Britart?
 c Britart conquers the USA
 d Continuing debates
 e The beginnings of Britart

4 Find the phrases in paragraphs 1–3 of the text and explain them in your own words.
 1 conceptual artists
 2 shock tactics
 3 strange materials
 4 unusual subject matter
 5 a keen art collector
 6 a major exhibition
 7 a wide audience
 8 in bad taste

5 🎧 3.02 Listen to two people talking about the works of art in the photos. Which works does the man like? Which works does the woman like?

6 🎧 3.02 Listen again. Complete the sentences. Who says them, the man (M) or the woman (W)?
 1 I don't think it's a _____.
 2 But she's trying to do something d_____. It makes you t _____.
 3 I think it's i_____.
 4 It's r_____.
 5 It's very c_____. The artist is trying to make us think about death in a new w_____.
 6 But where is the s_____ in putting a shark in a tank?
 7 I could do that m_____.
 8 Artists are always a_____ of their time.
 9 I know modern art isn't to everybody's t_____.

7 **SPEAKING** Work in pairs. Discuss the questions, then share your ideas with the class.
 1 Do you like the works of art in the photos? Why?/Why not?
 2 In general, do you like modern art, or do you prefer traditional painting and sculpture?
 3 Do you remember any modern work of art that you loved or hated? What was it? Describe it.
 4 Can anything be a work of art if it's in an art gallery? Why?/Why not?

Unit 10 • Inspiration

10D GRAMMAR
Determiners: *all, each, every, few, little,* etc.

I can use different determiners with nouns.

1 Read the text and answer the question in the title.

Can ballet change lives?

In 2006, a TV programme called *How Ballet Changed My Life* showed 60 young people taking part in a special performance of the ballet *Romeo and Juliet*. All of the participants were from disadvantaged families, with little money and few opportunities. Some participants had already been in trouble with the law. Each young person tells his or her story as part of the TV programme, which follows every step of their 18-month preparation. Before taking part in the programme, most of them had no experience of ballet. By the end, after much hard work and many hours of rehearsal, every one of them felt that the experience had led to some improvement in their attitude to life. A few of them might even become professional performers.

2 Look at the words in blue in the text and complete table 1.

Determiners: table 1	
every, _____	+ singular countable noun
few, a few, _____	+ plural noun
little, a little, _____	+ uncountable noun
all, most, _____, any, no	+ countable or uncountable noun

3 Look at the words in red in the text. What is the missing word in table 2?

Determiners: table 2			
all, most, some, any, (a) few, (a) little much, many, each, every one, none	_____	the, a/an my, your, etc. this, that, etc. us, it, them, you, etc.	+ noun

Remember the same rules in table 1 apply to the nouns and pronouns that follow the determiner, e.g. *much of* + uncountable noun.

●● Grammar Builder 10.2: Determiners: p. 126

4 Choose the correct words in the text.

In the TV programme *The Choir*, a conductor called Gareth Malone takes 30 teenagers who have never sung in a choir before and prepares them for an international choir competition in China. ¹**All / Every** of the teenagers are from a secondary school near London. Gareth was surprised to find that there were ²**no / none** music lessons at the school, and ³**most of / most** the students had ⁴**few / little** experience of classical music. In their auditions, ⁵**many / much** of the students chose to sing R&B songs! Nearly ⁶**all / each** of the students at the school took part in the auditions, but only a ⁷**few / little** of them were good enough for the choir. There wasn't ⁸**much / much of** time for rehearsal – only nine months – but the choir performed well and ⁹**every one / every** of the students grew in confidence as a result of the experience.

Look out!

We use *few* and *little* (rather than *a few* and *a little*) when we want to emphasise the smallness of the number or quantity. It usually has a **negative meaning**. Compare:
She enjoyed the party. She had a little food and chatted with a few nice people.
She hated the party. There was little food and few nice people.

5 Read the *Look out!* box. Complete the sentences with *few, a few, little* or *a little*.
1 They cancelled the concert because _____ tickets had been sold.
2 On Saturday, I went for a meal with _____ friends.
3 He's very lazy and spends _____ time working.
4 Do you mind if I ask you _____ questions?
5 I can afford to buy a new phone because I've earned _____ money working in my uncle's shop.
6 It's Liszt's most difficult work for piano and _____ pianists can play it well.
7 This soup tastes good, but it needs _____ salt.

6 Complete the sentences about your classmates with the phrases in the box. Try to guess the truth.

all	a few	many	most	none	some

1 _____ of them have seen a ballet performance on stage.
2 _____ of them have sung in a choir.
3 _____ of them walked to school this morning.
4 _____ of them enjoy dancing.
5 _____ of them like chocolate.
6 _____ of them had a shower this morning.

7 **SPEAKING** Read your sentences from exercise 6 to the class. Find out if they are correct.

Unit 10 • Inspiration 97

10 E READING
Urban art

I can understand and react to a magazine article about two artists.

BANKSY

'Banksy' is the name of a graffiti artist from Britain. Nobody knows his real name and few people have seen him. He has become famous for his street art, which has appeared in London and in other cities around the world. He has to stay unknown because graffiti is illegal. Nobody has caught him yet.

His images are very striking and often funny, and their message is usually anti-war, anti-capitalism and pro-freedom. He has claimed responsibility for a number of famous stunts over the past few years. For example, in 2001 he climbed into the penguin area at London Zoo and wrote 'We're bored of fish' in two-metre high letters on the wall. In May 2005, he made a primitive cave painting, showing a human hunting animals with a shopping trolley. He hung it secretly on the wall at the British Museum. ¹☐ In August of the same year, he painted nine images on the Palestinian side of the Israeli West Bank wall, including a picture of children digging a hole through the wall.

Nowadays, Banksy does some paid work for charities such as Greenpeace. He refuses to work for big businesses or do advertising. He has also started painting pictures. He has done a series of paintings based on famous works of art, such as Monet's *Water-Lily Pond*, except with rubbish floating in the water and a shopping trolley sticking out. ²☐

Pavement Picasso

'Pavement Picasso' is another name for Julian Beever, a chalk artist from Britain. He has been creating chalk drawings on the pavement for over ten years now. He has worked in cities all over the world, from Brussels to New York.

He works in chalk, so his art, which takes about three days to complete, can easily be destroyed by a shower of rain. The most important thing for him is to get a photo at the end before that happens.

He first started pavement drawing with copies of famous paintings like the *Mona Lisa* in the streets of Europe. Then he painted portraits of famous people; for example, when Princess Diana died, he did a portrait of her on a London pavement. ³☐

1 **SPEAKING** Look at picture 3. Describe what is happening using the words in the box to help you. Which part of the picture is real, and not drawn?

cars   climb   crouch   fall   ledge   look up/down
neighbour   pavement   rescue   Spiderman
road   window

2 Read the texts quickly. Decide which two of the pictures (1–4) are by Banksy, and which two are by Pavement Picasso. Which pictures do you prefer? Give reasons.

3 Match the sentences with gaps 1–4 in the text. There is one sentence that you do not need.
 a He sells them in a small gallery in London, but you'll never see him there.
 b He earns money by charging people to see his pictures.
 c He usually puts himself in the painting when he takes a photo of his work.
 d The Museum has since allowed it to stay there.
 e He also painted Bill Clinton on a New York sidewalk when he became President of the United States.

4 Decide if the sentences are true or false for each artist.

	Banksy	Pavement Picasso
1 He's British.	☐	☐
2 He works outside.	☐	☐
3 People know his real name.	☐	☐
4 Some of his work is illegal.	☐	☐
5 He does advertisements.	☐	☐
6 He sells his work.	☐	☐
7 His work is political.	☐	☐
8 His work disappears if it rains.	☐	☐
9 He has done work based on famous works of art.	☐	☐

5 Find adjectives in the text that mean:
 1 against the law (line 6)
 2 very interesting and unusual (line 7)
 3 belonging to a very early, simple society (line 14)
 4 incredible (line 41)
 5 very big (line 43)
 6 very detailed and complicated (line 45)

6 Find six present participle clauses and one past participle clause in the second and third paragraphs of the Banksy text.

7 **SPEAKING** Work in pairs. Choose one of the pictures (2–4). Make notes about what you can see. Then describe the picture to the class.

8 **SPEAKING** Discuss the question with the class. Use the phrases in the box to help you. Then have a class vote.
Graffiti: is it art or vandalism?

Expressing opinions
In my opinion, …   I think …
I agree.   Yes, that's right.
I don't agree.   I don't think that's right.
That may be true, but …   I see your point, but …

●●● Vocabulary Builder 10.2: Compound nouns (3): p. 137

But he is most famous for his amazing 3D images, which he started doing a few years ago. He can do a painting on the pavement which looks like a gigantic bottle of Coke standing in the road when you look at it
45 from a certain angle. ⁴☐ Some of his most elaborate 3D images show someone diving into a swimming pool, or being rescued from a building by Spiderman!

Nowadays, Beever is often paid by companies to advertise their products, but he still works on the
50 pavement. He says, 'My art is for anybody, it's for people who wouldn't go into an art gallery. It's art for the people.'

Unit 10 • Inspiration   99

10F EVERYDAY ENGLISH
Evaluating an experience

I can describe and give my opinion of an event.

Lucy	What did you do at the weekend?
Tara	I went to see a ballet with my aunt. We got a train down to London and then went to the theatre at Sadler's Wells.
Lucy	What was the ballet like?
Tara	It was fantastic! I loved every minute of it.
Lucy	Really? What was so good about it?
Tara	Everything, really. The music was wonderful, and the dancers were awesome. They were so athletic!
Lucy	It sounds great.
Tara	And I loved the male lead. He was such a brilliant dancer – and so handsome! You should come with me next time I go.
Lucy	Yes, I'd love to.

1 🎧 **3.03** Read and listen to the dialogue. What did Tara like about the ballet? Tick (✓) the things that she mentions.

- the costumes ☐
- the music ☐
- the story ☐
- the male lead ☐
- the scenery ☐
- the special effects ☐
- the dancing ☐
- the female lead ☐

2 Find five adjectives in the dialogue which mean 'extremely good'.

3 Imagine that Tara hated everything about the ballet. Rewrite the dialogue using some of the adjectives below and changing other words where necessary.

appalling   atrocious   awful   dreadful   pathetic
terrible   unattractive

4 Read the *Learn this!* box. How many examples of *so* and *such* are in the dialogue in exercise 1?

> **LEARN THIS!**
> **so and such**
> We can use **so** or **such** to intensify the meaning of an adjective or adverb. We use them in these structures
> 1 *be + so + adjective*
>   I'm so tired!
> 2 *so + adverb*
>   They all danced so brilliantly.
> 3 *such + adjective + plural noun/uncountable noun*
>   She's got such beautiful eyes/hair.
> 4 *such + a/an + adjective + noun*
>   He's got such an amazing voice.

5 Complete the sentences with *so*, *such* or *such a(n)*.
  1 The songs were _____ wonderful!
  2 The main character was _____ atrocious actor!
  3 I'd never seen _____ amazing scenery!
  4 The special effects were _____ brilliant!
  5 The actors were all wearing _____ beautiful costumes!
  6 The orchestra played _____ well!

👉 Grammar Builder 10.3: *so* and *such*: p. 127

6 🎧 **3.04** **PRONUNCIATION** Listen and repeat the sentences in exercise 5. Try to copy the intonation.

7 🎧 **3.05** Listen to four dialogues. Match what the people are talking about with the events in the box.

a musical   an opera   a film   a modern dance

8 🎧 **3.05** Listen again. Which of the aspects (a–g) does each speaker mention? Put a tick (✓) for a positive comment, and a cross (✗) for a negative comment.

	1	2	3	4
a the costumes				
b the music	✓			
c the story	✗			
d the scenery				
e the dancing				
f the male lead				
g the female lead				

9 **SPEAKING** Work in pairs. Prepare a dialogue about a real or imaginary show that you thought was very good or very bad. Comment on some of the aspects in exercise 8 and use your own ideas.

10 **SPEAKING** Act out your dialogue to the class.

100   Unit 10 • Inspiration

10G WRITING — A discursive essay

I can write an essay discussing a theoretical issue.

1 Read the essay and look at the essay plan below. Which paragraph in the plan is missing from the finished essay?

How does art affect our everyday lives?

Art does not just refer to paintings in a museum. There are many different kinds of art. Advertising and architecture are both kinds of art too, in my opinion, and they both have an effect on our lives. Even people who are not interested in going to art galleries are still affected by these other kinds of art.

Posters and other forms of advertisements are all around us, especially in towns and cities, and we cannot help seeing them. If they are successful advertisements, they affect our opinions and behaviour; they make us want to buy certain products. In addition, adverts often make the streets more colourful and attractive.

Buildings are not just places where we live and work – they are also part of our environment. Architecture has an effect on the way we feel. For example, living or working in a bright, attractive building makes people feel more optimistic, whereas dark, ugly buildings can make people feel gloomy.

To sum up, I believe that different forms of art are all around us and have a big effect on our everyday lives. Unfortunately, most cities and towns have parts which are ugly and depressing. What they need are beautiful buildings and colourful advertisements.

1 Introduction – art = not just paintings – also architecture, ads, etc.
2 ads – part of environment
   make us want to buy
   colourful, attractive
3 architecture – affects how we feel
   e.g. bright buildings → optimism ugly buildings → depression
4 fashion – not just 'designer' clothes – also 'street' fashion
   clothes affect how we judge sb
   e.g. unusual clothes → interesting person
5 sum up – ugly cities need beautiful buildings + colourful ads

> **Writing tip**
>
> It is not necessary to write full sentences in an essay plan. You can use key words, abbreviations and symbols.
>
> ~~A good job often means a high salary.~~
>
> good job = $$$

2 Read the writing tip. Then find abbreviations and symbols in the essay plan in exercise 1 which mean:
1 equals, is the same as
2 and other similar things
3 advertisements
4 for example
5 cause, lead to
6 somebody
7 and

> **LEARN THIS!**
>
> **Nominal subject clauses**
> We sometimes emphasise particular information in a sentence by beginning with a *what* clause followed by *be*.
> I'm looking for a more colourful outfit.
> **What I'm looking for is** a more colourful outfit.
> She needs a new job.
> **What she needs is** a new job.

3 Read the *Learn this!* box. Find an example of a *what* clause in the essay in exercise 1.

4 Rewrite the sentences using nominal subject clauses starting with *what*.
1 I prefer unusual clothes.
2 I like modern architecture.
3 I really hate grey tower blocks.
4 We need a new attitude to urban architecture.
5 It shows how important art can be.
6 They're looking for a more attractive house.

●● Grammar Builder 10.4: Nominal subject clauses: p.127

5 Read the essay question below. Make a plan using the suggestions in the box below and your own ideas. Remember to use abbreviations and symbols.

In what ways can films make our lives better?

> entertainment   learn about the world   historical films
> documentaries   fashion and film stars
> ideas of the future (sci-fi)   music in films

6 Write an essay using your plan from exercise 5. Write 200–250 words and remember to check your work for mistakes when you have finished.

Unit 10 • Inspiration 101

LANGUAGE REVIEW 9–10

Vocabulary

1 Complete the phrases with the verbs in the box.

| afford | borrow | buy | pay | save | waste |

1 _____ a bargain in the sales
2 _____ money on something you'll never use
3 _____ up to go on holiday
4 _____ £20 from a friend
5 _____ to buy a new car
6 _____ money into a bank account

Mark /6

2 Solve the anagrams to make words connected with art and performance art.

1 otrrptai
2 hstekc
3 unedeiac
4 talicer
5 lomedy
6 gjuglign

Mark /6

Grammar

3 Put the words in the correct order.

1 hair / is / black / his / Michael / dyed / having
_____
2 her / has / reduced / nose / Natasha / had
_____
3 living room / going / decorated / have / to / We're / our
_____
4 pierced / eyebrow / yesterday / Alisha / had / her
_____
5 new TV / their / having / tomorrow / delivered / They're
_____

Mark /5

4 Complete the text with the past or present participle form of the verbs in brackets.

Our school play was a huge success this year. The script ¹_____ (write) by Mr Hill, the English teacher, was really funny, and the actors, ²_____ (wear) costumes donated by the local theatre, performed really well. The audience joined in with all the songs ³_____ (sing) on stage and laughed at all of the jokes. The scenery, ⁴_____ (make) by the art department, was really beautiful, and, finally, the students ⁵_____ (play) in the band were excellent.

Mark /5

5 Use the prompts to write sentences. Add *of* if necessary.

1 Lots of snow fell on most / towns in my area.
_____
2 A few / my / friends had to walk to school.
_____
3 Most / the / students arrived late.
_____
4 None / our / teachers / could drive their cars.
_____
5 Many / students stayed at home.
_____
6 Every one / us expected to be sent straight home.
_____

Mark /6

Everyday English

6 Complete the sentences with the words in the box.

| mean | point | still | strongly | suppose |

1 I _____ you could be right.
2 I take your _____, but on the other hand we're broke.
3 I see what you _____, but I think it's too late now.
4 Whatever you want. I don't feel _____ about it.
5 I _____ think I'm right.

Mark /5

7 Put the lines (a–e) in the correct order to complete the dialogue.

a It sounds great.
b It was. You'll have to come with me next time.
c It was excellent. I loved every minute of it.
d Really? What was so good about it?
e The script, the actors, the scenery. Everything, really.

Nathan   What was the play like?
Poppy   ☐
Nathan   ☐
Poppy   ☐
Nathan   ☐
Poppy   ☐
Nathan   I'd love to.

Mark /5
Total /38

EXAM CHALLENGE Workbook pages 94–97

Skills Round-up 1–10

Reading

1 Read the e-mail and look at the photo. Why has Sarah taken this photo of Marek?

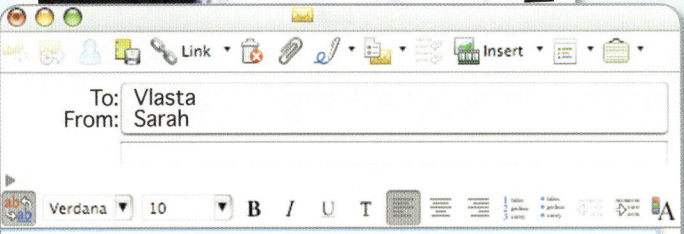

2 Are the sentences are true or false?
1 Sarah has painted some pictures for an exhibition.
2 James is pleased that Marek has found a flat.
3 There are three people living in Marek's new flat.
4 Sarah wants to know how Marek and Suzanne met.
5 Marek might be having a relationship with Suzanne.

Listening

3 🎧 3.06 Listen. Do you think Marek and Suzanne are boyfriend and girlfriend, or just friends? Give reasons for your answers.

4 🎧 3.06 Listen again and choose the correct answers.
1 Sarah's exhibition starts on
  A Saturday.   B Sunday.   C Monday.
2 It lasts for
  A one day.   B two days.   C three days.
3 Entrance to the exhibition costs
  A £5.   B £2.   C nothing.
4 The venue for the exhibition is
  A the town hall.   B the art college.
  C a gallery in London.
5 In the entrance hall, the exhibition has
  A a sculpture.   B a security camera.
  C a video installation.

Speaking

5 Work in pairs. You need to agree on something to do together tomorrow afternoon. (Look back at page 90, exercise 5 for phrases to help you.)
A You want to go to Sarah's art exhibition. Thinks of reasons why it is a good thing to do, and try to persuade B.
B You want to go to the cinema. Think of reasons why it is a good thing to do, and try to persuade A.

Writing

6 Write a short review of a film that you have seen recently. Give your opinion of:
- the story
- the main actors
- the music, costumes or special effects

To: Vlasta
From: Sarah

Dear Vlasta

Hi! I hope you're well. I've been really busy preparing an exhibition with some other students from Art College. It's going to be a mixture of photographs, paintings and drawings connected to the theme 'Changing Britain'. I'm contributing some photos of Marek! It was difficult taking them – he hates having his photo taken!

As you probably know, Marek has found a flat and moved out of our house – at last! Actually, I really enjoyed having him here, and I miss him. But I don't think James (my boyfriend and Marek's boss) would have been very pleased if he'd stayed here much longer. Anyway, Marek is now sharing a flat with two friends – Tom and Suzanne. Has he told you about Suzanne? He met her on a train to Edinburgh, and then bumped into her again in the Princes Street Gardens at dusk. How romantic! If he hadn't spilt her coffee on the train, she probably wouldn't have remembered him! Now they're really close friends – or maybe more than friends. He won't tell me! Has he told you?

I hope work is going better and you aren't feeling so tired. What you need is a holiday in England!

Love

Sarah

Get ready for B2 Exams 1

1 **Get ready to READ** Look at the Reading exam task in exercise 2. What building is the text about? Where is it?

2 Do the Reading exam task.

READING exam task

Read the text. Six sentences have been removed from the text. Choose from sentences A–G the one that best fits each gap. There is one extra sentence that you do not need.

Opera by the bay

Sydney's rich artistic heritage is beyond doubt, stretching back to Aboriginal engravings and drawings. So it seems only fitting that this city was chosen as the setting for the Australian Opera. **1**☐ Until the 20th century this was a military site which then was used as a tram depot. As trams were phased out, the building became redundant and was demolished in 1958 to make way for the Sydney Opera House.

Eugene Goossens, who in 1946 became the resident conductor of the Sydney Symphony Orchestra, was the first to bring up the subject of building an Opera House. **2**☐ In 1956, the government announced an international competition for the design of two concert halls attracting 233 entries from all over the world. A young Danish architect, Jørn Utzon, saw the competition advertised in a Swedish architectural magazine and sent in his ten drawings. On 29 January 1957 he was declared the winner. **3**☐ And this, unquestionably, has happened. One of the most recognisable images in the world today, the Opera House is the ultimate symbol of Sydney and Australia.

The Opera House building, its unique shape resembling a ship at full sail, graces Sydney's harbour. But it took years to construct. **4**☐ The works began in 1959 and it was 1961 before Utzon worked out the problem of the roof. **5**☐ Utzon said of his roof the the 'interplay is so important that together with the sun, the light and the clouds, it makes a living thing. In order to express this liveliness, these roofs are covered with glazed tiles'.

The final cost of the Sydney Opera House, excluding the organ, was $102 million. **6**☐ The Opera House has four halls and was opened by Queen Elizabeth II on 20 October 1973.

A The majority of the sum was raised by the specially created Opera House lottery.

B His drawings were said to present a concept of an Opera House which was capable of becoming one of the great buildings of the world.

C In order to do so, he drew inspiration from nature, in particular the palm leaf and the orange fruit.

D It took over ten years for his dream to even have the chance of becoming a reality.

E This was because, at the time of its design, the magnificent roof was, arguably, beyond the capabilities of the engineers of the time.

F He rightly believed the project would make him rich and famous.

G Yet it was a long time before it became the home of music.

3 **Get ready to SPEAK** Look at the photos. What kinds of art are they? What adjectives would you use to describe them?

4 Do the Speaking exam task.

SPEAKING exam task

Look at the photos, and talk about art, discussing the following questions.

1 How would you compare the four types of art shown in the pictures?
2 Who do various forms of art appeal to? Do they appeal to you? Give reasons.
3 Do you agree with the following statement?
  Art is less important in our lives today than it used to be.

Get ready for B2 EXAMS 2

1 **Get ready to LISTEN** Look at the Listening exam task. Who are you going to hear about?
  a an actor and a director
  b a painter and an art dealer
  c a model and a painter

2 🎧 3.07 Do the Listening exam task.

LISTENING exam task

You are going to hear a conversation about one of Picasso's muses, who often sat for the artist in her teens. In 1–6, choose the correct option: A, B, C or D.

1 Lydia Corbett
   A used to live in the south of France.
   B once visited a friend called Sylvette in France.
   C used to live in Devon but now lives in France.
   D became an artist's model at the age of 72.
2 How did Sylvette first meet Picasso?
   A Her mother introduced her to him.
   B Sylvette went to Picasso's studio.
   C Picasso invited her to his house.
   D Picasso came to her mother's house.
3 What was Picasso's first impression of Sylvette?
   A She was very shy.
   B She looked like a witch.
   C Her hair was very messy.
   D She was very beautiful.
4 As a result of that first meeting
   A Sylvette was fascinated by the great artist.
   B Sylvette's boyfriend started working for Picasso.
   C Picasso was inspired to paint a portrait.
   D Sylvette decided to change her hairdo.
5 Later,
   A Picasso taught Sylvette to paint.
   B Sylvette and Picasso were lovers.
   C Sylvette posed for numerous pictures.
   D Picasso took photos of Sylvette.
6 What is true about Sylvette?
   A She started painting under the name Lydia Corbett.
   B Picasso didn't appreciate her artistic talent.
   C She signed her pictures with various names.
   D Her husband was an English artist.

3 Look quickly through the text in the Use of English exam task below, ignoring the gaps. What is it about?
  a A robbery that has never been solved.
  b A robbery that took years for the police to solve.
  c A carefully planned robbery which was a failure.

4 Do the Use of English exam task.

USE OF ENGLISH exam task

Read the text and fill in each gap with a suitable word. Write one word only in each gap.

The year was 1990. The robbery was deliberately planned to ^{1}_____ place on the busiest day for the police in Boston: 17 March, St Patrick's Day. Two men pretending to be Boston police officers made their ^{2}_____ into Boston's Isabella Gardner museum, tied ^{3}_____ the security guards, and made off with thirteen pieces of art ^{4}_____ about half a billion dollars.

^{5}_____ the stolen paintings included five by Degas, three Rembrandts and a Manet, the canvas that is most often mentioned ^{6}_____ the greatest loss is Vermeer's *The Concert*. It is one of only 35 Vermeers ^{7}_____ existence and is now considered the world's most valuable painting ever to have ^{8}_____ stolen.

Around twenty years later, and in spite ^{9}_____ a $5 million reward, the art is still missing and the police are no nearer to making an arrest. ^{10}_____ short, the police investigation has been a failure. In the meantime, the Gardner museum has spent a fortune improving its security!

5 Work in pairs. Discuss what benefits the visual arts (painting, sculpture, etc.) might provide for (a) the artist and (b) the viewer. Use the words in the box and your own ideas. Give examples where possible.

> beauty/beautiful   inspiration/inspirational   original
> self-expression   therapeutic   thought-provoking

6 Do the Writing exam task.

WRITING exam task

Read the statement below. Then write 200–250 words presenting the arguments for and against the statement. Include your own opinion.

> Art should be made a compulsory subject in all types of schools.

Get ready for B2 exams 2

Get ready for B2 Exams 3

1 **Get ready to READ** What art festivals do you know? What kind of art do they celebrate?

2 Do the Reading exam task.

Reading exam task

Read the text. In 1–6, choose the best option: A, B, C or D.

Liverpool had done it before and really wanted to do it again. However, the Archdruid put his foot down and refused. He even went so far as to say that he would deny them his presence. Liverpool insisted. The Archdruid persisted. He believed somewhere in Wales was a more suitable choice. What was the squabble all about? The hosting of the time-honoured Welsh art festival – the National Eisteddfod of Wales.

The festival's roots can be traced back to 1176 when the first Eisteddfod (literally 'sitting' festival) is said to have been held at Lord Rhys' castle in Cardigan. It was a grand gathering of poets and musicians from all over the country with the prize of a chair at the Lord's table awarded to the best artists.

The idea caught on in no time, and the Eisteddfod became a folk tradition across Wales. However, when the Eisteddfod was officially associated with the Gorsedd of Bards at the beginning of the nineteenth century, it firmly established itself as a great artistic occasion. The Gorsedd of Bards is made up of the most distinguished Welsh artists who, to this day, participate in the festival. At their head is the Archdruid, who is responsible for conducting the ceremonies during Eisteddfod week and for choosing the venue. The ceremonies are still held to honour literary achievements amongst Welsh poets and prose writers.

Three ceremonies are held during the Eisteddfod week, the Crowning ceremony to honour the finest free verse poet, the Prose Medal ceremony and the Chairing ceremony for strict metre poetry. During the ceremonies, members of the Gorsedd of Bards gather on the Eisteddfod stage along with the Archdruid. But the indisputable highlight of the week is when the Archdruid reveals the identity of the winning poet, who is then honoured by a children's floral dance.

In its purest form an eisteddfod is simply a series of music and poetry competitions and there are hundreds of small local and school eisteddfodau (plural of eisteddfod) throughout Wales all year round. However, it is the national Eisteddfod that is the main event being held in a different spot each year and hosted by the Bards in their historic ceremonial robes. The venue turns into a vast sea of tents providing a roof for the artists and visitors who come to enjoy the performances as well as the craftsmen and traders surrounding the event.

1 According to the first paragraph
   A Liverpool hosted the first Eisteddfod.
   B the Archdruid thought the festival should take place in Wales.
   C the Archdruid refused to make a choice.
   D Liverpool did not want to host the festival.
2 The first Eisteddfod took place
   A in a castle.
   B all over the country.
   C around a large table.
   D in a large theatre.
3 What is true about Eisteddfod?
   A It quickly became very popular in Wales.
   B Prominent artists did not have time for it.
   C It became unpopular at the start of the 19th century.
   D It was only for Lords and the wealthy.
4 Nowadays, Eisteddfod
   A is held in the town of Gorsedd.
   B has awards in two categories.
   C includes a dance competition with flowers.
   D is held where the Archdruid decides.
5 A floral dance is held to celebrate
   A the victory of the winning poet.
   B the end of the Eisteddfod week.
   C the arrival of the Archdruid on stage.
   D all of the week's highlights.
6 The national Eisteddfod
   A takes place at the same time as hundreds of small, local competitions.
   B is only for artists who have already won their local eisteddfod.
   C in the most famous of many competitions which happen all through the year.
   D travels from one venue to another throughout the year.

3 **Get ready to SPEAK** Work in pairs. Look at the list of topics and decide how important the influence of America is to each one in your country. Give examples.

cinema
television
popular music
classical music
food in the home
fast food
fashion/clothes
language

4 Do the Speaking exam task.

Speaking exam task

Read the statement below, and decide if you agree or disagree. Work in pairs. Discuss the statement, presenting your arguments, and responding to your partner's counter-arguments.

Many people see the influence of American culture as a threat to their own national traditions.

Get ready for B2 Exams 4

1 **Get ready to LISTEN** Look at the Listening exam task, and answer these questions.
1 Which cities are you going to hear about?
2 What do they have in common?

2 🎧 3.08 Do the Listening exam task.

LISTENING exam task

Listen to the recording about four capital cities. Match the cities to questions 1–8. Write the correct letter after each question.

L=London   D=Dublin
W=Washington DC   C=Canberra

Which city
1 has seen a lot of bloody conflicts? ☐
2 was designed to include the green areas which were already there? ☐
3 aims to improve its political status? ☐
4 used to be two separate cities? ☐
5 was chosen to settle a dispute between two other cities? ☐
6 contains one of the largest green areas in the world? ☐
7 was damaged extremely badly? ☐
8 has something for those fascinated by science and technology? ☐

3 Do the Use of English exam task.

USE OF ENGLISH exam task

Read the text and fill in each gap with a suitable word. Write one word only in each gap.

London became the administrative capital of Britain mainly because it was the largest and most important city in the country. However, before becoming capital of Spain in 1561, Madrid was not a major city, or ¹_____ a large town. For centuries, the capital of Spain ²_____ considered to be wherever the Spanish monarch and his court lived. For many years, Toledo was the capital and today the 'old city', ³_____ its beautiful castle and cathedral, is a World Heritage Site. ⁴_____ Toledo, Seville became the next capital, another city full of beautiful ⁵_____ historic architecture. So why, in 1561, ⁶_____ king Philip II of Spain decide to choose Madrid ⁷_____ the new capital? There was no cathedral there, no university, no trade – nothing of interest ⁸_____ all. Its only real quality was its location in the very centre ⁹_____ the country. Philip decided this was the only way he could be in a position to govern all of his kingdom. Of course, once it ¹⁰_____ become the capital, Madrid grew. However, even today, Madrid is quite a small city when you compare it with other European capitals.

4 **Get ready to WRITE** Look at the essay below. Complete the text with the missing phrases.

| All in all | As a result | However |
| It is commonly believed | Therefore | What is more |

As the world moves towards what is essentially a global village, the need for effective communication is stronger than ever before. ¹_____, the number of people studying foreign languages is increasing, and the effectiveness of various language courses is becoming a vital issue. One of the questions most frequently discussed is whether or not language courses should include the study of the culture of the country where the language is spoken.

²_____ each language is deeply rooted in the culture where it operates. ³_____, full understanding is often impossible without some knowledge of certain elements of its history, literature and traditions. Besides, studying cultures different from one's own increases international awareness and understanding, which in turn stimulates the language learning process.

⁴_____, some people argue that in business contexts, the language is just a tool and, as long as both sides clearly understand the technical vocabulary they use, no cultural background is necessary. ⁵_____, it would be impossible to define what particular culture should be taught, as many internationally used languages are spoken in different countries whose cultures differ significantly from one another.

⁶_____, it seems that the role of the cultural component in a language course should depend on the learner's goals. Those who need the language for technical or business purposes, will probably find the historical and literary elements less important than those for whom this language is something more than just a means of communication.

5 Do the Writing exam task.

WRITING exam task

Read the statement below. Write an essay in 200–250 words, discussing your views.

When studying a foreign language, it is important to learn translation skills both in writing and speaking.

GRAMMAR BUILDER AND REFERENCE

1.1 Order of adjectives

1 Put the words in the correct order to make sentences.

1 wearing / shoes / elegant / black / She's / high-heeled
   She's wearing elegant black high-heeled shoes.
2 a / That's / stripy / shirt / smart / cotton
3 dress / wearing / cotton / an / awful / She's / flowery
4 wool / at / mini-skirt / check / Look / beautiful / that
5 stripy / blue / like / your / hoody / I / baggy
6 shiny / is / roll neck / great / This / nylon / a
7 leggings / tight / wearing / ridiculous / She's / furry

The order of adjectives before a noun depends on their meaning.

	opinion	size	age	colour	origin	material/ type/ purpose	
a	lovely	big	old	blue	French	leather	bag
a	nice	tall	young		English		man

1.2 Present tense contrast

1 Decide if the sentences are correct or not. Correct the sentences that are incorrect.

1 The plane **is taking** off tomorrow morning at eight o'clock.
2 It's quite warm today. I **don't take** a jacket.
3 What **do you read** at the moment?
4 I **live** with a family in Ireland for a month.
5 She's a writer so she**'s always working** from home.
6 They **don't go** to the party on Saturday night.
7 **Are you** usually **wearing** jeans to school?
8 My sister**'s always borrowing** my clothes! It's really irritating!

2 Complete the pairs of sentences with the present simple or present continuous form of the verbs in brackets.

1 a My cousin _____ (live) in London. She was born there.
   b My sister _____ (visit) her at the moment.
2 a My dad _____ (not drive) to work. He usually takes the train.
   b Today the trains are on strike, so he _____ (drive).
3 a I need to translate a letter. _____ you _____ (speak) French?
   b Excuse me for interrupting, but what language _____ you _____ (speak)?
4 a Paul _____ (have) toast for breakfast today.
   b He usually _____ (have) cereal.
5 a Where _____ you _____ (meet) Linda tonight?
   b What time _____ the film _____ (start)?
6 a I'm getting fed up with my boyfriend. He _____ (always leave) the kitchen in a mess!
   b He _____ (not wash) the dishes and he never clears the table!

We use the present simple to talk about:
- habits and routines.
  I usually get up at eight o'clock.
- a permanent situation or fact.
  Jack lives in London. It's his home town.
- timetables and schedules.
  The train leaves at 6.30 tomorrow morning.

Notice the third person form of the present simple.
- Add -s to the verb.
  I start.   It starts.
- Add -es (after -ch, -ss, -sh or -o).
  They teach.   She teaches.
  We don't teach.   He doesn't teach.
- Take away -y, then add -ies (after verbs ending with -y after a consonant).
  I study.   He studies.

We use the present continuous to talk about:
- things that are happening now.
  We're watching a movie right now. Come over!
- annoying behaviour with *always*.
  He's always talking about himself.
- arrangements in the future.
  Sally and Tom are flying to Rome next Friday.

Notice how the present participle -ing is formed.
- Add -ing to the verb.
  I wait.   She's waiting.
- When verbs end with -e, take away -e then add -ing.
  They smile.   We're smiling.
- When verbs have one vowel followed by -m, -g, -p or -t, double the final consonant, then add -ing.
  You stop.   They're stopping.

108 Grammar Builder and Reference • Unit 1

GRAMMAR BUILDER AND REFERENCE

1.3 State and dynamic verbs

1 Complete the sentences the correct form of the verbs in the box.

| belong know not like need rain not remember |
| wait want |

1 Sorry, I _____ your name.
2 Tom's shoes are worn out. He _____ some new ones.
3 Jason _____ dancing very much.
4 It _____ and I haven't got an umbrella.
5 Those trainers _____ to me. Give them back!
6 _____ you _____ where my dictionary is?
7 'Where are you?' 'We _____ for the bus.'
8 I'm tired and I _____ to go home now.

2 Choose the correct words.

1 I **enjoy / 'm enjoying** this party.
2 She **thinks / 's thinking** you're right.
3 Jack **has / 's having** a shower.
4 I **feel / 'm feeling** stupid in this skirt.
5 They **consider / 're considering** moving house.
6 I **forget / 'm forgetting** people's names very easily.

3 Complete the pairs of sentences with the present simple or present continuous form of the 'state' verbs.

1 *smell*
   a What are you cooking? It _____ delicious!
   b Ryan _____ all the perfume samples to try and find the right one for his girlfriend.
2 *look*
   a That dress _____ nice. Where did you buy it?
   b Can you help me? I _____ for a denim jacket.
3 *taste*
   a This meat _____ a bit strange. Is it OK?
   b 'What are you doing?' 'I _____ the sauce to make sure it has enough salt.'
4 *feel*
   a Your shirt _____ really smooth. Is it cotton?
   b The doctor _____ my brother's leg to make sure it isn't broken.

Dynamic verbs are verbs that describe actions. They can be used in simple and continuous forms.
I run ten kilometres every day.
I'm running in a race at the moment.

Verbs that describe a state or situation are not usually used in continuous tenses.
I don't understand you. (a state of mind)
NOT *I'm not understanding you.*
This book belongs to me. (a possession)
NOT *This book is belonging to me.*

Common state verbs:

| like love hate prefer understand believe |
| remember forget want need belong |

Be careful. Sometimes, state verbs can be used with a 'dynamic' meaning.

This cheese tastes nice. (a 'state' of the cheese)
I'm tasting cheese at the moment. (an action)

1.4 Verb patterns

1 Complete the sentences with the correct form of the verbs in brackets.

1 They agreed _____ (not spend) all their money.
2 Kate can't face _____ (go) to the gym tonight.
3 She pretended _____ (not see) me.
4 My parents refuse _____ (buy) me a motorbike.
5 I feel like _____ (eat) out tonight.
6 He suggested _____ (do) more exercise.
7 They hope _____ (not arrive) late for the play.
8 We avoid _____ (drive) in the city centre at the weekend.

Some verbs are followed by an infinitive.
John managed to finish his homework.

Some verbs are followed by the *-ing* form.
Sally fancied going away for the weekend.

verb + infinitive	verb + *-ing* form
agree	avoid
decide	can't face
expect	can't help
fail	can't stand
happen	enjoy
hope	fancy
manage	feel like
mean	imagine
pretend	spend (*time*)
promise	suggest
refuse	
seem	
want	

Note that *like, love, prefer* and *hate* can be followed by the infinitive or the *-ing* form without changing the meaning.
I hate to get up early.
I hate getting up early.

Grammar Builder and Reference • Unit 1   **109**

GRAMMAR BUILDER AND REFERENCE

1.5 Verbs that change their meaning

1 Complete the dialogue with the correct form of the verbs in brackets.

A Why are you walking like that, Brian?
B I've been playing football and I've hurt my leg.
A I thought you'd stopped ¹_____ (play) football!
B No. I only stopped ²_____ (study) for my exams.
A Oh, I see. Have you tried ³_____ (take) a painkiller?
B Yes, but it still hurts.
A Poor you! Are you going to be OK for Mum's birthday?
B I think so. Did you remember ⁴_____ (make) a cake?
A Yes, I made the cake. But I forgot ⁵_____ (buy) any champagne. Can you get some?
B OK. I'll try ⁶_____ (get) some on the way to the party. I'm looking forward to it!
A Me too. I'll never forget ⁷_____ (dance) with Dad last year. He really enjoyed it. And I've bought Mum a really nice blouse for her birthday.
B Again?
A Sorry?
B Don't you remember ⁸_____ (give) her that pink shiny one last year?
A Oh no, you're right! I've just got time to change it! Bye!

Some verbs change their meaning depending on whether they are followed by an infinitive or the *-ing* form.

I remember living in Paris when I was young.
Meaning: this is a memory in which 'living' happened before 'remember'.

Did you remember to phone Jenny?
Meaning: this is an action that needed doing – 'remember' happened before 'to phone'.

I'll never forget swimming with all those sharks.
Meaning: this is a memory in which 'swimming' happened before 'forget'.

Patrick forgot to go to football practice.
Meaning: this is an action that needed doing – 'forgot' happened before 'to go'.

Please stop talking!
Meaning: end this action.

Karen stopped to ask for directions.
Meaning: stop in order to do something else.

Sarah went on writing her novel.
Meaning: continued doing it.

Joe went on to record another rock album.
Meaning: did something else later.

We tried hitting it with a hammer but we couldn't open it.
Meaning: did it in order to solve a problem.

Sophie tried to save some money but she spent it all.
Meaning: attempted it/did her best.

2.1 Past tenses

1 Complete the sentences with the past simple or the past continuous form of the verbs in brackets.

1 Will _____ (break) his leg while he _____ (play) football.
2 The sun _____ (shine) so we _____ (decide) to go to the beach.
3 We _____ (have) dinner when we _____ (get) home.
4 She _____ (wait) for the train when she _____ (see) her boyfriend with another girl.
5 I _____ (listen) to my MP3 player, so I _____ (not hear) the phone.
6 It was difficult to see because it _____ (get) dark.

2 Combine the sentences. Use the words in brackets and both the past simple and the past perfect.

1 Pete broke the television. Dad shouted at him (because)
   Dad shouted at Pete because he had broken the television.
2 Kate played football. Then she had a shower. (after)
   Kate _____.
3 We forgot to water the plants. They died. (because)
   The plants _____.
4 We did our homework. We went out. (after)
   We _____.
5 I lost my mobile phone. I bought a new one. (because)
   I _____.
6 They didn't buy any petrol. Their car stopped. (because)
   Their car _____.
7 I left the house. Then I locked the door. (after)
   I _____.

We use past tenses to narrate past events.
- We use the past continuous to set the scene.
  The birds were singing in the trees that morning.
- We use the past simple for actions or events that happened one after the other.
  Joanna walked down the road, turned left, then saw the house for the first time.
- We use the past continuous to describe a background event, and the past simple to describe an action or event that interrupted it.
  While we were staying at the campsite, somebody stole Fiona's camera.
- We use the past perfect to talk about an event that happened before another event in the past.
  I wasn't hungry because I had already eaten lunch.

Notice that with regular verbs the past simple and the past participle form of the past perfect are the same.
It crashed.   It had crashed.

However, with irregular verbs the past simple and the past participle form of the past perfect are often different.
I saw Peter.   He'd already seen me.

(There is a list of irregular past simple forms and past participle forms on page 120 of the Workbook.)

GRAMMAR BUILDER AND REFERENCE

2.2 used to

1 Make questions. Use the prompts and phrases in the box and *used to*.

when it was your birthday?	~~when you were a child?~~
before they got married?	where you could play?
before you started school?	when you got up?
before you went to bed?	at the weekend?

1 you / eat vegetables
  Did you use to eat vegetables when you were a child?
2 What / your grandparents / give you
3 there / be / a park / near your house
4 Where / your parents / live
5 you / watch TV / on Saturday mornings
6 Who / your family / visit
7 your mother / read to you
8 you / get up early

2 Complete the sentences. Use the affirmative or negative form of *used to* and the verbs in brackets.

1 Mia *used to go* (go) to my school, but now she doesn't.
2 Aidan _____ (be) very tall, but now he is.
3 Ali _____ (work) in a factory, but she doesn't now.
4 We _____ (play) football at the weekend, but now we don't.
5 There _____ (be) a market every Friday, but now there isn't.
6 They _____ (wear) a uniform to school, but now they do.
7 Christopher _____ (drink) coffee, but now he does.

We use *used to* + infinitive to describe past situations or habits that are different now.
I used to live abroad. (for a long time in the past but not now)
I used to work in a newspaper shop at weekends. (regularly in the past but not now)

Affirmative	Negative	Question form
Sally used to live in Scotland.	Sally didn't use to live in England.	Did Sally use to live in Ireland?

2.3 Exclamatory sentences

1 Choose the correct words.

1 Someone stole my wallet yesterday.
  What / How a nightmare!
2 My aunt was rushed to hospital last night.
  What / How terrible!
3 I thought someone had broken into my house!
  What / How a shock!
4 Sharon was wearing the same party dress as me!
  What / How funny!
5 My parents are going to pay for my holiday!
  What / How wonderful!
6 Why don't we organise an end-of-term trip?
  What / How a great idea!
7 Our flight to New York has been cancelled!
  What / How a pain!
8 My mobile keeps ringing at three o'clock every night.
  What / How strange!

We use exclamatory sentences beginning with *What* or *How* to react strongly to something. They always end with an exclamation mark.
- We use *How* with an adjective.
  How wonderful!
- We use *What* with a noun or an adjective followed by a noun. Notice that we say *What a ...* with a countable noun and *What ...* with plural or uncountable nouns.
  What a day! What a lovely person! What wonderful weather!

3.1 Defining relative clauses

1 Choose the correct words.

1 He's the man **who / which** interviewed me for the job.
2 That's the hospital **where / whose** my sister works.
3 She works as part of a team **where / which** is in Paris.
4 Gina's the pianist **who / whose** accompanies the show.
5 They're the neighbours **who / whose** car was stolen.
6 That's the woman **whose / who** is in charge of paying the salaries.
7 A laboratory is **which / where** scientists work.
8 Unskilled work is work **which / who** requires no training.

GRAMMAR BUILDER AND REFERENCE

2 Complete the sentences with relative clauses using the phrases in the box.

they repair bicycles	there are a lot of parks there
it makes furniture	his job is similar to a doctor's
they play jazz	his classes are so interesting
my brother works there	~~the new hospital will be there~~

1 They work on the building site where the new hospital will be.
2 A paramedic is a person _____.
3 Tom works for a design company _____.
4 We live in a district _____.
5 They're looking for musicians _____.
6 Do you know any mechanics _____?
7 He's the lecturer _____.
8 That's the bank _____.

Defining relative clauses come immediately after a noun and give vital information about that noun.
He's the doctor. (Which doctor?)
He's the doctor who helped my grandmother.

They can go in the middle or at the end of sentences.
The man who told me about this place was old.
I met the young woman who cuts your hair.

Defining relative pronouns are different depending on whether they refer to people, places, things or possessions.

Defining relative pronouns	
who (that)	people
where	places
which (that)	things
whose	possessions

Who or *which* can replace the subject or object of a sentence. When they replace the object, it is possible to omit *who* or *which*.
She's the girl who works here. (subject)
She's the girl who I met. (object)
She's the girl I saw on the bus. (omission)

We often use *that* instead of *which*, and can use *that* instead of *who* in informal English.
Here's the book that you wanted.
Did you see the guy that kissed Mary?

3.2 Non-defining relative clauses

1 Rewrite the sentences. Use the sentences in brackets to form non-defining relative clauses.
1 My sister works in the local hospital. (She's a nurse.)
   My sister, who's a nurse, works in the local hospital.
2 My dog's vet is very good with animals. (Her surgery is very near.)
3 Stockholm is the capital of Sweden. (It's in Scandinavia.)
4 Martin Scorsese received an Oscar in 2007. (His films include *Taxi Driver* and *Raging Bull*.)
5 Next month we're going to Cardiff. (My uncle lives there.)
6 The headmaster is retiring. (I've known him for several years.)

2 Invent relative clauses to complete the sentences. Use the questions to help you.
1 Shakespeare, who wrote 'Romeo and Juliet', was born in Stratford upon Avon. (What did Shakespeare write?)
2 Switzerland, _____, is in Central Europe. (What's Switzerland famous for?)
3 Feta cheese, _____, is delicious in salads. (Where is Feta produced?)
4 Nicole Kidman, _____, was born in Hawaii. (Who is her ex-husband?)
5 The White House, _____, has 132 rooms and 35 bathrooms. (Who lives there?)
6 Jennifer López, _____, was born in New York. (What does she do?)

Non-defining relative clauses come immediately after a noun and give extra information about that noun.

Harrods is a famous department store.
Anything else?
Harrods, which is in Knightsbridge in London, is a famous department store.

Q is a magazine about pop music.
Anything else?
Q, which is published monthly, is a magazine about pop music.

They can go in the middle or at the end of sentences, and start with a comma and end with a comma or full stop.
Abraham Lincoln, who was president of the United States in the nineteenth century, was shot while he was attending a play.
Kingston is the capital of Jamaica, which is an island in the Caribbean.

Non-defining relative pronouns are different depending on whether they refer to people, places, things or possessions.

GRAMMAR BUILDER AND REFERENCE

Non-defining relative pronouns	
who	people
where	places
which	things
whose	possessions

We cannot omit non-defining relative pronouns, and we cannot replace *who* or *which* with *that*.

4.1 Past simple and present perfect

1 Complete the dialogue with the present perfect form of the verbs in brackets.

Nick Hello Linda!
Linda Nick! I ¹_____ (not see) you for ages! How are you?
Nick Not bad at all! What are you doing in London?
Linda I ²_____ (move) to London to live with my boyfriend. We want to buy a house, but we ³_____ (not find) one yet. What about you?
Nick I ⁴_____ (come) to visit an old school friend. Do you remember Chris?
Linda Yes, I remember him.
Nick Well he ⁵_____ (just get) married, and he wanted to show me the wedding photos.
Linda Nick, you're looking really good! ⁶_____ (lose) weight?
Nick Yes, I have. And you ⁷_____ (change) your hair. It looks great!
Linda Thanks. We should catch up sometime.
Nick Good idea. I'd like that.

2 Complete the sentences with the past simple or present perfect form of the verbs in brackets.

1 Leah and Tom _____ (move) house a year ago.
2 We _____ (know) each other since we were children.
3 So far I _____ (not fail) any of my exams.
4 My little sister _____ (be born) in 1999.
5 Grace _____ (break) her leg last week.
6 They _____ (not go) to school yesterday.
7 _____ you _____ (finish) your homework yet?
8 Rhys had dinner and then he _____ (go) to bed.

We use the past simple to talk about:
• completed events in the past.
  I visited my aunt last weekend.

We use the present perfect to talk about:
• how long current situations have existed.
  I've been at this school for six years.
• experiences in the past (when the exact time is not important).
  My sister has met Brad Pitt.
• events that are connected with the present.
  I've lost my watch. Have you seen it?
  Jane has already done her homework. Here it is.

Notice that we often use finished past time expressions with the past simple (*yesterday, three months ago, last week, in 1999*), but unfinished past time expressions with the present perfect (*for, since, already, just, yet*).
I went to Paris in 2006.
I haven't been to Paris yet.
She's been here since Tuesday.

We form the present perfect with *have/has* + the past participle.
(There is a list of irregular past simple forms and past participle forms on page 120 of the Workbook.)

4.2 Present perfect simple and present perfect continuous

1 Complete the pairs of sentences with the present perfect simple and the present perfect continuous form of the verbs.

1 cut
  a Sarah needs a plaster because she _____ her hand.
  b Dad's crying because he _____ onions.
2 watch
  a We _____ a new series on TV. It's great!
  b _____ you _____ a live football match before?
3 tidy
  a I _____ my room, but there's still a lot to do.
  b Jack _____ his room. It looks much better.
4 read
  a Clare _____ that book four times.
  b I _____ the latest *Harry Potter* book all day. I'm dying to know what happens in the end!
5 run
  a Margaret _____ never _____ in the London marathon before.
  b Larry is red in the face because he _____.
6 study
  a Jimmy can go out when he _____ for the exam.
  b Kim's in her room. She _____ all day.

Grammar Builder and Reference • Unit 4   113

GRAMMAR BUILDER AND REFERENCE

2 Complete the sentences with the present perfect simple or the present perfect continuous form of the verbs in brackets.

1 I'm so sorry! I _____ just _____ the car! (crash)
2 The ground is wet because it _____. (rain)
3 _____ you ever _____ a well-known actor? (meet)
4 I _____ never _____ why you're going out with Alfie. (understand)
5 Something smells good! _____ you _____? (cook)
6 We _____ painting the house. After lunch we're going to do the living room. (not finish)
7 How exciting! I _____ always _____ to go to Rome! (want)
8 Where is your homework? Don't tell me you _____ again. (not do)

We use the present perfect continuous to talk about:
- an action that began in the past and is still in progress.
  I've been working for this company since 2002.
- an action that has recently stopped and which explains the present situation.
  David has been playing tennis so he's really tired.

Notice that we only use the present perfect continuous with actions which happen over a period of time. With finished and complete actions we use the present perfect simple.
We have been living in London for twelve years.
(We're still there now.)
They've lived in Moscow, Berlin and Madrid.
(They aren't there now.)

We often use the present perfect continuous with *how long*. If we ask *how often* or *how much/many* we use the present perfect simple.
How long has she been sleeping?
How often have you worn that suit?
How many English lessons have you had?

We form the present perfect continuous with *have/has + been + the -ing* form.

5.1 Zero conditional

1 Use the prompts to make zero conditional sentences.

1 you / not use / sun cream / you / get burnt
2 the beaches / be full / you / go / on holiday / in August
3 I / understand / my English teacher / she / speak / slowly
4 I / not put away / my clothes / my mum / get angry
5 I / eat / too much / my stomach / hurt
6 Matt / take / his medicine / he / not cough

2 Complete the sentences with the correct form of the verbs in the box.

use	switch off	not have	crash	discover	give

1 If your computer _____, you can call the hotline.
2 If anyone _____ your password, you should change it.
3 If you press that button, the monitor _____.
4 You can _____ the Internet if you have a router.
5 If I _____ you my address, you can send me an e-mail.
6 You can't download music if you _____ broadband.

We use the zero conditional to say that one thing follows automatically or naturally from another.
If you press the button, the machine comes on.
If you eat too much chocolate, you feel ill.

We form the zero conditional by using the present simple in both the conditional *if* clause and result clause.

Conditional clause	Result clause
If you **don't wear** socks, (present simple)	your feet **get** cold. (present simple)

5.2 Speculating and predicting

1 Write sentences using *will*, *may*, *might not* or *won't* and the prompts.

1 Perhaps / it / rain this afternoon
  It may rain this afternoon.
2 I'm sure / we / not win the match tonight
  We _____
3 Perhaps / Chris / not be at home right now
  Chris _____
4 Perhaps / Abigail / know the answer to the homework
  Abigail _____
5 I'm sure / I / pass my driving test first time
  I _____
6 Perhaps / Megan / not come to our party
  Megan _____
7 I'm sure / my parents / pay for my holiday
  My parents _____

GRAMMAR BUILDER AND REFERENCE

2 Complete the first conditional sentences with the correct form of the verbs in brackets.
1. If the bus _____ (not come) soon, I _____ (be) late for school.
2. We _____ (go) for a picnic at the weekend if it _____ (not rain).
3. My parents _____ (be) upset if I _____ (not pass) my exams.
4. I _____ (not go) to the party if I _____ (not get) an invitation.
5. If I _____ (get) a job I _____ (move) out of my parents' house.
6. They _____ (not win) the match if they _____ (not play) better.
7. She _____ (not buy) him a new phone if he _____ (lose) this one.
8. He _____ (make) me really happy if he _____ (send) me some roses.

We use the first conditional to make predictions about the future.
If global warming gets much worse, the climate will change.

We form the first conditional by using the present simple in the conditional *if* clause and *will* + base form in the result clause.

Conditional clause	Result clause
If scientists **cure** disease, (present simple)	people will **live** very long lives. (*will* + base form)

The conditional *if* clause usually comes first, but it can come after the result clause.
Many people will have nowhere to live if the sea levels rise.

The modal verbs *may*, *might* and *could* can be used instead of *will* or *won't* in the result clause.
We may experience very hot summers in Europe if we don't do anything about global warming.

5.3 Future perfect and future continuous

1 Complete the sentences with the future perfect or the future continuous form of the verbs in brackets.
1. My driving test is on 3 March. (have)
   By April I *will have had my driving test*.
2. My brother is starting work on 5 September. (start)
   In September he _____
3. They're moving house on 15 February. (move)
   By March they _____
4. We're going on holiday on 2 August. (go)
   In August we _____
5. Our plane lands in New York at 10 o'clock. (land)
   At 10 o'clock we _____
6. My exams are in May. (finish)
   By June I _____
7. My sister is getting married in October. (get married)
   By November she _____

2 Complete the sentences with the future perfect or future continuous form of the verbs in brackets.
1. I _____ (read) your book by the end of the week.
2. We always have dinner at eight o'clock, so we _____ (finish) if you come round at nine o'clock.
3. My cousins _____ (sit) on the plane to Australia this time tomorrow.
4. You'll recognise her because she _____ (wear) a bright yellow hoody.
5. We _____ (wait) for you when you arrive at the station.
6. I hope he _____ (find) a job by the end of the month.

We use the future perfect to refer back from a future point in time to a completed action also in the future.

X——————————X ?——————————X→
NOW   hotel built   2015

By 2015, we will have built a hotel on the moon.

We use the future continuous to talk about an action in progress at a time in the future.

X——————————————————————X→
NOW   2016 living on moon

In 2016, we will be living on the moon.

We form the future perfect with *will* + *have* + the past participle.
*By Friday afternoon, we **will have finished** all the exams.*
(There is a list of past participle forms on page 120 of the Workbook.)

We form the future continuous with *will* + *be* + *-ing* form of a verb.
*This time next month, I **will be sitting** on a beach.*

Grammar Builder and Reference • Unit 5   115

GRAMMAR BUILDER AND REFERENCE

5.4 will, going to and present continuous

1 Choose the correct words.
1. My foot hurts, so **I'll go / I'm going** to the doctor's this evening.
2. Our car is really old, so **we'll buy / we're going to buy** a new one.
3. Let's go to the cinema tonight. **I'll meet / I'm meeting** you outside at eight o'clock.
4. **I'll play / I'm playing** tennis with John this afternoon, so I'd better take my tennis racket.
5. Harry **'ll get up / 's going to get up** early tomorrow to study for the exam.
6. **I'll call / I'm calling** you later about Saturday night.
7. They can't come to my party because **they're flying / they'll fly** to Paris that weekend.
8. **I'm going / I'll go** to the hairdresser's tomorrow at 5.15.

We use *will* + infinitive for things we decide to do as we are speaking (instant decisions, offers, promises).
Bye John. I'll call you later.
That looks heavy. I'll help you carry it.

We use *going to* + infinitive for things we have already decided to do before speaking (intentions).
I've already decided on Tim's birthday present. I'm going to get him a new mobile phone.

We use the present continuous for things we have already agreed to do, usually with somebody else (arrangements).
We've booked the flight. We're flying to Barbados in February.

5.5 Future time clauses

1 Join the two sentences with *when*.
1. I'll get home. I'll call you.
   I'll call you when I get home.
2. Liz will arrive. She'll tell us her news.
3. I'll go on holiday. I'll send you a postcard.
4. He'll get up. He'll have a shower.
5. We'll go shopping. We'll pick up some bread.
6. I'll get paid. I'll give you the money.
7. It'll stop raining. We'll go out.

2 Complete the sentences with the correct form of the verbs in brackets.
1. I _____ the windows before I _____ the house. (close / leave)
2. Sophie _____ us as soon as she _____. (tell / arrive)
3. We _____ eating until Karl _____ here. (not start / get)
4. I _____ you know the moment I _____ my results. (let / get)
5. Ruby _____ her boyfriend while he _____ away. (miss / be)
6. I _____ home when I _____ 21. (leave / be)

In future time clauses with *when*, *while*, *before*, *until*, *as soon as* and *the moment*, we normally use the present simple, not *will*.
*I'll phone you **when** Peter arrives.*
*Sue will be doing her homework **while** we're at the party.*
*I'll go and get some popcorn **before** the film starts.*
*We won't make coffee **until** Fiona gets here.*
*They'll go home **as soon as** the match finishes.*
*Paula will kiss Tom **the moment** he walks through the door.*

6.1 must have, might have, can't have

1 Use the prompts to make sentences with *must have*, *might have* and *can't have*.
1. The thief / might / enter / through the back door.
   The thief might have entered through the back door.
2. He / can't / have / a key.
3. He / might / find / an open window.
4. He / must / be / very quick.
5. The neighbours / can't / see / him.
6. The family / must / go / out.
7. He / might / escape / through the garden.

2 Rewrite the sentences using *must have*, *might have* or *can't have*.
1. I'm sure Millie gave out the invitations.
   Millie must have given out the invitations.
2. Perhaps Elizabeth went to the doctor's.
3. I'm sure Amelia didn't forget about the party.
4. Perhaps Tyler went on holiday.
5. I'm sure Archie missed the train.
6. Perhaps Alex fell off his bike.
7. I'm sure Amy didn't get lost.

GRAMMAR BUILDER AND REFERENCE

We use *must have*, *might have* and *can't have* to speculate about past events.
We use *must have* to say that it seems **certain** that something that happened in the past is true.
The only place I haven't looked for my keys is the car. I **must have** left them there.

We use *can't have* to say that it seems **impossible** that something that happened in the past is true. It has the opposite meaning to *must have*.
I've checked the car – under the seats and everywhere. You **can't have** left your keys there.

We use *might have* to say that it seems **possible** that something that happened in the past is true.
Perhaps they're at home. I **might have** left my keys at home.

We can use *may have* and *could have* with similar meanings to *might have*.
I don't know where the keys are. I **could have** dropped them. I **may have** left them in the restaurant.

We form these structures with a modal verb (*must, can't, might, may, could*) + *have* + the past participle.

6.2 Reported speech (statements)

1 Complete the sentences in reported speech.

1 'We saw a strange man in the garden,' they told their son.
They told their son that _____ a strange man in the garden.
2 They told him, 'We've never seen anyone there before.'
They told him that _____ anyone there before.
3 They said, 'We didn't go out last night.'
They said that _____ the night before.
4 They said, 'We're thinking of calling the police.'
They said that _____ of calling the police.
5 The woman said, 'I'll call them in the morning.'
The woman said that _____ them in the morning.
6 Their son said, 'I can explain everything.'
Their son said that _____ everything.
7 He said, 'I often forget my key.'
He said that _____ his key.
8 'I climbed up the drainpipe,' he told them.
He told them that _____ up the drainpipe.

2 Complete the reported speech with the correct time expressions.

1 'We're staying in tonight,' said Emily.
Emily said that they were staying in _____.
2 'We've been out all day today,' she said.
She said that they had been out all day _____.
3 'We're going on holiday next week,' she said.
She said that they were going on holiday _____.
4 'We went to work yesterday,' she said.
She said that they had been to work _____.
5 'We didn't go out very much last month,' she said.
She said they hadn't been out very much _____.

3 Rewrite what Emma says using the correct time expressions.

1 We nearly moved house last year.
2 Last month we bought a new house.
3 We packed our books into boxes yesterday.
4 Today we're moving the furniture.
5 Tonight we're sleeping in our new bedroom.
6 We're having a house-warming party next week.

1 Emma said that they had nearly moved the year before.
2 Emma said that _____
3 She said _____
4 She _____
5 _____
6 _____

4 Complete the sentences with *said* or *told*.

1 He _____ his girlfriend that he had bought a ring.
2 She _____ him that she didn't like it.
3 He _____ that it had cost a fortune.
4 She _____ him that she didn't care.
5 He _____ her that he would change it.
6 She _____ that she wanted diamonds.

Grammar Builder and Reference • Unit 6   117

GRAMMAR BUILDER AND REFERENCE

We use reported speech to report what someone has said without using their exact words.

When we change direct speech to reported speech, we often make the verb form go one tense back.
'Tom **lives** in Germany,' said Claire.
Claire said that Tom **lived** in Germany.

Direct speech	Reported speech
Present continuous →	Past continuous
'She's sleeping,' he said.	He said she was sleeping.
Past simple →	Past perfect
'He fell over,' he said.	He said he had fallen over.
Present perfect →	Past perfect
'They've lost their money,' he said.	He said they had lost their money.
can →	could
'She can swim,' he said.	He said she could swim.
will →	would
'They will be late,' he said.	He said they would be late.

- The pronouns often change.
  'I'm tired,' she said.
  She said she was tired.   (I → he/she)
  'We're upset,' they said.
  They said they were upset. (we → they)
  'You're late,' he said.
  He said I was late.   (you → I)

- Time expressions often change.
  'I saw Tom yesterday.'
  He said he had seen Tom the day before.

Direct speech	Reported speech
today	that day
tonight	that night
next week	the next week
yesterday	the day before
last month/year	the month/year before

6.3 Reported speech (questions)

1 Complete the reported questions with the correct pronouns.
1 'Where have you been?' our parents asked us.
   ____ asked ____ where ____ had been.
2 'What time did you arrive home?' my dad asked me.
   ____ asked ____ what time ____ had arrived home.
3 'Did you see the thief?' the policewoman asked Jack.
   ____ asked ____ if ____ had seen the thief.
4 'What did he take?' we asked our mum.
   ____ asked ____ what ____ had taken.
5 'Why have you got my camcorder?' Dad asked Jack.
   ____ asked ____ why ____ had his camcorder.
6 'Did you forget about our play?' we asked everybody.
   ____ asked ____ if ____ had forgotten about their play.

2 Report the questions.
1 'What did you see?' John asked Emma.
2 'Will you clean my room?' Sean asked his mum.
3 'Have you done your homework?' Amy's dad asked.
4 'Where are you going?' Megan asked Joe.
5 'Do you like jazz?' Lily asked Robert.
6 'Can you help me?' Oscar asked Katie.

When we change direct questions to reported questions, the verb form often goes one tense back, pronouns change, and time expressions often change.
'Did **you see** the football match **yesterday**?'
She asked me if **I had seen** the football match **the day before**.

We use the reporting verb *ask* when reporting questions. In *yes/no* questions, we use the structure '(somebody) asked (me/him/them/etc.) if…'
'Did you go out?'
She asked me if I had gone out.

In *wh-* questions, we use the structure '(somebody) asked (me/him/them/etc.) + question word (where, what, how, etc.)…'
'Where did you go?'
She asked me **where I had gone**.

Notice that in a reported question the subject comes before the verb, and auxiliary verbs like *do* or *did* are not used.
'What do you like?'
She asked me **what I liked**.

GRAMMAR BUILDER AND REFERENCE

6.4 Verbs with two objects

1 Rewrite the sentences with the indirect object as a pronoun. Do not use *to* or *for*.
1 Mia's boyfriend made dinner for Mia last night.
   Mia's boyfriend made her dinner last night.
2 Tom's mum bought a new shirt for Tom.
3 Daisy owes £50 to her dad.
4 Beth's neighbour sold his car to Beth.
5 Patrick wrote a letter to his sister.
6 Scott sent a text message to Julie.
7 Dad booked a flight to Paris for us.

Some verbs can be followed by both an indirect object (usually a person) and a direct object (usually a thing).
              [indirect object]   [direct object]
Peter gave   Penelope   his keys.

If we want the direct object to come first, we must put *to* or *for* before the indirect object.
              [direct object]   [indirect object]
Peter gave   his keys   to Penelope.

              [direct object]   [indirect object]
Peter cooked   dinner   for Penelope.

Notice that English avoids having a pronoun as a direct object at the end of the sentence.
Peter gave them to Sally.
NOT Peter gave Sally them.

7.1 Comparison

1 Correct the sentences.
1 I think my friend is prettyer than me.
2 But I'm more tall than she is.
3 She's got longest hair than me.
4 My eyes are beautifuller, though.
5 I'm not as slim than her.
6 My legs are longer that hers.
7 She's the goodest student in the class.
8 I'm funniest person in the class.

2 Rewrite the sentences using *less* or *least*.
1 Shannon and Jade are more popular than Leah.
   Leah is _____ of the three girls.
2 Leah is more intelligent than Shannon.
   Shannon _____ Leah.
3 Jade is more hard-working than Leah.
   Leah is _____ Jade.
4 Joshua and James are more confident than Callum.
   Callum is _____ of the three boys.
5 Callum is more polite than James.
   James is _____ Callum.
6 James and Callum are more generous than Joshua.
   Joshua is _____ of the three boys.

3 Use the prompts to make comparative sentences with *than*.
1 Ellie / arrives / early / Jessica.
2 Vicky / writes / neatly / Lewis.
3 Alex / does the science experiments / well / Isabella.
4 Michael / sits / quietly / Brandon.
5 Abigail / speaks / softly / Lauren.
6 Ella / shouts / loudly / Grace.

4 Complete the sentences with the superlative form of the adverbs in brackets.
1 Of all our class David studies _____ (hard).
2 Holly finishes exams _____ (quick).
3 Alfie runs the 100 metres _____ (fast).
4 Jacob always gets up _____ (late). He's so lazy.
5 Bethany speaks _____ (clearly) of all of us.
6 Finlay sings _____ (beautifully).

5 Put the words in the correct order to make comparative sentences.
1 used to / than / confident / be / she / She's / more
2 last week / was / is / That shirt / than / it / cheaper now
3 was little / he was / as / not / He's / when he / fat as
4 faster / drive / used to / than / you / You / now
5 we did / further / We live / than / from the centre / before
6 than / at school / We arrive / do / our friends / earlier

The comparative and superlative forms of adjectives and adverbs with one syllable are formed by adding *-er* or *-est*. The same is true of adjectives with two syllables ending in *-y*.

subject + verb	comparative form		object
John is	old (+ *er*) older	than	Sue.
	slim (+ *m* + *er*) slimmer		
	busy (*y* + *ier*) busier		
John runs	fast + *er* faster		

Grammar Builder and Reference • Units 6–7   119

GRAMMAR BUILDER AND REFERENCE

subject + verb	superlative form
John is	(the) + old (+ est) the oldest
	(the) + slim (+ m + est) the slimmest
	(the) + busy (y + iest) the busiest
John runs	(the) + fast (+ est) the fastest

The comparative and superlative forms of adjectives and adverbs with two syllables or more are formed by putting *more* or the *most* before the adjective or adverb.

subject + verb	comparative form		object
John is	*more* + famous more famous	than	Sue.
	more + popular more popular		
John talks	*more* + clearly more clearly		

noun	superlative form
John is	(the) + most + popular the most popular
John talks	(the) + most + clearly the most clearly

We can also form comparatives and superlatives of adjectives and adverbs with *less* and *the least*.
Less is the opposite of *more*. *Least* is the opposite of *most*.

subject + verb	comparative form		object
Sue is	*less* + slim less slim	than	John.
	less + famous less famous		
Sue talks	*less* + clearly less clearly		

subject + verb	superlative form
Sue is	(the) + least + popular the least popular
Sue talks	(the) + least + clearly the least clearly

We can make comparisons with clauses as well as nouns.
Peter is taller than he used to be.

We often use a superlative with the present perfect and *ever*.
It was the best holiday we've ever had.

We can compare two things, using *as ... as* to say that they are the same.
Jill is as old as Julie.

Remember irregular comparative and superlative forms.

adjective	comparative	superlative
good	better	the best
bad	worse	the worst
far	further	the furthest

7.2 Second conditional

1 Complete the second conditional sentences with the correct form of the verbs in brackets.

1 If my boyfriend _____ (go out) with another girl, I _____ (not talk) to him again.
2 I _____ (not chat up) a boy if I _____ (not fancy) him.
3 If my girlfriend _____ (not like) my friends, I _____ (stop) seeing her.
4 I _____ (not go out) with my best friend's brother if he _____ (ask) me.
5 I _____ (try) speed dating if I _____ (know) where to go.
6 If she _____ (split up) with her boyfriend, she _____ (be) really upset.
7 Their parents _____ (be) really happy if they _____ (get engaged).
8 If Charlie _____ (get) a job in another city, Chloe _____ (go) with him.

120 Grammar Builder and Reference • Unit 7

GRAMMAR BUILDER AND REFERENCE

We use the second conditional to talk about an imaginary situation or event, and its result.
If I had a billion dollars, I'd live on a desert island.

We form the second conditional by using the past simple in the conditional *if* clause and *would* + base form in the result clause.

Conditional clause	Result clause
If **I had** a billion dollars, (past simple)	**I would** buy a castle. (*would* + base form)

Notice that you can use *were* instead of *was* in the conditional clause with *I*, *he* and *she*. Both *was* and *were* are generally acceptable, although using *were* is considered more correct, especially in formal situations.
If I were you, I'd give the money to charity.
If he were older, he'd understand what I'm saying.

7.3 I wish, If only, I'd rather

1 Complete the sentences about imaginary situations.
1 I haven't got a boyfriend.
  If only I **had** a boyfriend!
2 I live in a small flat.
  If only _____ in a bigger flat.
3 I can't find a job.
  I wish I _____ a job.
4 Please don't call me any more.
  I'd rather _____ me any more.
5 Please stop complaining all the time.
  I wish _____ complaining all the time.
6 My boyfriend's moving to another city.
  If only _____ moving away.
7 Please don't smoke in my room.
  I'd rather _____ smoke in my room.
8 I can't stand it when you borrow my clothes.
  I wish _____ my clothes.
9 I'd prefer to have dinner at home tonight.
  I'd rather _____ at home tonight.

We use *I wish …* or *If only …* with the past simple to say that we really want a situation to be different.
I wish it were Sunday.
If only I had more money.

We use *I wish …* or *If only …* with *would* + base form to say that we really want somebody's (or something's) behaviour to be different.
I wish you wouldn't smoke.
I wish this machine would work.

We use *I'd rather* with a base form to express a preference.
'Do you want a cup of tea?' 'I'd rather have a coffee.'

We use *I'd rather* with the past simple to say that we really want somebody's (or something's) behaviour to be different.
I'd rather you didn't leave your bag there.

7.4 Question tags

1 Add question tags to the statements.
1 You're going out with Luke, _____?
2 They've split up, _____?
3 Ryan asked you out, _____?
4 You wouldn't prefer to eat out, _____?
5 Adam really looks down on his sister, _____?
6 You fancy Cameron, _____?
7 You won't tell anyone, _____?
8 Sam can't dance, _____?

We use question tags when we want somebody to confirm something that we are saying. A statement with a question tag often sounds more polite than a direct question or a plain statement.
You have a brother and a sister, don't you?

When the main verb is affirmative, the question tag is negative, and vice versa.
You were on holiday, weren't you?
You weren't tired, were you?

We use the verb *be*, auxiliary verbs (*do*, *have*) or modal verbs (*will*, *would*, etc.), depending on the tense of the verb in the statement.

tense	statement	tag
Present simple	You like chocolate,	don't you?
Present continuous	He's skiing,	isn't he?
Past simple	She lost her purse,	didn't she?
will	You'll be here soon,	won't you?
Present perfect	He's been away,	hasn't he?
would	He'd miss her,	wouldn't he?

Grammar Builder and Reference • Unit 7   121

GRAMMAR BUILDER AND REFERENCE

7.5 *in*, *at* and *on* with time

1 Complete the sentences with *in*, *at* and *on*.
1. I'm meeting Freya tonight ___ 7.30.
2. We play tennis after school ___ Tuesday evenings.
3. We're going to Paris together ___ Christmas.
4. Amy and Ethan are going dancing ___ the weekend.
5. Max doesn't like going out ___ night.
6. William and Olivia like going skiing ___ the winter.
7. They've got their final exams ___ June.
8. We got married ___ 2006.
9. It's my birthday ___ 22 September.
10. We're driving to the beach ___ the morning.

We use *at* with:
- clock times.
  He arrived at nine o'clock.
- festivals and holidays.
  We go to my parents at Christmas.
- the weekend, night.
  At night, we close all the windows.

We use *in* with:
- parts of the day (the morning, the afternoon, the evening).
  She got up early in the morning.
- seasons.
  In summer, we play tennis.
- months.
  My birthday is in April.
- years (2005, 1492, etc.).
  Tom was born in 1989.

We use *on* with:
- days of the week.
  I'll see you on Monday.
- dates (12 May, 1 April, etc.).
  The party is on 2 December.

8.1 The passive

1 Rewrite the questions using the passive. Use *by* where necessary.
1. Who wrote that poem?
   Who was that poem written by?
2. Who painted that picture?
3. How will they drive trains in the future?
4. What causes traffic jams?
5. Where have they taken your car?
6. Why did they cancel the train?
7. Who had cleaned the room?

2 Complete the sentences using the verbs in brackets. Use the affirmative or negative form of the passive and the correct tense.
1. The meeting next week _____ (change) from Monday to Friday.
2. Cows _____ (not eat) in India.
3. Harriet eventually found her car. It _____ (not steal) by car thieves.
4. The painting *Sunflowers* _____ (paint) by Van Gogh.
5. The shopping centre _____ (open) next Monday by the mayor.
6. The Narnia books _____ (not write) by J K Rowling.

3 Choose the correct words.
Mobile phones [1] **use / are used** by over 2 billion people all over the world today. But who [2] **were they invented / did they invent** by?
Mobile phone technology [3] **was first developed / developed first** by American telecommunications company AT&T, but the inventor of the first hand-held mobile phone [4] **considered / is considered** to be Martin Cooper of Motorola. He [5] **made / was made** the first mobile phone call on 3 April 1973.
Since then mobile phones [6] **have become / have been become** cheaper and much more accessible to the general public. In the United States mobile phones [7] **owned / are owned** by 50% of children and nearly 3 billion dollars per year [8] **spends / is spent** on commercial ring tones.

We make passive forms with the verb *be* + the past participle.
(There is a list of past participle forms on page 120 of the Workbook.)

Tense	Passive form
Present simple	Sweets **are made** of sugar.
Present continuous	A new supermarket **is being built**.
Past simple	The TV **was invented** in 1926.
Present perfect	My car **has been repaired**.
Past perfect	The keys **had been lost** earlier.
Future with *will*	Your dress **will be cleaned** soon.

In passive constructions, we use *by* when we want to say who (or what) performed the action.
The jet engine was invented by Frank Whittle.

Grammar Builder and Reference • Units 7–8

GRAMMAR BUILDER AND REFERENCE

8.2 Indefinite pronouns

1 Use *some-*, *any-* and *no-* to complete the sentences in each group.

1 -body
   a Does _____ know where the bus stop is?
   b That cab is empty. There's _____ in it.
   c We arrived in plenty of time because _____ gave us a lift.

2 -thing
   a That suitcase is very light because there's _____ in it.
   b I didn't buy _____ in the duty free shop.
   c The flight attendants gave us _____ to eat during the flight. It was delicious.

3 -where
   a Let's go _____ different on holiday this year.
   b There's _____ to sit on this bus. It's packed.
   c We never go _____ nice at the weekend.

2 Correct the incorrect sentences.

1 There isn't nobody on the train.
2 I haven't got something to wear.
3 Freya doesn't want somebody to see her crying.
4 Can I have anything to drink?
5 I want to spend our holidays somewhere hot.
6 Please sit nowhere.
7 Has somebody seen my sunglasses?
8 Would you like something to drink?

We form indefinite pronouns with *some-*, *any-* and *no-*.

people	someone/somebody anyone/anybody no one/nobody
places	somewhere anywhere nowhere
things	something anything nothing

We use pronouns with *some-* in affirmative sentences and in offers and requests.
Somebody has eaten my lunch.
Can I do something to help?

We use pronouns with *any-* in negative and interrogative sentences.
I haven't got anything to wear.
Did you meet anyone interesting?

We can also use pronouns with *any-* in affirmative sentences when we mean 'it doesn't matter who/what/where …'.
Ask anybody round here and they'll help you.

We use pronouns with *no-* with affirmative verbs as the meaning is already negative.
Nobody likes losing.

8.3 Indirect questions

1 Rewrite the direct questions as indirect questions using the words in brackets.

1 What type of car was it? (Have you any idea …)
   Have you any idea what type of car it was?
2 Could you describe the robbers for me? (I wonder …)
3 What were they wearing? (Can you remember …)
4 What did they do with the bags they were carrying? (Would you mind telling me…)
5 Where did the car go? (Did you notice …)
6 When did you phone the police? (Can you tell me …)
7 Could you come back tomorrow and answer some more questions? (I wonder …)

We make indirect questions with phrases like *Can you tell me…?* and *Do you know…?* We use them to ask politely for information.
Excuse me. **Can I ask you** what time it is?

To make a *yes/no* question into an indirect question, we use *if*.
Could you tell me **if** the film has started yet?

To make a *wh-* question into an indirect question, we use the question word.
Would you mind telling me **where** the bank is, please?

The word order and verb forms in an indirect question are the same as in a statement.
Do you know if **there is a seat free** on the flight to London?

Grammar Builder and Reference • Unit 8   123

GRAMMAR BUILDER AND REFERENCE

8.4 Introductory *it*

1 Put the words in the correct order to make sentences.
1. we checked / departure time / job / It's / our / a good
2. to sit / nowhere / there's / a shame / It's
3. a trolley / getting / worth / It / isn't
4. changing / if the track's / blocked / trains / no use / It's
5. the right / to find / ages / It took / us / platform
6. in the / It's / to get / impossible / to the centre / rush hour

2 Rewrite the sentences to make them sound more natural using introductory *it*.
1. To do my homework took me over an hour.
   It took me over an hour to do my homework.
2. To repair my bike is impossible.
3. That you failed your driving test is a shame.
4. What you get me for my birthday doesn't matter.
5. That we brought some sandwiches was a good idea.
6. Taking the car to the centre isn't worth it.

We often use *it* in sentences referring to time, weather, temperature and distance.
It's seven o'clock.
It's Friday.
It took two days to travel from Europe to Australia.
It's sunny and it's 27°C.
It's 100km from here.

We can use *it* when we want to avoid starting a sentence with an infinitive, *-ing* form or clause, which often sounds unnatural or very formal.
It's great being here. (= Being here is great.)
It's hard to say exactly what I mean. (= To say exactly what I mean is hard.)
It's a shame that she had to go home early. (= That she had to go home early is a shame.)
It doesn't matter where you go. (= Where you go doesn't matter.)

9.1 *have something done*

1 Rewrite the sentences with the correct form of *have something done*.
1. The shoe repairer is mending Chloe's shoes.
   Chloe's having her shoes mended.
2. The hairdresser has dyed my hair.
   I _____
3. The painters painted their house last year.
   They _____
4. The mechanic is repairing Tom's car.
   Tom _____
5. The builders are changing my neighbour's windows.
   My neighbours _____
6. The photographer is going to take my photo.
   I _____
7. The optician tested Olivia's eyes last week.
   Olivia _____
8. The dry cleaner has cleaned Harvey's coat.
   Harvey _____
9. The plumber is going to install our new shower.
   We _____

2 Complete the dialogue using the prompts in brackets and the correct form of *have something done*.

Lauren Look at Keira! What do you think of her new look?
Hannah I think she looks awful. [1]_____?
(she / cut / her hair)
Lauren Yes, I think so. And [2]_____
(she / dye / it), too.
Hannah And her face looks different. [3]_____
(she / not reduce / her nose), has she?
Lauren I don't know. Maybe. There's something strange about her mouth, too. [4]_____?
(she / whiten / her teeth)
Hannah Yes, that's it! And her lips are bigger, too.
Lauren But what about that dress? [5]_____
(she / make / it) especially for the party?
Hannah That's what she said. Do you like it?
Lauren Not really. I think it makes her look older. And I don't know where [6]_____
(she / do / her make up) because it's really bad.
Hannah What a waste of money! I think she looked better before.

124 Grammar Builder and Reference • Units 8–9

GRAMMAR BUILDER AND REFERENCE

We use the structure *have* + object + past participle to say that you arranged for somebody to do something for you. (You didn't do it yourself.)
I had my car cleaned last week.
You need to have your room redecorated.

You can also use the structure for unpleasant things that have happened to you (which you didn't arrange).
I had my mobile phone stolen yesterday.
He had his leg broken while he was playing football.

9.2 Reflexive pronouns

1 Write a suitable response. Use a reflexive pronoun.
1. Do you have your clothes ironed?
   No, I iron them myself.
2. Does your mum have her hair dyed?
   No, _____
3. Do your friends have their rooms cleaned?
   No, _____
4. Does your dad have his chest shaved?
   No, _____
5. Do you have your nails painted?
   No, _____
6. Do you and your friends have your bikes repaired?
   No, _____
7. Do you and your brothers and sisters have your meals cooked for you?
   No, _____

2 Complete the sentences with the verbs in the box and a reflexive pronoun.

burn   cut   get   hurt   look after   turn

1. Ethan _____ _____ when he fell off the stepladder.
2. She warned her children not to _____ _____ on the hot frying pan.
3. Our parents went away for the weekend and left us to _____ _____ .
4. I _____ _____ while I was shaving my legs.
5. Sophie takes such a long time to _____ _____ ready every morning.
6. Our heating has a timer switch and can _____ _____ on and off.

We use reflexive pronouns when the object of a verb is the same as the subject.
He hurt himself.

Subject pronoun	Reflexive pronoun
I	myself
you	yourself
he	himself
she	herself
it	itself
we	ourselves
you	yourselves
they	themselves

We use reflexive pronouns to add emphasis.
They painted the bedroom themselves.

9.3 Third conditional

1 Write third conditional sentences.
1. Jacob spent all his money. He was broke.
   If Jacob hadn't spent all his money, he wouldn't have been broke.
2. Holly forgot her credit card. She didn't buy a new TV.
   If _____
3. We bought a new car. We asked for a bank loan.
   We _____
4. Amy went to the sales. She found a bargain.
   If _____
5. Samuel didn't save up. He borrowed the money for the present.
   Samuel _____
6. Daisy had enough money. She lent Benjamin £50.
   If _____
7. Joseph didn't look in the sales. He didn't find a cheap leather jacket.
   Joseph _____

2 Use the prompts to write third conditional questions.
1. What / you / eat / last night / if / you / have / the choice?
   What would you have eaten last night if you'd had the choice?
2. What / you / do / if / you / feel ill / this morning?
3. Where / you / go / if / today / be / Sunday?
4. Where / you / stay / if / you / go away / last weekend?
5. Which film / you / see / if / you / go / to the cinema / last night?
6. Who / you / visit / last night / if / you / have / the time?
7. What / you / buy / yesterday / if / you / have / the money?

Grammar Builder and Reference • Unit 9   125

GRAMMAR BUILDER AND REFERENCE

3 **SPEAKING** Work in pairs. Ask and answer the questions in exercise 2.

> What would you have eaten last night if you'd had the choice?

> I'd have eaten lasagne and garlic bread in my favourite restaurant. How about you?

We use the third conditional to talk about the imaginary result of things that didn't happen.
If I'd driven faster, we would have arrived before six.

We often use it to express criticism or regret.
You would have passed if you hadn't been so lazy!
If I'd been more careful, I wouldn't have hurt myself.

We form the third conditional with *if* + past perfect, *would have* + past participle.
*If John **had arrived** earlier, he **would have seen** the start of the film.*

We can also put the *if* clause at the end of the sentence.
*I'd have invited you **if** I'd known you liked fancy dress parties.*

Notice the short forms used in third conditional sentences. The short form of both *had* and *would* is *'d*.
If I'd had more money, I'd have paid for you.

10.1 Participle clauses

1 Combine the two sentences using a participle clause.

1 A picture was stolen by art thieves. It was painted by Munch.
   A picture painted by Munch was stolen by art thieves.
2 You can see Velazquez in this painting. He is standing in the background.
3 The sculpture represents the biblical King David. It was carved in the early 1500s.
4 *Cats* is one of the longest-running musicals in Britain. It was written by Andrew Lloyd Webber.
5 *The Matrix* was released in 1999. It stars Keanu Reeves.
6 An exhibition has been extended by a month. It features works by M C Escher.
7 The play is about social justice. It was written by Bertolt Brecht.

We use participle clauses to give more information about a noun. They can be described as shortened relative clauses (defining or non-defining).
*There's a woman **carrying a baby**.* (= who is carrying a baby)

They contain either a present participle or past participle.

- Clauses with a present participle (*-ing* form) replace an active verb. The verb they replace can be in any tense.
  *He worked in a shop **selling shoes**.* (= which sells shoes)
- Clauses with a past participle replace a passive verb. The verb they replace can be in any tense.
  *A valuable statuette, **made of gold**, will be sold tomorrow.* (= which is made of gold ...)

10.2 Determiners

1 Choose the correct words.

1 **Most / Most of** people enjoy the cinema.
2 **Some / Some of** modern art is difficult to understand.
3 **A few / A few of** my friends are going to art college.
4 Eleanor didn't like **any / any of** those portraits.
5 Isabelle looked through **every / every one** of the postcards before she bought one.
6 They had **no / none** time to buy souvenirs.
7 They spent **a little / a little of** their pocket money on sweets.
8 There wasn't **much / much of** the play left by the time they arrived.

2 Complete the sentences with *many*, *much*, *a few* or *a little*.

1 'How _____ friends have you made?'
  'Just _____. I've only been here for a week.'
2 'How _____ time have we got?'
  'Just _____. We'll have to run.'
3 'How _____ sandwiches do you want?'
  'Just _____. I'm not that hungry.'
4 'How _____ milk would you like in your coffee?'
  'Just _____. I don't like it very milky.'
5 'How _____ people are coming to the party?'
  'Just _____. Everyone's away that weekend.'
6 'How _____ money have you got?'
  'Just _____ coins, but it's enough for an ice cream.'

3 Correct the mistakes with *any*, *no* or *none*.

1 Any of the people complained about the price.
2 We haven't got no paint.
3 No of my classmates has been to the opera.
4 I haven't read none books by Virginia Woolf.
5 Any art expert should miss the Vermeer exhibition.
6 There aren't no tickets left.

Each and *every* are followed by a singular countable noun. *Each* is used when all the people or things it refers to are seen individually. *Every* is used to refer to all the people or things.
Each egg is painted in different colours.
Every egg can be purchased for ten euros.

126 Grammar Builder and Reference • Unit 10

GRAMMAR BUILDER AND REFERENCE

Few and *a few* are followed by a plural noun. *Few* has a negative meaning. *A few* has a neutral or positive meaning.
Few people came to the concert. It was very disappointing.
A few students stayed behind to help me.

Little and *a little* are followed by an uncountable noun. *Little* has a negative meaning. *A little* has a neutral or positive meaning.
People on this housing estate have little money and no future.
I have a little money – let's go out.

Many is followed by a countable noun. *Much* is followed by an uncountable noun.
There aren't many people here.
I haven't got much time to work.

All, most, some, any and *no* can be followed by either a countable or an uncountable noun.
Most people here have no free time at the weekend.
Some books are missing but all the CDs are here.

We can use determiners with *of* before another determiner and a noun.
A few of my friends came to the party. (plural noun)
All of the milk has been drunk. (uncountable noun)

When we use *no* and *every* with *of*, they change to *none* and *every one*. We use a plural noun with *every one*.
Every one of the students passed the exam.

10.3 *so* and *such*

1 Compete the dialogue with *so* or *such*.

Robert What did you do for your birthday?
Lily We went to see the opera *Nabucco*. It was ¹_____ good.
Robert But it's ²_____ long, isn't it?
Lily Yes, three hours. But it was ³_____ fantastic that the time flew by.
Robert What about the singing?
Lily Amazing. And *Nabucco* has ⁴_____ beautiful music, too. I really enjoyed it.
Robert Where did you see it?
Lily Oh, it was ⁵_____ an incredible venue. An open air theatre on the edge of town. And we were sitting under the stars. It was ⁶_____ romantic!
Robert It sounds fantastic. I might come with you next time.

We can use *so* or *such* to intensify the meaning of an adjective or adverb.
be + *so* + adjective
I'm so happy!
so + adverb
They all ran so quickly.
such + adjective + plural noun / uncountable noun
She's got such beautiful eyes / hair.
such + *a* / *an* + adjective + noun
She's got such an attractive face.

10.4 Nominal subject clauses

1 Put the words in the correct order to make sentences.

1 need / right now / on holiday / to go / What / I / is
2 I'm / my exams / What / is / finishing / looking forward to
3 to have / I'd like / a lie-in / What / is / to do / tomorrow
4 a trip / What / is / I'm / planning / thinking about / together
5 have / we're / party / What / an end-of-term / is / going to do
6 watch TV / I / tonight / to do / What / is / want / instead of / revising

2 SPEAKING Work in pairs. Complete the sentences.

1 What we need right now is _____.
2 What we're looking forward to is _____.
3 What we'd like to do tomorrow is _____.
4 What we're thinking about is _____.
5 What we're going to do this weekend is _____.
6 What we want to do tonight is _____.

We sometimes emphasise particular information in a sentence by putting it in a *what* clause followed by the appropriate form of the verb *be*.
We are looking for volunteers.
What we are looking for **is** volunteers.
I really like action films.
What I really like **is** action films.

VOCABULARY BUILDER

1.1 Clothes

1 Underline the odd word out. Explain why it is different.

1 boots   shoes   jacket   trainers
  You don't wear a jacket on your feet.
2 shorts   sandals   T-shirt   coat
3 shirt   jeans   tracksuit bottoms   trousers
4 blouse   tie   dress   skirt
5 jumper   T-shirt   socks   top
6 suit   jeans   shirt   tie

2 Label the pictures with the words in the box.

| combat trousers | fleece | hoody | leggings |
| mini skirt | polo shirt | roll-neck | v-neck |

a   b   c   d   e   f   g   h

3 **SPEAKING** Work in pairs. Decide what are the best clothes to wear:

1 to go to a party
2 to go running
3 to go out in the snow
4 to play football
5 to go on holiday
6 to go dancing

What would you wear to a party?

I'd wear a stylish, stripy top and jeans. What about you?

1.2 Compound adjectives

Look out!

A compound adjective is a single adjective made up of two or more words. These words are linked together with a hyphen to show that they are part of the same adjective.

short-sleeved   blue-eyed

1 Match the words in A and B to make compound adjectives.

A	B
high-	looking
hard-	heeled
old-	working
good-	fashioned

A	B
bad-	haired
well-	known
easy-	going
long-	tempered

2 Complete the definitions with the compound adjectives in exercise 1.

1 A person who isn't very fashionable is old-fashioned.
2 Someone who is always relaxed is _____.
3 Shoes that make you taller are _____.
4 A person who does a lot of work is _____.
5 Someone who is always angry is _____.
6 An attractive person is _____.
7 Famous people are very _____.
8 A person who doesn't often go to the hairdresser's is _____.

3 Complete the sentences with a compound adjective from exercise 1.

1 My sister's always found long-haired men attractive.
2 People recognise him everywhere he goes. He's so _____.
3 That dress is _____. It must be at least 50 years old.
4 He's so _____ he could be a model!
5 She can't walk in those _____ shoes.
6 It's difficult to have fun with Markus. He's so _____.
7 She's very _____. She studies every night until midnight.
8 Nothing worries David. He's very _____.

128   Vocabulary Builder • Unit 1

VOCABULARY BUILDER

2.1 Noun formation

LEARN THIS! We use the suffixes -ment, -ion and -ness to form nouns from adjectives. Sometimes the spelling changes.
amusement   depression   happiness

1 Read the *Learn this!* box. Use a suffix to form nouns from the adjectives in the box and write them in the correct column of the chart.

~~confused~~   disappointed   embarrassed   excited
frustrated   homesick   irritated   nervous   sad

-ment	-ion	-ness
1	1 confusion	1
2	2	2
3	3	3

2 Complete the sentences with nouns from exercise 1.
1 Imagine my _____ when my trousers fell down!
2 Brett's favourite band were only playing one concert that summer, so it was a big _____ when it was cancelled.
3 There was a lot of _____ over the technology project because the instructions weren't clear.
4 You could see the _____ on the children's faces when we told them about the holiday.
5 Do you suffer from _____ when you're away from your family?
6 They felt a deep _____ when their dog died.

2.2 Adjective prefixes

LEARN THIS!
1 We use the prefixes un-, dis-, in-, im-, il- and ir- to make negative adjectives.
uncomfortable   dissatisfied   incredible
2 Before *m* and *p* we usually use *im-*: impossible
3 Before *r* we usually use *ir-*: irresponsible
4 Before *l* we usually use *il-*: illogical

1 Read the *Learn this!* box and find three negative adjectives in the first paragraph of the text on page 16.

2 Rewrite the sentences using a prefix to make the adjectives negative.
1 My mum's very patient.
2 My bedroom's quite tidy.
3 My writing's always legible.
4 My life is quite organised.
5 I eat at regular times.
6 I think I'm quite sensitive.

3 **SPEAKING** Work in pairs. Tell your partner which sentences are true for you.

> My mum's very patient. Is yours?
> No, she's really impatient.

2.3 Adjectives + prepositions

LEARN THIS! Some adjectives are followed by certain prepositions before a noun or pronoun.
John is **nervous about** his exam.
I'm **fed up with** this book.
Jane's parents are very **proud of** her.

1 Read the *Learn this!* box. Then match the two parts of the sentences.
1 Kurt is really happy
2 I'm surprised
3 They were sad
4 Lydia was upset
5 Kevin and Megan were bored
6 He's ashamed
7 Jack's parents were worried
8 She's scared

a of heights.
b about their son.
c of his behaviour yesterday.
d with watching TV, so they went out.
e at the news he was leaving.
f about her bad exam results.
g at you! You're not usually so rude!
h with his new mobile phone.

2.4 -ed/-ing adjectives

1 Choose the correct words.
1 She was really **shocked** / **shocking** after the accident.
2 I dropped all my books as I was going into class. It was very **embarrassing** / **embarrassed**!
3 His parents were very **disappointed** / **disappointing** by his school report.
4 The film was really **excited** / **exciting**. I was on the edge of my seat all the way through.
5 Alistair is really **irritated** / **irritating**! He keeps borrowing things and then doesn't give them back.
6 I don't know how to use this new program. The manual is really **confused** / **confusing**.

Vocabulary Builder • Unit 2   **129**

VOCABULARY BUILDER

2.5 Phrasal verbs

LEARN THIS!
1 Phrasal verbs consist of a verb and one or two prepositions. Some phrasal verbs are transitive, which means they are used with an object.
We turned on the light.
2 Other phrasal verbs are intransitive, which means they are used without an object.
The plane took off.

1 Read the information in the *Learn this!* box and tick (✓) the correct sentence in each pair.

1 a He was looking after the baby. ☐
　b He was looking after. ☐
2 a Isaac and Louise are going out. ☐
　b Isaac and Louise are going out home. ☐
3 a Our car broke down. ☐
　b Our car broke down the engine. ☐
4 a My grandmother is getting over. ☐
　b My grandmother is getting over her operation. ☐
5 a Zoe tried on the jacket. ☐
　b Zoe tried on. ☐
6 a My alarm clock didn't go off. ☐
　b My alarm clock didn't go off the alarm. ☐

2 Rewrite the sentences using the phrasal verbs in the box. All the verbs are transitive.

call back　call off　look after　look for
look forward to　put away　put on　run out of

1 We **haven't got any** food!
2 You'd better **wear** a coat because it's cold outside.
3 Please can you **take care of** my plants?
4 They're **very excited about** the holidays.
5 They **cancelled** the football match because of the rain.
6 She's **trying to find** her purse.
7 I'd like you to **tidy** your clothes.
8 Can you **return my phone call**?

3.1 Jobs and gender

1 Complete the sentences with the jobs in the box.

architect　chef　estate agent　mechanic　nanny
nurse　surgeon　travel agent

1 A _____ is an experienced cook.
2 A _____ takes care of sick people.
3 A _____ repairs car engines.
4 An _____ designs buildings.
5 A _____ sells holidays.
6 A _____ looks after children.
7 A _____ performs operations.
8 An _____ sells houses.

LEARN THIS!
1 The suffix *-ess* indicates that the person doing a job is a woman.
actress　manageress　air hostess
2 However, it is now more usual to use the same term for both men and women.
actor　manager　flight attendant
3 The neutral words *assistant*, *worker*, *person* or *officer* are now often used instead of *-man* or *-woman*.
police officer　spokesperson　factory worker

2 Read the *Learn this!* box and rewrite the sentences using a more neutral word for the job.

1 The policeman was running down the street.
2 The air hostess gave us a drink.
3 The manageress was very friendly.
4 The chairman opened the meeting.
5 She's a really good actress.
6 The spokeswoman explained the company's decisions.

VOCABULARY BUILDER

3.2 Agent nouns

LEARN THIS!

1 We can use the following suffixes for people who do particular jobs or activities: *-er*, *-or*, *-ist*, *-ant*, *-ician*
farmer   actor   journalist   applicant   musician

2 Agent nouns ending in *-er* sometimes have a corresponding form finishing in *-ee*.
-er is the person who does the action.
-ee is the person who is affected by the action.
employer–employee   trainer–trainee

1 Read the *Learn this!* box. Find examples of agent nouns in the text on page 26.

2 Complete the sentences. Use an agent noun formed from the word in brackets.
1 Fran's dream is to become a well-known _____ (music).
2 Mel loves chemistry and physics, so she wants to be a _____ (science).
3 Matt enjoys reading and writing and he'd like to be an _____ (edit).
4 Vince is good at explaining things so he's going to be a _____ (teach).
5 Danny likes working with numbers, so he's hoping to become an _____ (account).
6 Jill's ambition for the future is to be a bank manager. At the moment she's a _____ (train).

3.3 Phrasal verbs: separable and inseparable

LEARN THIS!

1 Some transitive phrasal verbs are separable, which means there are two possible positions for the object.
She **picked up** some bread on the way home.
She **picked** some bread **up** on the way home.

2 However, when the object is a pronoun, it always goes between the two parts of a separable phrasal verb.
She **picked** it **up** on the way home.

3 Other transitive phrasal verbs are inseparable, and the object always follows the phrasal verb.
He **gets on** well with his mother.
He **gets on** well with her.

4 Your dictionary will tell you if a phrasal verb is separable or not.

1 Read the *Learn this!* box and rewrite the sentences using a pronoun instead of the phrase in **bold**. Use a dictionary to check if the phrasal verbs are separable or inseparable.
1 Why don't you take off **your coat**?
  Why don't you take it off?
2 They've employed a nanny to look after **the children**.
  They've employed a nanny _____.
3 He made up **the excuse** so she didn't get angry.
  He _____ so she didn't get angry.
4 I'm looking forward to **our trip**.
  I'm _____.
5 When they got home they put away **the shopping**.
  When they got home they _____.
6 Kieran worked out **the answer**.
  Kieran _____.
7 The teacher gave out **the exams**.
  The teacher _____.

4.1 Parts of the body

1 Solve the anagrams to make parts of the body.
1 neek   5 elg   9 ohumt
2 shect   6 hsmtcoa   10 sneo
3 eto   7 abkc
4 gfienr 8 eey

2 Choose the correct words.
1 My friends always pull my **knee** / **leg** about my red hair.
2 Greg is head over **heels** / **ankles** in love with Sandra.
3 I wasn't going to lend Mick any money, but he twisted my **elbow** / **arm**.
4 He really put his **foot** / **hand** in it when he asked her about her cat. It died last week!
5 I called her because I needed to get something off my **chest** / **stomach**.
6 'We won the basketball match 78–76.'
  'It was 78–77, actually.'
  'Stop splitting **hairs** / **fingers**! We won, didn't we?!'

VOCABULARY BUILDER

4.2 Inside the body

1 Match the parts of the body in the box with the pictures.

| artery | bone | brain | heart | liver | lungs | muscle |
| ribs | skin | skull | spine | stomach | vein |

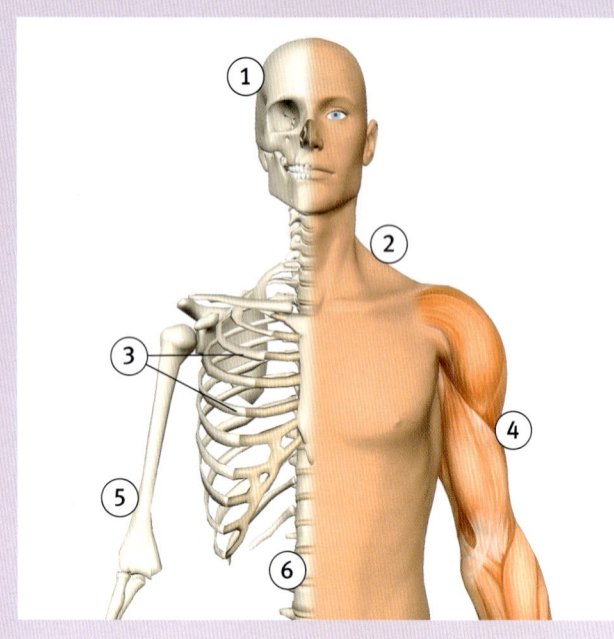

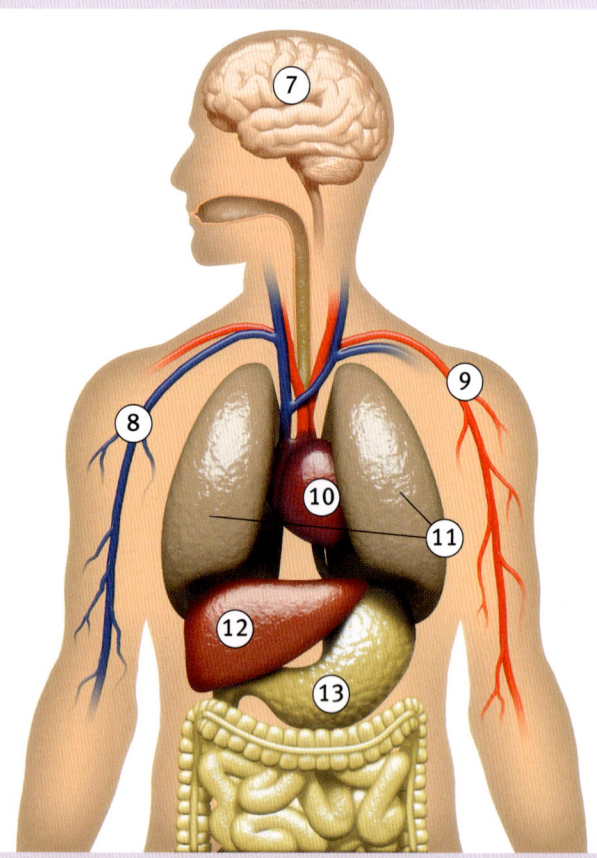

4.3 Aches and pains

LEARN THIS!
1 You can say you have **a pain** in a part of your body.
   He's got a pain in his shoulder.
2 You can also say a part of your body **aches**.
   His back aches because he's been moving the furniture.
3 There are special words for aches and pains for some parts of the body.
   backache   earache   toothache   a headache

1 Read the *Learn this!* box and complete the sentences using *He's got*.

1 ankle   *He's got a pain in his ankle.*
2 head   *He's got a headache.*
3 stomach _____
4 arm   _____
5 leg   _____
6 tooth   _____
7 knee   _____
8 ear   _____
9 neck   _____
10 back   _____

5.1 Noun prefixes

LEARN THIS!
We can use the following prefixes to change the meaning of nouns.

mono-	one or single	micro-	small
multi-	more than one	pseudo-	not true
semi-	half or partly	sub-	less than
auto-	of or by yourself	ex-	former

Your dictionary will tell you if you need to use a hyphen or if the noun with prefix is written as one word.

1 Read the *Learn this!* box. Complete the sentences using the words in brackets and the correct prefix.

1 He's got so much money he's a _____ (millionaire).
2 RFID tags contain a small _____ (chip).
3 We sit in a _____ (circle) in our English class.
4 He talks in a really boring _____ (tone). It makes you fall asleep!
5 Some people regard astrology as a _____ (science).
6 Robbie Williams wrote his _____ (biography) at the age of 28!
7 He's going out for dinner with his _____ (girlfriend) tonight. I wonder if they'll get back together.
8 I like watching films in English if they have _____ (titles).

132 Vocabulary Builder • Units 4–5

VOCABULARY BUILDER

5.2 Compound nouns (1)

LEARN THIS!
1 Compound nouns are formed by joining two nouns
 username sound card
 or by joining an adjective and a noun
 software hard disk
2 You need to check in a dictionary whether a compound noun is written as one word or two words.

1 Read the *Learn this!* box and find more compound nouns in the text on page 46.

2 Match 1–10 with a–j to make compound nouns used to talk about the environment.

1 solar	a species
2 GM	b rain
3 carbon	c effect
4 global	d layer
5 endangered	e disposal
6 greenhouse	f emissions
7 acid	g forest
8 waste	h foods
9 ozone	i power
10 rain	j warming

3 Complete the sentences with compound nouns from exercise 2.
1 Many forests have been damaged by _____.
2 The _____ is causing the earth's atmosphere to heat up.
3 _____ will cause the icebergs to melt.
4 The Amazon _____ is in the Amazon Basin of South America.
5 The _____ helps to protect the earth from harmful radiation from the sun.
6 Coal-burning power stations are a source of _____.
7 Some _____ can only be seen in zoos.
8 _____ is a renewable source of energy.

5.3 Verb + noun collocations

1 Choose the correct words to make sentences about ideas that would help the environment.
1 Developing countries should **avoid / promote** the mistakes made by developed countries.
2 Local councils should **promote / ban** the recycling of household waste.
3 Multinational companies should **improve / increase** conditions in their factories in developing countries.
4 Teachers should **ban / discuss** environmental issues with their students.
5 Governments should **ban / improve** the use of CFC gases.
6 Governments should **prevent / increase** investment in renewable sources of energy.
7 If governments don't **achieve / prevent** global warming, more natural disasters will occur.
8 Governments should try to **avoid / achieve** the targets for carbon emissions that they agree on.

6.1 House and garden

1 Complete the mind map with the words in the box. Some of the words can be used more than once.

armchair basin bath bedside table bookcase
chest of drawers coffee table desk dishwasher
fireplace flowerbed ~~fridge~~ hedge microwave
mirror path shower stepladder wardrobe
washing machine

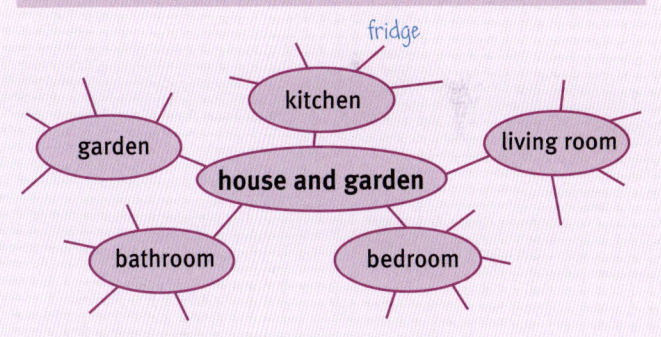

fridge
kitchen
garden
living room
house and garden
bathroom
bedroom

2 **SPEAKING** Work in pairs. Ask and answer questions about your ideal house.

What's in your living room?

There are two big red sofas around a big coffee table. There's a large picture above the fireplace and an amazing flat screen television on another wall. How about you?

Vocabulary Builder • Units 5–6 **133**

VOCABULARY BUILDER

6.2 Compound nouns (2)

LEARN THIS!
Compound nouns: nouns functioning as adjectives
Some compound nouns are formed by joining two nouns. The first noun defines the second noun so it functions as an adjective.
music room   flowerbed

1 Read the *Learn this!* box. Complete the pairs of compound nouns with the nouns in the box.

| brush | door | game | lamp | pan | player | room | table |

1 coffee _____
   dining _____
2 front _____
   cupboard _____
3 guest _____
   bed _____
4 desk _____
   table _____
5 CD _____
   DVD _____
6 sauce _____
   frying _____
7 video _____
   computer _____
8 paint _____
   hair _____

2 Match the definitions with the compound nouns from exercise 1. Use a dictionary to check whether the compound noun is written as one or two words.

1 Soup is made in a _____.
2 We all sit at the _____ for Sunday lunch.
3 She needed a _____ because her hair was a mess.
4 We turned on the _____ to watch a film.
5 The main entrance is through the _____.
6 When my aunt visits, she always sleeps in the _____.
7 We've got a new PC, but my _____ don't work on it.
8 I couldn't study because there wasn't enough light in my room, so my parents bought me a _____.

6.3 Intransitive phrasal verbs

LEARN THIS!
Intransitive phrasal verbs
Some phrasal verbs are intransitive. They do not take a direct object and you cannot separate the verb and the preposition.
carry on   wake up   break down   get up
I asked him to stop, but he carried on walking.

1 Read the *Learn this!* box. Rewrite the sentences using the correct form of the intransitive phrasal verbs in the box.

| come back | fall through | give up | go out | grow up |
| hold on | stand up | stay in |

1 When he **becomes an adult** he wants to be a fire fighter.
2 'What are you doing this weekend?' 'I'm **going to a party** with some friends.'
3 He told me to **wait** while he fetched his jacket.
4 We **returned home** from the match exhausted.

5 She wasn't enjoying the lessons so she decided **to stop** learning to play the piano.
6 They **remained in the house** because it was raining.
7 They **got to their feet** and left the room.
8 His plans for the weekend **didn't happen** because of the bad weather.

2 Decide if the sentences are correct or not. Correct the sentences that are incorrect.

1 He sat down **the chair** and began to read his book.
2 She told us to hold on **while she called a doctor**.
3 They grew up **their childhood** in a village in Sicily.
4 Jay and Mia got up **themselves** and went to school.
5 Courtney woke up **late this morning**.
6 Madison stood up **the room** and started to speak.
7 Please don't come back **late tonight**.
8 The plane didn't take off **the runway** until midnight.

7.1 Three-part phrasal verbs

LEARN THIS!
Three-part phrasal verbs
Some phrasal verbs have more than two parts. These phrasal verbs are used with an object and they are inseparable.
run out of   split up with

1 Read the *Learn this!* box. Complete the three-part phrasal verbs with the words in the box. Then match them to their meaning.

| away | down | on | out | out | up | up | up |

1 get _____ with   a be someone's girlfriend/boyfriend
2 fall _____ with   b think you are better than someone
3 get _____ with   c have a good relationship
4 put _____ with   d not be punished for
5 look _____ on   e think of something
6 come _____ with   f have an argument
7 look _____ to   g tolerate something
8 go _____ with   h admire someone

2 Complete the sentences with the correct form of the three-part phrasal verbs in exercise 1.

1 Ivan _____ people who have achieved a lot in life.
2 Millie has _____ Theo again, so they aren't talking to each other.
3 Hannah _____ a fantastic idea for the school trip.
4 Dominic doesn't keep in touch with his brothers because he doesn't _____ them.
5 I think Declan's in love. He's _____ Mia for 3 months.
6 Charlotte _____ her younger sister because she didn't go to university.
7 Billy _____ not doing his homework. The teacher didn't notice.
8 How do you _____ him? He's so bad-tempered.

134   Vocabulary Builder • Units 6–7

VOCABULARY BUILDER

8.1 Travel and transport

1 Complete the mind map with the words in the box. Some of the words can be used more than once.

aisle   arrive   bay   ~~cabin~~   carriage   check-in desk
departure lounge   driver   flight attendant   gate
journey   land   leave   luggage rack   motorway
overhead lockers   pilot   platform   runway
take off   ticket inspector   track   waiting room

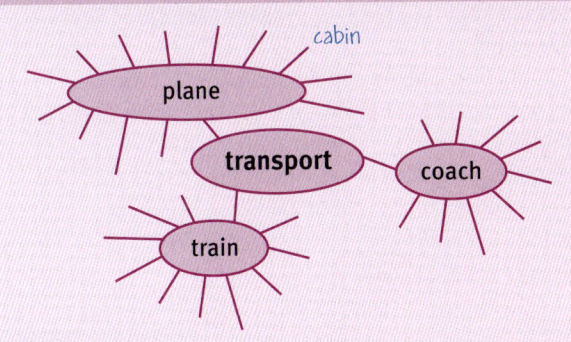

- plane — cabin
- transport
- coach
- train

2 Complete the sentences with words from exercise 1.
1 The coach to Oxford leaves from _____ 14.
2 We bought some presents from the shops in the _____ before we went to the gate to board.
3 We took our bag onto the coach and put it on the _____.
4 The _____ brought us some free drinks because the flight was so late taking off.
5 Our journey was very comfortable because we had seats in the first-class _____.
6 There were no seats left on the train, so we had to stand in the _____ for the whole journey.
7 There was no traffic on the _____ so the coach arrived early.
8 We couldn't find our tickets when the _____ asked for them, so we had to pay again.

8.2 Tourism and travel

1 Choose the correct words.
1 We prefer cooking our own meals, so we usually stay in a self-catering **apartment** / **hotel** on holiday.
2 We didn't enjoy our last trip to our usual ski **resort** / **village** in the Alps. There wasn't any snow!
3 The guided **tour** / **trip** of the cathedral took two hours, but it was really interesting.
4 Our package **holiday** / **break** included the flights, the accommodation, the excursions and all our meals.
5 Our trip to Amsterdam was a bargain because we went on a charter **flight** / **plane**.
6 We went to the beach for a long **Saturday** / **weekend** last month. We stayed from Friday to Monday.
7 We went on a day **travel** / **trip** to the zoo last Sunday.
8 My parents are on a city **break** / **holiday** in Prague.

8.3 Verbs + prepositions

LEARN THIS! Verbs + prepositions
1 Some verbs are often followed by certain prepositions.
*Let's listen **to** some music.*
*She smiled **at** her mother.*
2 In questions, we often put the preposition at the end.
*What are you waiting **for**?*

1 Read the *Learn this!* box and complete the pairs of sentences with the same preposition.
1 They're on the platform waiting _____ the train.
  We apologised to her _____ arriving late.
2 They argued _____ him about the price.
  She agreed _____ me about the poor service.
3 He's always boasting _____ his second home.
  I dreamed _____ you last night.
4 She's concentrating _____ the audio guide.
  He insisted _____ taking a taxi.
5 People always laugh _____ Sam's jokes.
  What are you staring _____ ?
6 That suitcase belongs _____ me.
  They listened _____ the announcement carefully.

9.1 Money and payment

1 Match words in A and B to make phrases to complete the sentences.

A	B	A	B
buy	of money	be	in cash
save up	a bargain	afford	overcharged
a waste	broke	pay	a loan
be	for a laptop	ask for	a new car

1 Jessica's PC is very old. She's going to _____.
2 Matthew's going to earn some money at last. He doesn't want to _____ any more.
3 Make sure you count your change. You don't want to _____ again!
4 We couldn't _____ so we bought a second-hand one.
5 When Lucy goes shopping in the sales she always manages to _____.
6 My MP3 player stopped working after two days. What _____!
7 The corner shop on my street doesn't take credit cards. You have to _____.
8 Harry didn't have enough money to open his own business, so he had to _____ from the bank.

Vocabulary Builder • Units 8–9

VOCABULARY BUILDER

2 Complete the dialogue with the words in the box.

| afford bargain borrow debt discount lend |
| saving up waste |

Ben Did I tell you I was ¹_____ for a digital camera?

Jay Are you? I can ²_____ you some money, if you want.

Ben Thanks, but I'd rather not. I hate being in ³_____.

Jay I know what you mean. What do your parents think?

Ben They think it's a ⁴_____ of money. They say I should use theirs instead of buying my own.

Jay Well maybe you can buy a ⁵_____ in the sales.

Ben That's what I'm hoping. I should be able to buy a good one even if I can't ⁶_____ the best one in the shop.

Jay You need to look around and see what ⁷_____ the shops are offering.

Ben Good idea. Do you want to come with me?

9.2 Prepositions + noun phrases

Look out!

Some nouns are used in expressions with a fixed preposition.
by cheque   **by** credit card   **in** cash

1 Complete the pairs of noun phrases with the prepositions in the box.

| at by for from in on out of under |

1 ___ fun	5 ___ first sight
___ a change	___ his own expense
2 ___ chance	6 ___ control
___ mistake	___ her breath
3 ___ the phone	7 ___ touch
___ holiday	___ pocket
4 ___ trouble	8 ___ scratch
___ a mess	___ A to Z

2 Complete the sentences with preposition + noun phrases from exercise 1.

1 Lewis invited all his friends to his holiday villa _____. They didn't have to pay a thing!
2 She told her friend the answer _____ so that the teacher couldn't hear.
3 James and Ryan are away for the party. They're _____ that week.
4 I wasn't expecting to see Jake in Berlin, so it was a lovely surprise when we met _____ in a bar.
5 Megan's room's _____ again. She never tidies it.
6 Cameron's a bit _____ with his friends at the moment because he's moved to another town.
7 We had to start the project _____ when Abigail's computer crashed and we lost all the data.
8 We never do anything exciting at the weekend, so we decided to go to the theme park _____.

9.3 Small and large numbers

Look out!

1 In English, thousands, millions and billions are written with commas.
425,950   9,310,896   2,856,487,000
2 Decimals are written with a decimal point. When we use a decimal we say each number to the right of the decimal point individually.
4.75 = 'four point seven five' **NOT** 'four point seventy-five'

1 **SPEAKING** Work in pairs. Write down three numbers larger than 1,000 and three numbers with a decimal point. Read out the numbers for your partner to write down. Then swap roles.

You say:

> One million two hundred and thirty thousand.

Your partner writes: 1,230,000

2 Write the fractions in numbers and complete the percentages.

1 ½	half	50 %
2 ___	a quarter	___ %
3 ___	three tenths	___ %
4 ___	three quarters	___ %
5 ___	a fifth	___ %
6 ___	a tenth	___ %
7 ___	a twentieth	___ %

VOCABULARY BUILDER

10.1 Artists and artistic activities

1 Complete the chart with the words in the box.

cartoonist	composes	dancer	draws	film
instrument	novelist	performs	playwright	pictures
poems	song	screenplays	sculptures	songwriter

	Artist	Activity
Performing arts	musician	plays an _____ / plays a piece of music
	_____	dances / _____ a dance
	actor	acts / appears in a play or _____
	singer	sings a _____
Visual arts	painter	paints _____ / _____ pictures
	_____	draws cartoons
	sculptor	sculpts _____ / creates / makes _____
Music	composer	_____ music / writes music
	_____	writes songs
Literature	_____	writes plays
	poet	writes _____
	_____	writes novels
	scriptwriter	writes _____

2 Complete the sentences with the words from the chart in exercise 1.

1. The sculptor Botero creates enormous _____ of overweight figures.
2. Do you prefer the _____ of the romantic or the modern poets?
3. Arthur Miller is one of the most famous American _____. He wrote the play *Death of a Salesman*.
4. It must be difficult for a _____ to convert the words of a novel into the screenplay for a film.
5. The composer Tchaikovsky _____ some very moving symphonies.
6. The novelist Thomas Hardy wrote some fairly depressing _____.

10.2 Compound nouns (3)

> **Look out!**
> We can form compound nouns from two nouns or from an adjective and a noun.
> *stage musical   abstract painting*

1 Look at the text about Banksy on page 98 and find at least four compound nouns.

2 Match words in A and B to make compound nouns.

A	B
electric	kit
backing	vocals
classical	music
drum	guitar

A	B
heavy	song
European	singer
love	tour
lead	metal

3 Choose the correct words.

1. I can never tell what abstract **paintings** / **art** are supposed to represent.
2. The **stage** / **scenery** musical *We will rock you* tells the story of the rock band Queen.
3. **Performance** / **Acting** artists are very common in contemporary art exhibitions nowadays.
4. The stage **hands** / **arms** helped move the scenery.
5. His drum **apparatus** / **kit** takes up a lot of space.
6. Andy Warhol became a **household** / **family** name in the sixties.
7. Expensive works of art are often put in glass **cases** / **boxes** for exhibitions.
8. The **subject** / **topic** matter of her paintings is often disturbing.

Vocabulary Builder • Unit 10   137

OXFORD
UNIVERSITY PRESS

Great Clarendon Street, Oxford OX2 6DP

Oxford University Press is a department of the University of Oxford.
It furthers the University's objective of excellence in research, scholarship,
and education by publishing worldwide in

Oxford New York

Auckland Cape Town Dar es Salaam Hong Kong Karachi
Kuala Lumpur Madrid Melbourne Mexico City Nairobi
New Delhi Shanghai Taipei Toronto

With offices in

Argentina Austria Brazil Chile Czech Republic France Greece
Guatemala Hungary Italy Japan Poland Portugal Singapore
South Korea Switzerland Thailand Turkey Ukraine Vietnam

OXFORD and OXFORD ENGLISH are registered trade marks of
Oxford University Press in the UK and in certain other countries

© Oxford University Press 2008

The moral rights of the author have been asserted

Database right Oxford University Press (maker)

First published 2008

2013 2012 2011 2010
10 9 8 7

No unauthorized photocopying

All rights reserved. No part of this publication may be reproduced,
stored in a retrieval system, or transmitted, in any form or by any means,
without the prior permission in writing of Oxford University Press,
or as expressly permitted by law, or under terms agreed with the appropriate
reprographics rights organization. Enquiries concerning reproduction
outside the scope of the above should be sent to the ELT Rights Department,
Oxford University Press, at the address above

You must not circulate this book in any other binding or cover
and you must impose this same condition on any acquirer

Any websites referred to in this publication are in the public domain and
their addresses are provided by Oxford University Press for information only.
Oxford University Press disclaims any responsibility for the content

ISBN: 978 0 19 455181 6 Book
ISBN: 978 0 19 455182 3 CD-ROM
ISBN: 978 0 19 455180 9 Pack

Printed in China

ACKNOWLEDGEMENTS

The publisher and authors are grateful to the many teachers and students who read and piloted the manuscript, and provided invaluable feedback. With special thanks to the following for their contribution to the development of the Solutions series:
Zinta Andzane, Latvia; Irena Budreikiene, Lithuania; Kati Elekes, Hungary; Danica Gondová, Slovakia; Ferenc Kelemen, Hungary; Natasha Koltko, Ukraine; Mario Maleta, Croatia; Juraj Marcek, Slovakia; Dace Miška, Latvia; Anna Morris, Ukraine; Hana Musílková, Czech Republic; Zsuzsanna Nyirő, Hungary; Eva Paulerová, Czech Republic; Hana Pavliková, Czech Republic; Rita Rudiatiene, Lithuania; Dagmar Škorpíková, Czech Republic).

The publisher and authors would like to extend special thanks to Jane Hudson *for the additional material she contributed to this level.*

The publisher and authors would like to thank: Zoltán Rézműves *for the part he played in developing the material.*

The authors and publisher are grateful to those who have given permission to reproduce the following extracts and adaptations of copyright material: p9 'Somebody's Watching Me'. Words and Music by Rockwell © 1983 Jobete Music Co Inc. EMI Music Publishing Ltd, London W8 5SW. Reproduced by permission of International Music Publications Ltd (a trading name of Faber Music Ltd). All Rights Reserved. p26 'Cream of the crop: Matt Keating meets the new, high-achieving generation of Polish migrant workers' by Matt Keating, 20 May 2006, from *The Guardian* © Guardian News & Media Ltd 2006. Reproduced by permission. p38 'The day I met the memory man' by Laura Barton, 17 June 2003, from *The Guardian* © Guardian News & Media Ltd 2003. Reproduced by permission. p66 *When You Are Old* by WB Yeats. Reproduced by permission of A. P. Watt Ltd on behalf of Gráinne Yeats. p68 'Are Online Relationships Real?' by Linda F. Johnson, from HYPERLINK "http://www.personal-computer-tutor.com" www.personal-computer-tutor.com. Reproduced by kind permission of the author. p69 'Hero' Words and Music by Enrique Iglesias, Paul Barry, and Mark Taylor © 2001 Enrique Iglesias Music, Rive Droite Music Ltd and Metrophonic Music Ltd (50%) EMI Music Publishing Ltd, London W8 5SW. Reproduced by permission of International Music Publications Ltd (a trading name of Faber Music Ltd). All Rights Reserved.

(45%) Published by Crosstown Songs UK Ltd. (MCPS/PRS) Sub-Published by Fintage Publishing & Collection B.V. Reproduced by permission. p78 'Small spectator, big game in Africa' from *The Sunday Times*, 3 December 2006. Reproduced by permission of NI Syndication. p89 'Everything I Own' Lyrics by David Gates © Sony/ATV Tunes LLC. Administered by Sony/ATV Music Publishing. All rights reserved. Used by permission. p92 'Friendlier Footprints' by Jenny Hontz, from *Newsweek* April 10-17 2006. Reprinted by permission of the author.

Sources: p27 'One millionaire's strange cry – tickets, please!' by Vincent Mallozzi from *The New York Times* 14 April 2005. p84 HYPERLINK "http://www.quoteworld.org" www.quoteworld.org p86 www.tes.co.uk

Thanks to: Helen Reilly of www.arnosdesign.co.uk for managing all illustrations and researched and commissioned photography

Illustrations by: Claude Bordeleau/Agent002 pp54, 64; Joy Gosney p128; David Oakley/Arnos Design Ltd p53 (replica of a tree fridge), Andy Parker pp48, 49, 57, 132.

The publisher would like to thank the following for their permission to reproduce photographs: Alamy pp4 (man wearing cape), 18, 24 (secretary. doctor), 33 (librarian), 37, 38 (cards), 44 (scanner, Playstation), 46, 67, 69, 75 (plane), 76 (skiing), 77 (safari trip), 81, 83 (zoo, Museum of Childhood, Dynamic Earth), 90, 91 (bicycle), 94 (art installation, piano recital, still life), 104 (sculpture), 104 (ballet/Redferns); Arnos Design Ltd pp5, 23, 26 (graphs),44 (computer game), 63, 103, 117; BBC Photo Library pp97 (still from The Choir); Camera Press pp66 (Adam Mickiewicz/Ullstein Bild); Sarah Coles HQ, London p96 (Beer Can Penis 1993-2004 by Sarah Lucas); Corbis pp4 (woman wearing baggy suit), 6, 10, 11 (horse riding), 14 (cross), 17 (teenager, ghost town), 20, 21 (band/Erik Isakson), 24 (plumber), 27 (toy maker), 30, 34, 45 (Reuters), 53 (craftsman/Christophe Boisvieu, cars/Charles O'Rear), 56 (Loch Ness), 60, 61 (women,house), 66 (W.B Yeats), 70, 72 (yoga/Ron Chapple, weights/ Catherine Wessel), 73 (Brad and Angelina), 75 (car), 76 (beach scene),77, 78 (elephants), 84 (currency), 88, 92 (King Pacific Lodge/Richard T. Nowitz), 93 (both), 96 (Shark/Damien Hirst), 98 (CND by Banksy), 100, 128, 137; Dreamstime p16 (war memorial/Uolir); Empics pp98 (men with Bananas/ Banksy), 99 (Spiderman and swimming pool street drawings by Julian Beever), 104 (grafitti); Fotolia p44 (keyboard/Tommy Ingberg), p84 (piggy bank), 87, 91 (tent); Getty Images pp4 (model with red socks), 7 (TAXI/VCL/ Spencer Rowell), 12 (tailor/Don Smetzer), 14 (upset, bored, pleased ,excited), 15 (Thom Lang). 16 (poppy day/Getty/AFP), 17 (village), 29, 38 (Andi Bell), 39, 40, 50, 56 (sasquatch/Photonica), 73 (The Beckhams), 74 (traffic- jam), 85 (both), 86, 94 (gig); Istock pp26 (polish flag/Ufuk Zivana, uk flag/Christopher Steer), 36 (fast food), 43 (all), 44 (laptop, monitor, printer, mouse/Donald Swartz), 78 (leopard), 83 (Edinburgh castle); Mary Evans Picture Library pp25 (link boy); 58 (Tichborne, Orton); Photolibrary pp33 (Japan Travel Bureau); Nintendo p72 (brain game/The Red Consultancy); PA Photos p52 (boxing/Michael Villagran/AP) 72 (woman playing game/Kevin P. Casey/AP); Punchstock pp8 (CCTV camera/Image Source), 11 (siblings), 12, 24 (police woman/Peter Dazely), 41; Rex Features Ltd pp4 (model wearing tracksuit), 8 (monitoring screens), 19, 28 (midwife/John Selby), 35, 65, 74 (airport scene, underground scene), 80, 94 (buskers, performance art), 96 (My Bed/Tracey Emin), 101; Science Photo Library p47, 53, 56 (Nessie), 130;Still Pictures p133 (Michel Gunther/BIOS); Telegraph Media Group/David Howells p27 (Walter Rourke);The Art Archive p25 (water caddy) Musée Carnavalet Paris/ Gianni Dagli Orti);The Bridgeman Art Library p95 (Sunday Afternoon on the Island of La Grand Jatte 1884-86 by Seurat, Georges Pierre/The Art Institute of Chicago IL, USA), 104 (Branch Hill Pond Hampstead by John Constable 1776-1837/The Victoria & Albert Museum London UK); The Forest Wake Print Collection USA p95 (Lunch with Lautrec/Warrington Colescott 1921-); UK Government Art Collection pp58 (The Tichborne Claimant trial scene); Stewart Wood p97 (still from How Ballet Changed My Life).

Solutions Intermediate MultiROM

In your computer
- Interactive activities to practise the grammar and vocabulary in the Student's Book
- Exercises to help improve your writing and listening
- Games to help you revise what you've learned

In your CD player
- Audio tracks for listening exercises in Solutions Intermediate Workbook:
1 Listening 1, pages 20–21
2 Listening 2, pages 38–39
3 Listening 3, pages 56–57
4 Listening 4, pages 74–75
5 Listening 5, pages 92–93